Helping Children Cope with Death

Helping Children Cope with Death

Guidelines and Resources

Second Edition

Edited by
HANNELORE WASS
University of Florida, Gainesville
and
CHARLES A. CORR
Southern Illinois University, Edwardsville

● **HEMISPHERE PUBLISHING CORPORATION**
Washington   New York   London

DISTRIBUTION OUTSIDE THE UNITED STATES
McGRAW–HILL INTERNATIONAL BOOK COMPANY
Auckland   Bogotá   Guatemala   Hamburg   Johannesburg
Lisbon   London   Madrid   Mexico   Montreal
New Delhi   Panama   Paris   San Juan   São Paulo
Singapore   Sydney   Tokyo   Toronto

To
BRIAN,
KEVIN,
KAREN,
and SUSAN

HELPING CHILDREN COPE WITH DEATH: Guidelines and Resources, Second Edition

1 2 3 4 5 6 7 8 9 0   E B E B   8 9 8 7 6 5 4 3

*This book was set in Baskerville by Hemisphere Publishing Corporation.
The editors were Christine Flint and Janet Mais; the production supervisor
was Miriam Gonzalez and the typesetter was Shirley J. McNett.
Edwards Brothers, Inc., was printer and binder.*

Library of Congress Cataloging in Publication Data

Main entry under title:

Helping children cope with death.

   (Series in death education, aging, and health care)
   Audiovisual resources: p.
   Bibliography: p.
   1. Children and death. 2. Children and death—Abstracts.
I. Wass, Hannelore. II. Corr, Charles A. III. Series.
BF723.D3H44   155.9'37   83-22622
ISBN 0-89116-369-7
ISSN 0275-3510

∞∞∞

CONTENTS

∞∞∞

CONTRIBUTORS

Sandra L. Bertman, M.A.
Associate Professor, Program of Ethics, Values, and Medical Humanities,
University of Massachusetts Medical School, Worcester, Massachusetts

Charles A. Corr, Ph.D.
Professor, Philosophical Studies, School of Humanities,
Southern Illinois University at Edwardsville, Edwardsville, Illinois

Edgar N. Jackson, Ph.D.
Minister, Writer, and Consultant, Washington Road, Corinth, Vermont

Richard A. Pacholski, Ph.D.
Professor and Chairman, Department of English,
Millikin University, Decatur, Illinois

Hannelore Wass, Ph.D.
Professor, Educational Psychology and Human Development,
Department of Foundations of Education, University of Florida,
Gainesville, Florida

PREFACE

In this second edition to *Helping Children Cope with Death: Guidelines and Resources,* as in the first, our goal was to produce a volume that offers valuable suggestions and resources for effective helping.

The response to the first edition was immediate and positive and has encouraged us to prepare this second edition. From the section, "Guidelines," the three chapters "Children's and Others' Thoughts and Expressions about Death," "The Pastoral Counselor and the Child Encountering Death," and "Helping with Death Education"—each unique, stimulating, and helpful—have been retained with little change. We have, however, greatly expanded the scope of this volume by the addition of an extensive new chapter "Parents, Teachers, and Health Professionals as Helpers." The chapter first describes some basic requirements for effective helping, then provides, in condensed form, research and clinical findings concerning death and the child. Next it considers common problems that result when the child encounters death in various contexts, and offers specific guidelines and suggestions to health professionals, parents, and teachers for helping children cope with these problems. Death-related issues are discussed separately for the typical child, the dying child, and the bereaved child. This chapter offers additional resources and indicates how they can be used. The emphasis in this chapter is on the *practical.*

The section, "Resources" has been revised to include most recent titles. Also, distributors of audiovisual materials and their addresses have been checked and updated.

We hope our readers will find this new edition a dependable source for helping children cope with death.

Hannelore Wass and Charles A. Corr

∞∞

PREFACE TO THE FIRST EDITION

∞∞

As more and more parents, teachers, and other adults face up to the pressing need to help our young cope with death, it becomes apparent that guidelines and resources for effective helping are also needed. In this supplementary volume we have attempted to provide these.

Part One of our book, Guidelines, consists of three chapters. In the chapter by Sandra Bertman, the reader can see some of the richness of children's relationships with the phenomenon of death and some stunning verbal and artistic expressions of their death concerns. The chapter also gives illustrations of the sensitivity to children's needs found in the creative literature. Edgar Jackson shares insights he has gained from counseling children. He suggests specific ways in which a counselor, especially a pastoral counselor, can help, and offers a set of basic guidelines for effective counseling. Both chapters may stimulate the reader to explore further the considerable wealth of knowledge that now exists about death and the child. Charles Corr not only presents a carefully reasoned discussion of opportunities and responsibilities for death education, but also deals with the complex question of goals; he suggests a variety of forms that death education for children can take and ways in which various resources can be used effectively.

In Part Two of our volume we offer a comprehensive listing of a variety of resources that we consider helpful for those who want to be effective helpers. Here Charles Corr presents an annotated bibliography of 44 books for adults. Hannelore Wass provides an annotated bibliography of 156 books about death for children and adolescents. Richard Pacholski provides an annotated mediagraphy consisting of 136 entries.

We hope this volume will be useful to parents, teachers, counselors, and other adults who interact with children.

Hannelore Wass and Charles A. Corr

INTRODUCTION

HANNELORE WASS AND CHARLES A. CORR

In his oft-quoted book, *The Prophet,* Kahlil Gibran says: "If you would indeed behold the spirit of death, open your heart wide unto the body of life. For life and death are one, even as the river and the sea are one" (1, p. 80). This insight is fundamental and many writers have expressed it in various ways. To the extent that we are able to gain insight into the meaning of death before it actually comes to us individually, we must do so through an understanding of life. That is not so unusual, for the human condition as we know it is to have to view things from the perspective of the only life that we now have to live. Further, an appreciation of transitoriness and finitude, of separation and loss within life, is one way of approximating the final cessation and limitation of life. And much of what we commonly speak of as "death" is really a mode of *living* that immediately precedes or follows that event. For example, references to the "death" of a person often actually concern his or her *dying,* and comments about difficulties with the "death" of a spouse may actually have to do with the mate's *bereavement.* Thus, as Gibran tells us, the correct approach to a human understanding of death is properly seen as a study of life in all of its fullness.

This is worth mentioning because it is sometime suggested that learning about death is a kind of extraordinary or odd adventure. On the contrary, learning about death is actually at the same time learning about life. This is to repeat Gibran's observation and also to bring into focus its obverse. As argued elsewhere:

On the one hand, death will be thought to be unimportant wherever we lack the imagination or the sensitivity to see and to

1

feel the importance of life. And on the other hand, by distancing ourselves from death and losing respect for its significance, we also find ourselves drawing away from a sense of the value of life. (2, p. 37)

We cannot grasp or evaluate correctly the proportions and the significance of life if we do not bring death into the picture. Just as death must be construed through life, so also life must eventaully be seen in the context of death. Certainly, death is not the only perspective from which to understand life. But it is an essential one, and in the long run, it is indispensable as a constitutive element of human existence. That is why death can become, as Herman Feifel once said, a "piloting force" in our lives. Consistently to keep death out of an account of life is to misperceive our human mode of being in a way that is fundamental and not otherwise correctable.

Acknowledging that death and life are inextricably intertwined need not, however, be an exercise of daily confrontation. In fact, many of us race, hurdle, or stumble through each day, often overwhelmed by the moment-to-moment demands of living, imprisoned by routine and endless detail, worried about tasks unfinished and plans yet to be realized. But it is imperative that every so often we take time out to look back, look forward, and look within in order to move beyond the current moment and discover or rediscover the larger picture. Often it takes a personal crisis such as a death to force us to stop and ponder in this way. Many times a child's probing questions are the impetus for us to reflect on meanings and purposes in life and death.

For today's children, death is more remote than ever before. During the 19th century and the early part of the 20th, the experience of a death in the family was common to children. Most witnessed the death of at least one sibling, and many before reaching adulthood also lost one or both parents. Because most people died at home, children were intimately acquainted with all aspects of dying. They often helped care for the dying family member, witnessed the moment of death, and participated in the funeral. Thus, children lived with the fact of death from infancy and there was nothing strange about it. With rapid advances in medical science and technology, infant mortality has been drastically reduced; many infectious diseases have been conquered to a large degree; and many others can be cured. As a consequence, average life expectancy has increased from about 47 years at the turn of the century to about 76 years today. In fact, the past two generations are the first in history in which many people in our society have reached middle age without having experienced the death of a close family member (3).

As *direct* personal experience with death has become more limited, *indirect* experience through the media, especially television, has vastly increased. The amounts of time children spend in front of a television set are unprecedented, and the extent of the impact of this medium is something with which we have to reckon. We know as yet relatively little about the long-range effect that television may have on our young, but early indications are that its influence may be formidable. There is at least one television set in 98 percent of American households, and children are television's heaviest users (4). The view of death presented by television programs is highly distorted. Often death is portrayed as something that does not happen at all. For example, Wiley Coyote on "Road Runner" gets tossed into a ravine, shot, stabbed, blown up, and run over—yet he instantly returns to life and the chase resumes. In "The Bionic Man" and "The Bionic Woman," two ordinary people become practically indestructible because they are superhuman in strength and endurance. When death does occur on television, it is often without visible pain, blood, or tears. Most television deaths are the result of violent acts; few people die a natural death; honest bereavement is rarely depicted; and actors who have long been dead are frequently resurrected through reruns. What notions of the nature of dying and death can a child glean from such exposure? Obviously it will be up to adults to make certain that such misperceptions are replaced with facts. Psychologists and educators are urging parents to seek a better balance for their children between fantasized portraits of death on television and direct personal experience or constructive accounts in literature.

Parents and teachers are important people in the lives of children. Raising and educating a child is a great responsibility and challenge. Even though this is often a joyful and gratifying venture, we are sometimes reminded of how awesome a task it is. There is no denying the fact that our responsibilities on behalf of children are difficult. They require continued goodwill, genuine caring, and personal maturity, along with knowledge of the child's world and a deep sensitivity to the child's needs. Though all of us were once children, it is all too easy to forget what that was like. And it is difficult at one and the same time to carry out our adult responsibilities and to put ourselves in the child's place. Nevertheless, this is what we must be able to do to be most effective in helping the child grow and develop in a healthy manner.

If we want to help children understand and interpret direct or indirect death-related experiences, if we want to help alleviate fears and provide comfort for children, we need to know something of their thoughts and feelings about death. But this immediately presents obstacles for many of us. First of all, the terms *children* and *death* seem contradictory. To associate them seems to violate our sense of appropriateness. Children symbolize life and growth and the future, whereas death marks decay, the end of growing, and what is now past. Bringing the two together seems morbid. But death is a natural part of life, a dimension with special power to help us appreciate the preciousness of life. When we realize this and free ourselves from misguided thinking, we will have overcome the primary obstacle. The second obstacle is also difficult to overcome. It concerns our natural tendency to shield and protect our children. We want to shield children from the harsh reality of death and thereby from frightening thoughts about death. The problem is that, no matter how hard we may try to do this, in the long run we cannot. Perhaps we can for a while, but as children grow older we cannot control and restrict their experiences. Indeed, we might ask: Should we even try? Mental health specialists have long noted that overprotection is as harmful to the child as neglect. Both stunt normal growth. Death is a natural and normal part of life. It creates fears and anxieties, but adults can comfort children and assist them to cope with such realities.

Other obstacles include misconceptions and erroneous notions about the thoughts and feelings that children have in relation to death. We need to overcome some common misunderstandings by using knowledge about both childhood and death—knowledge that has come from research and clinical observation over the last several decades. What are some of these misconceptions and what are some of the true facts? One common misconception holds that children are not interested in death, and if they are, they need psychiatric care. This is not so. On the contrary, it is a sign of normal, healthy development when children want to know about death. Children have a need to know and understand themselves, others, and the world around them. Given the opportunity and a supportive, responsive atmosphere, children begin asking fundamental existential questions at a very early age. Often we adults do not recognize these questions for what they are. For example, the question Where do babies come from? or the more pointed question How are babies made? is, when asked by a very young child, often misinterpreted as an unhealthy and inappropriate interest in sex. Nothing could be further from the truth. The child is concerned with the origin of her or his existence. Such questions are in the same category as: What are we before we are born? Are we air or dust or ants? Where are we before we are born? Or these questions: Why do people die? What happens when people die? Where do you go when you are dead? These are all quite proper and natural questions about the basic meaning of life and death that are likely to arise in childhood.

A related misconception is that children do not think about death on their own. Thus, unless we tell them, they will not have any idea about what death is. Wrong again. Through numerous studies conducted over a period of more than 40 years, we know that children's understandings of death depend to a large extent on their level of cognitive development, their experiences, and their perception of events in the world. Further, we know that children's thinking is qualitatively different from that of adults and that concepts of death usually develop in an orderly sequence. This sequence proceeds from nonconceptualization of death in infancy; to the concept in late infancy and early childhood that death is a reversible event, a temporary restriction, departure, or sleep; to the comprehension during middle childhood and preadolescence that death is irreversible but capricious; to the understanding during adolescence that death is irreversible, universal, and personal but distant. These concepts develop in close relation to a child's experiences. Today's child may not be exposed to the death of a close family member, but there are other deaths that may occur, such as the death of a relative, a neighbor, and sometimes a classmate. Most frequently, however, the child comes into contact with death through animals. These experiences touch off many questions that deserve honest answers. Being kept in the dark creates its own anxieties. In addition, if we adults hedge and evade such questions, we unintentionally communicate a powerful message to the child: "Death is such a horrible thing that it terrifies even adults so much that they can't talk about it." Such unspoken communication only intensifies perplexity and anxiety.

The misconceptions that we have mentioned lead logically to the mistaken belief that children do not have any fears of anxieties about death. The facts do not bear out this belief. Fears and anxieties develop early in infancy and take on many forms. The earliest fears are those that threaten the infant's survival, the fear of being separated from or abandoned by the nurturing one. Variations of this fear are fears associated with being left alone, not recognizing a familiar face, or being in a dark place. Young children have many fears that are related to personal danger. They fear monsters, wild animals, witches, ghosts. They worry about the dead being unable to breathe or to get out from under the ground when they wake up. As children's concepts of death become more realistic and children mature, death-related fears become increasingly more like those of adults.

There are a number of good sources of information related to children's death fears and anxieties. They are listed in Part II of this volume in the annotated bibliographies of books for adults and audiovisual resources. Much of what is written can be helpful to parents, teachers, counselors, and other adults as basic background information. But we must remember that each child is unique; to help a particular child cope with fears and anxieties, we must try to listen to this particular child with a "third ear," as Wilhelm Reich has suggested. By that, he means that we must be sensitive and tuned in to a child's thoughts, feelings, and actions. No adult will find comprehensive answers that will be universally valid for all children. But each can develop specific responses to individual needs in a process of personalized sharing with his or her child. Helping children in this way to cope with death in life more effectively is a worthwhile, rewarding, and challenging task. With that in mind we have attempted in this little book to alert adults to special needs of children, to offer guidelines for effective helping, and to direct attention to resources that can assist in that undertaking.

References

1. Gibran, K. *The Prophet.* New York: Knopf, 1972.
2. Corr, C. Reconstructing the changing face of death. In H. Wass (Ed.), *Dying: Facing the facts.* Washington: Hemisphere, 1979, pp. 5–43.
3. Stillion, J., & Wass, H. Children and death. In H. Wass (Ed.), *Dying: Facing the facts.* Washington: Hemisphere, 1979, pp. 208–235.
4. Wass, H., & Cason, L. Death anxiety and fears in childhood. In H. Wass & C. A. Corr (Eds.), *Childhood and death.* Washington: Hemisphere, in press.

GUIDELINES

∞∞

CHILDREN'S AND OTHERS' THOUGHTS AND EXPRESSIONS ABOUT DEATH

∞∞

SANDRA L. BERTMAN

University of Massachusetts Medical Center, Worcester

Death: Some Definitions

Death is

> "when a person can't live any longer"
> "old age"
> "when someone dies"

In other words, death is some sort of simple fact, biologically appropriate, with little psychological baggage attached.
    Death is

> "when you go to another place or world"

That is, death is movement and transition.
    Death is

> "someone dyeing [sic] and letting some room in the world for other living things"
> "when God says it is time to leave"

That is, death is an interpretation of the scheme of the universe—orderly and according to a prexistent master plan.
    Death is

> "when it doesn't hurt any more"

Death is, in other words, release from pain and suffering. Peace.

Death is

"when someone dies and all the people he knows come to
see him buried [sic] "
"the spooks"

Death is, then, ritual, being the center of attention, connectedness, a being together, a time, scarey.
Death is,

"when you don't have to take tests and school"
"when everybody hates you"

Death is relief and excuse; better than failing, being friendless,
and feeling uncomfortable and alone.

These definitions from a class of fifth graders cover a range
of interpretations that smudge psychologically ascribed developmental lines (1, 2) both with their startling simplicity and with
their sophistication. The youngster's criteria are more than
biologic and clinical. They bespeak of continuum and human
values, such as relief from pain and suffering; find meaning by
merging with a universe in which life and death coexist; exhibit
a degree of comfort and trust and a sense of connection with all
humanity, future and past. Coexistent with the rational search
for reasons, explanations, and meaning about the event of death
are feelings of being scared, sad, angry, out of step, alone, and
"all wrong with the world." Such ideologies and sentiments have
been the subject matter of the most mature philosophers, poets,
and artists of any era.

Definitions are skeletal, limited, and limiting. When embel-
lishment is called for—through visual or verbal media—other
concerns surface. A major preoccupation appears to be the life
of the dead one, or the living dead. Specifics about the new
environment, the changed body, activities of the dead, and
connection with the living claim much attention. License for
fanciful thought tends to pummel one's darker imaginings and
fears. The more unmentionable concerns have to do with the
contagion of death, one's murderous impulses, fantasies using

the threat of death as a means of controlling others, and viewing death as punishment or as stigma.

Life of the Dead One

Children's literature attempts to address the concerns that youngsters express about life after death. In *Anne and the Sand Dobbies,* a father explains to younger siblings that their sister, Annie, is dead, but in residence elsewhere: "The simplest way to put it, I guess, is to say she's with God. Some people say she's in heaven. I don't know exactly where she is. All we know is that she is living and that she's all right—wherever she is" (3, p. 64). In *The Magic Moth,* a minister consoles the family with his belief that when people die they step through the door into another place the living cannot see with their eyes (4, p. 46). At another time, in this same book, an older sibling explains that, wherever her sister is, it is "nice" (4, p. 17).

The strict designation, the literal location of this heaven, is a subject of concern not just for the very young. The jests of Woody Allen, a 20th century comic philosopher, expose his (adult) underlying anxiety. He envisions heaven as a cocktail party but fears "no one will know where it is being held" (5). Quite the contrary, Emily Dickinson, a 19th-century poet, likens this uncharted place to moors or seas, neither of which she has actually experienced in her lifetime. In tones of faith and affirmation, she states the analogy:

I never spoke with God
nor visited in heaven
yet certain am I of the spot
as if the chart were given. (6, p. 201)

The "burid" body is not readily discarded by youngsters. In children's literature, adult characters explain that the body is tired, worn out, sick, outgrown. Death is the sloughing off of a useless husk. In *Thank You, Jackie Robinson,* this image is the consolation: "That's just Davy's shell, there in the box left behind like an old snake skin" (7, p. 115). The snake symbol of regeneration is appropos when one can witness the metamorphic process. The newly skinned snake literally slithers away. Unlike the snake, however, the whereabouts of the newly dead person— the one skinned, as it were—is less dramatically visible.

The cremated body is even harder to fathom. Visualizing Annie in heaven or with angels, without her intact body, is just not possible for the younger siblings: " 'But Annie hasn't got any arms at all, has she?' I asked. 'They're going to burn those arms off. They're going to burn her all up. Isn't that right, Dad? How can she fly if she hasn't got any arms?' " (3, p. 76).

Nine-year-olds have studied the question of what is dead. One youngster defined dead as "when your heart stops beating, when you stop breathing, and when you don't sneeze or hiccup any more" (8). A 12-year-old explained that the dead person continues to have a body, but without physical power. Yet this loss of physical power is paradoxical. For though the embodied spirit cannot taste, hear, or smell, it can hover and it can see. In this youngster's drawing (Fig. 1), depicting a ghost approximately four months after death, the spirit is envisioned "hover-[ing] over the family member of it's choice . . . but once it's chosen the person it can't leave until the member has died . . . the 'ghost,' then, can't really communicate with the living until s/he, too, dies" (9). The dead body still is quite corporeal— clothed as in life, watching, hovering near by, patiently waiting

FIGURE 1

to communicate more directly and reunite when the living member subsequently dies.

The spirit of the dead watching, however, can be spooky. In *The Rock and the Willow,* Leeroy, following a chastisement about his behavior, wonders if his dead mama can see him (10, p. 158). Such rituals as holding one's nose when passing cemeteries or not walking on burial plots bespeak belief in goblins who are waiting to get one if one does not watch out. Even the young artist of this picture admonishes that usually you close your ears and eyes and hold your breath—"you try to block off all your senses. You think a dead person may come to haunt you if you have a sense left open, so to speak" (9). One is reminded of Gauguin's painting *The Spirit of the Dead Watching* (11, p. 76), in which a spirit is portrayed as a black-hooded figure seated at the foot of a bed. A female figure lying on the bed faces the opposite direction—avoiding the spirit. Is the live young woman distressed by or simply unaware of the deceased's presence? Is she turned away, deliberately, trying to hide from death? Would she be comforted if she faced the shrouded one, acknowledging death's presence?

In *Little Women,* Beth, the one dying, tries, with her courage at giving up life, to comfort her sister Jo. Her faith, however, is pierced when she admits the hardest part is leaving her family. To her assurances that she is not afraid and that she will be taken care of by God, Beth adds poignantly, "but it seems that I should be homesick for you even in heaven" (12, p. 339). In *A Taste of Blackberries,* the child-narrator looks at the clouds ("horses and lambs and floppy-eared dogs chased across the sky") (13, p. 36) and wonders whether his dead friend is playing with them or being lonesome in heaven. Even for the dead, then, it would seem being alone is the worst curse imaginable.

In *Anne and the Sand Dobbies,* the father, though adding a new dimension of saintliness to being dead, nonetheless views the afterlife in terms of the activities and values of the human framework as we know it: "One thing I do know . . . is that you can't be a lone wolf in heaven. . . . You can't even be a lone wolf here. . . . When you're in heaven you just do this perfectly all the time rather than in the half-baked way we do it here" (3, pp. 75–76).

The dead, then, are felt to be altered but very much alive. They exist somewhere and function somehow, living almost as usual in a different place. Perhaps they are drinking cocktails à la Woody Allen or being decent like Annie, or lonesome like Beth or Jamie, or goblin ghosts. Life may be diminished for them—less than it was when "alive"; some senses do not work; routines are certainly different. But "out-of-body" in whatever sense, the essence and presence of the one dead is strongly felt by the living. Annie's ashes are buried near the summer beach house where the family had its happiest time together. Annie now lives in a spiritual world where, like the sand dobbies who are invisible, she does not *do* anything, she just *is:* "Seeing sand dobbies is the same as being able to see people because they have bodies. But even when you can't see their bodies anymore, the sand-dobby part of them, the *real* part still goes on" (3, pp. 108–109).

The child-narrator of *A Taste of Blackberries* ultimately comes to feel that his dead friend Jamie, too, was glad "the main sadness was over." He wonders how fast "angels" or "whatever he was now" can move, as he continues to play with his dislocated friend. "Race you," he calls to Jamie as he runs up the hill (13, p. 75).

Ghosts are the external sense of presence. In another sense, they are an inside presence, as memory. A 10-year-old girl's role-playing response to the question of where a dead person goes emphasizes remembering in context of the good:

> I think that she goes in the ground and goes in a little pieces of the soil but the heart goes to the family and makes them think about the good times with the person who dies and finally they feel better and go out and just have a good time. And the person who dies stays in the other people so they don't forget her and always think of the good times. (9)

A character in children's literature, Sammy (in *Thank You, Jackie Robinson*), also comes to believe in an immortality of memory; his dead friend Davy will always be seen in his mind's eye. Although Sammy is speaking of Jackie Robinson, the reader knows Sammy's words apply to Davy and that Sammy has made peace with the death: "In my mind, where nothing ever dies, I can see him still, to this very day, running from base to base in the top of the seventh inning, between the second and third out, in a brand-new baseball game that will never, ever be over" (7, pp. 124–125).

A more generalized presence is experienced as a diffuse bond of good feeling. In a Christian funeral service (in *The Magic Moth*), Maryanne's body is commended to the earth from whence it came and her spirit to heaven, a place of light, "more like the kind you feel inside when you love someone, like Maryanne" (4, p. 46). This consolation and the sense of continued connection are remarkably akin to the words of the poet Dylan Thomas: "Though lovers be lost, love shall not/And death shall have no dominion" (14, p. 77).

Death Arouses Anger, Diffuse and Unlimited

How should one behave when confronted with death? And how do those behaviors reflect feelings and judgments about the event and about oneself? Not eating, not playing, not enjoying oneself are ways of expressing mourning.

In *Thank You, Jackie Robinson,* young Sammy lost his most adult friend, his father-surrogate, Davy. After Davy's funeral, Sammy shuts himself in his room, determined to just sit there feeling sorry for himself. He refuses to turn on the radio and angrily rejects his mother's suggestion that he listen to the ball game, that special activity once shared between Davy and Sammy: "Who did she think she was, interfering with my misery?" (7, p. 121). Sammy is further angered because she does not tell him some story about Davy's soul being in heaven: "She didn't know for sure one way or the other. She could have fibbed a little to make me feel better and maybe I could have believed her fib for a little while" (7, p. 121).

But Sammy is also angry at his friend. Sammy blames Davy for his empty and lonely feelings. After all, if he had not known and loved this man Davy, his death would not make any difference. "'Tis better to have loved and lost than never loved at all" would, at this moment, be empty rhetoric. The reader is privy to Sammy's reasoning: "I would be just the way I had been before I'd known him. I'd be better of than I was, because right then I thought the hole in my stomach was going to last the rest of my life" (7, p. 117).

Six-year-old Mark-O (in *The Magic Moth*) is angry at everyone. He expresses his rage by locking himself in his room and refusing lunch. Mark-O's frustration at disrupted life and his fury at the visitors talking, laughing, and making noise is voiced to his mother: "I can't play the record player, and I can't get out the game box and I can't beat my drums and I can't. . . . Anyway, they shouldn't be laughing when Maryanne is dead" (4, p. 47).

Strong reaction against the usual activities of living (talking, eating, listening to the radio, playing) are not just acts of protest; they may also be expressions of blame and self-punishment. In *A Taste of Blackberries,* the child-narrator interprets talking, eating, even moving as "just like things were the same" as being somehow disloyal. He will do penance by nonparticipation and by fasting. Finally, after the funeral, when he allows himself to eat, he is surprised at how good everything tastes and at how ravishingly hungry he is. When his father reassures him, giving permission even to wolf down the food, this youngster, aware that his father has read his mind, tries to stifle his smile: " 'It's okay to smile too,' my dad said. 'Jamie would want you to do both.' Well, that sure was the truth. Jamie would be the last one to want me to go around sad and starving. I ate three servings of everything" (13, p. 67).

Anger may be understood as the underpinning for guilty judgments about one's feelings. In *By the Highway Home,* a while after news of her brother's death in Vietnam, 13-year-old Catty feels guilty for wanting life to resume some normalcy and good feelings. After criticizing her parents for the unrelenting atmosphere of somberness at home, she exposes her shame: " 'I want to pretend he's gone around the corner for an hour and forget him sometimes'—She pulled out of her mother's arms and leaned her head back closing her eyes. 'I'm not nice, am I?' she said slowly" (15, p. 25).

Death lingers in sadness, apparent and repressed. Good and bad qualities of the deceased plague the thoughts of survivors. A way to facilitate the mourning process is to encourage review of the relationship, however painful. In *Blew and the Death of the Mag,* Blew senses the pressure from people to cover her feelings and pretend everything is fine. In her innocence, she is aware of being preoccupied with *both* painful and happy memories. She wants to remember, show, and share her feelings, not only by laughing at happy thoughts, but by *crying at awful thoughts* (16, p. 57). In *The Tenth Best Thing about Barney,* a youngster is encouraged to recall *good* memories (10 of them) of his dead cat (17, p. 24). Caveat: repressing anger and memories, especially negative, uncomfortable reminiscences, lest the exposure and relieving be too painful, inhibits grieving.

Death Is Stigma and Embarrassment

Death is not easily tolerable, for it can breed shame. Recently, a college student confessed in a class to his sense of diminishment with regard to his father's death. He reported through his journal:

> Something you said in class the other day *really* hit home. You said you were surprised to hear that a child might (did) lie about her parents being alive. I used to lie all the time. When a teacher would ask up to junior high school age, what does your father do for a living, I would rarely say he is deceased. I always hated the word. Many times I would simply say he owns a candy store. (He did when he was alive.) I felt ashamed and embarrassed because I was different from everyone else. If I said he was dead, they would all feel sorry for me. I couldn't stand that and would rather lie. (9)

In *A Grief Observed,* the bereaved husband is acutely aware of others. The author, C. S. Lewis, shares the awareness that his loss is a source of embarrassment to those he meets. It seems a situation with no possible positive solution. In such a state, no behavior of others with regard to the loss, be it acknowledgment or denial, is acceptable to the bereaved: "At work, at the club, in the street, I see people, as they approach me, trying to make up their minds whether they'll say something about 'it' or not. I hate it if they do and if they don't" (18, p. 10).

Death as Punishment

A fourth-grade youngster is frightened and terrified by the prospect of death. His misconduct, elevated almost to a level of sinfulness, resulted in a desperate contact with a just and terrible God. Scrawled on a paper towel was his note, which read: "Dear God Please I don't want to die. I'll stop teasing and temper" (9).

Western-world youngsters coming from strong Christian and Puritan backgrounds, are familiar with tales and stories that conclude with the moral that death is punishment for sins or behaviors. Grünewald's painting, *The Damnation of Lovers* (19), is a horrendously graphic and frightful depiction of animals devouring the very portions of the flesh so enjoyed by the lustful lovers. *Struwwelpeter* is filled with such tales as "The Dreadful Story of Harriet and the Matches" and "The Story of Augustus Who Would not Eat His Soup." The fates of both child protagonists, conveyed in painstaking detail (though charmingly) in verse and image, are most extreme. Harriet is burned to death

> *... with all her clothes,*
> *And arms, and hands, and eyes, and nose;*
> *Till she had nothing more to lose*
> *Except her little scarlet shoes;*
> *And nothing else but these was found*
> *Among her ashes on the ground. (20, pp. 6-7)*

Robust Augustus, who refused to eat his soup, is sketched getting skinnier and skinnier until he completely disappears.

> *Look at him, now the fourth day's come*
> *He scarcely weighs a sugar-plum;*
> *He's like a little bit of thread,*
> *And on the fifth day, he was—dead! (20, p. 17)*

The final illustration is of his gravestone, marked by a cross and soup tureen.

Death is fraught with implications of responsibility. Bad thoughts or words can eventuate in someone's death, holding the living in uneasy bondage. In Vogel's story *My Twin Sister, Erika,* the surviving twin tries to forget she had once told her sister in a fit of anger that she wished her dead. She even tries to make herself believe that she never actually said the words. As her grandmother often told her, prayers and good thoughts have great power. Would not the reverse be also true? She wonders: "Was it possible bad thoughts had great power, too? Was it possible I had caused Erika's death?" (21, p. 52). Blew, too (in *Death of the Mag*), agonizes over her responsibility for her imaginary companion's illness and death. She starts playing games with herself. Her guilty thoughts ("if only") become promises and bargains:

> *If only I hadn't ever yelled at her, maybe she wouldn't have gotten sick. . . .*
> *If only she gets better, I'll never hurt anybody ever. . . .*
> *If only she gets well, I'll become a doctor, and never let anyone die. . . .*
> *If only she lives, I'll never do anything wrong again. . . . (16, p. 33)*

Such reasoning, again, is not peculiar to children. In Kudret "Feast of the Dead," when Gulnaz hears the news of her husband's accidental death, she freezes, asking herself if this event is the punishment for her little tricks and her cheating. Her rationalizations to herself are clearly not convincing: "No, oh no, God could not be that cruel. This could not be anything but an accident. There were witnesses: he slipped, fell down, and died. Anybody could fall this way and die" (22, p. 162).

Death Is Controlling, Punishing

In turn, death can be punishment and the agency of revenge. Controlling others by the threat of suicide appears in film, song, and painting. Scene after scene in *Harold and Maude* (23) presents an adolescent son surprising his mother by suiciding in the bathtub, closet, anywhere to get her attention. In Elton John's popular favorite of the 1970s, "Suicide Rag," a teenager is taken with the idea of the scandal he would cause by shocking everyone with suicide. He fantasizes himself making the headline news. In the next-to-last stanza, the motivation for these thoughts becomes apparent:

> *A rift in my family,*
> *I can't use the car*
> *I gotta be in by 10 o'clock*
> *Who do they think they are? (24)*

Feeling impotent and angry at his parents' restrictions leads to a series of fantasies of acts that would cause them shame and remorse.

A 10-year-old expresses the power he has by the gesture of suicide. "They'll be sorry" is also the theme of Fig. 2. Just in time, the parent apologizes and thus aborts the event. In another drawing (Fig. 3), the suicide is successfully avoided by the (caring) parents' chastisement and punishment. Any concern, apology, or attention including that of anger, even hate, is welcome. Only indifference is unacceptable.

Young lovers, too, manipulate with the rescue fantasy. In Gilbert and Sullivan's marvelous parody "Tit-Willow," Ko-Ko wins Katisha with his tale of a poor bird downing himself in the name of unrequited love. Lest one missed Ko-Ko's intent in the

FIGURE 2

FIGURE 3

telling of such a maudlin story, the focus is switched from the bird to that of Katisha and quite clearly spelled out:

> *And if you remain callous and obdurate, I*
> *Shall perish as he did, and you will know why,*
> *Though I probably shall not exclaim as I die,*
> *"O Willow titwillow, titwillow!" (25)*

Roy Lichtenstein's *Drowning Girl* presents the same threat in painting. About to be engulfed by waves, a young woman, eyes brimming with tears, righteously, makes her thoughts known. Cartoon fashion, the blurb reads: "I'd rather sink than call Brad for help" (26).

A sequence drawing by a youngster (Fig. 4) dramatizes again the vengeful anger inherent in a suicide threat wherein the explanation that "they'll be sorry" is made explicit. Once again, one's personal death, an extraordinary price in terms of self-punishment, is envisioned as an instrument of controlling others.

FIGURE 4

Contagion of Death

Can one "catch" dying? Is the idea of death too much to bear close witness? Both Figures 5 and 6 suggest resistance and fear on the part of the visitor to the dying. In a 16-year-old boy's drawing (Fig. 5), the son wants to talk to his mother from a distance. One might speculate that not coming closer for this final conversation, or the cavalier attitude on his part, allows for denial of sorts: If the last words are not spoken, the death cannot yet happen. But the boy's response—words, stance, and distance—suggest fear of contamination or contagion.

In a 12-year-old's drawing (Fig. 6), the young visitor's thoughts are made explicit through the caption. He sees himself in the casket at his own funeral if he shares the soda offered by his friend with leukemia. Both these drawings expose another truth: Visiting the dying is exposure to the sadness of the

FIGURE 5

FIGURE 6

26

situation. One will be tainted by grief, feelings of self-pity, and sorrow as one bears the loneliness of the eventual separation.

Thinking about the dead is painful. In an unpublished manuscript, young Dusty is able only to think about his dead friend a little at a time. Sometimes his sadness is so great he feels his stomach hurting. As he tries to make sense of his friend's accidental death, the progression of thoughts leads directly to those concerning his own future: "I don't see why Dusty had to die. . . . I don't want to die. I want to get to be a grown-up so I'm taller than my Dad and I can be a deep sea diver or a veterinarian and stay up late" (27).

In the Gerard Manley Hopkins poem "Spring and Fall to a Young Child," the scenario is an inocuous situation. A youngster, Margaret, muses on the dying leaves of autumn, on "goldengrove unleaving." Her sigh is the realization all living things must die, and in the final couplet, she makes the association to her own inevitable death: "It is the blight man was born for/It is Margaret you mourn for" (28, p. 89). As no man is an island (29), no witness to dying can remain insular, invulnerable to sadness, distress, or confrontation with thoughts of his or her own mortality. One is touched by being in contact with death.

Murderous Impulses

If we are "afraid" of death's visage, what better way of mastering the fear than aligning oneself with the power of death-giving. But the murderous impulse is not readily borne without self-judgment.

"The Day of the Robin" (9) is a short story recalling the incident of stoning a bird to death. Skipping school with a friend, two fourth graders happen upon a bird with a broken wing, fluttering feebly, still trying to fly: "I have forgotten whose idea it was first. I hope it was Oliver's. We decided the robin must be put out of it's misery; it must be killed." The actual execution, ironically precipitated by the boy's memory of a picture of St. Stephen, was to be carried out with a stone. But the bird did not die as instantly as anticipated: "Then we grew frightened . . . and we took more stones and threw them as hard as we could at the robin. . . . The stones fell one upon the other until the bird was covered except for its head . . . and still it was not dead." After a final smash, the boys stand silently for a long time, physically separated by the pile of stones between them, unable even to face one another. Their shame and regret erupts in tears: "No sound but the distant shouts of our classmates playing on the lawn. The sun shone brilliantly: nothing had changed in the world, but without a word and at the same moment, we both began to cry."

In Steinbeck's novel *The Red Pony,* little Jody, motivated by boredom, baits a rat trap with stale cheese, intending to set it where a dog would get his nose snapped. Another time, Jody kills and dismembers a bird. As in "The Day of the Robin," the guilt, shame, and remorse occur after the frenzy of the activity. Jody did not care what older people would say if they had seen him kill the bird; but in retrospect, he was ashamed because of their potential opinion: "He decided to forget the whole thing as quickly as he could, and never to mention it (30, p. 63).

Feelings of aggression find expression in daring adventure. Such a bold act transformed the boys in "The Day of the Robin." Crying together was not the only outlet for the boys who stoned the bird; the author was able to "mention" the deed by the very act of writing the story. Not so for Jody, who has no chance to share his guilty secret. No confessional. No chance to do penance or transcend his shame. Jody is saddled with the added burden of repressing his uncomfortable feelings.

Traditionally, societies have provided outlets for such impulses and fantasies through the grimmest of horror stories and fairy tales. An African lullaby, "Simba-Ba," or "Mama's Baby," translates: "Twist his neck and hit him on the head/Throw him in the ditch and he'll be dead." Similarly, the Western lullaby "Rock-a-bye-baby" outlines an unhappy accident. Sleeping peacefully in a cradle fastened high in a tree, a baby falls when a bough breaks. Motifs not only of unhappy endings but of cruelty are evident:

> *There was a little man, and he had a little gun*
> *And his bullets were made of lead, lead, lead.*

And he went to the brook and shot a little duck
Right in the middle of the head, head, head.

Clarence Darrow's confession that he never wanted to see anybody die but that there were a few obituary notices he has read with pleasure helps us feel less lonely with our fantasies of having wished certain people dead. Gilbert and Sullivan's Lord High Executioner receives much applause and knowing chuckles as he enumerates in great detail his little list of those who never would be missed (31). Children sing with gusto of their one and only counselor who died committing suicide; "She did it just to spite us/It really did delight us." The limericks and aphorisms were intended neither to frighten nor to evoke feelings of sorrow, guilt, or remorse. Quite the contrary. Humor, irony, and such gestures of scorn as sick humor allow for release, albeit temporary, of pent-up anxieties.

Murderous impulses can be safely embedded in fiction, fairy tales, and drama. Being human, by definition, admits to behaviors other than the saintly. But merely naming the devil, as in the tale of Rumplestiltskin—just acknowledging one's destructive impulses—is not enough. One must face again and again their unsettling existence. In *After the Fall,* Arthur Miller, goes further than acceptance. The knowing is not all: "The wish to kill is never killed, but with some gift of courage one may look into its face when it appears, and with a stroke of love—as to an idiot in the house—forgive it; again and again . . . forever" (32, p. 128).

Conclusion

Children and others seem to view death in multiple ways. Death happens to people, and the event itself arouses concerns for ongoing living of the survivors as well as for ongoing living of the deceased. Children's images seem fancifully occupied with where the dead go; but adults, too, seem anxious to transmit their own convictions of the place of residence of the deceased. For all, death arouses need for connectedness and continuation of relationship.

Death is also an instrument of feelings. Shame, remorse, guilt, and anger, though common enough emotions, can be overwhelming. Literature and the arts help make such anguish bearable. The arts, reflecting life, are arenas where contradictions can coexist, where neither the bright nor the dark must eradicate the other's existence. They provide a sense of comfort and kinship as they give voice to the unmentionable and most inner torments.

Death gives one power. Again, the art forms, story and painting, provide insight into how children and others use a death threat for revenge, for control of others, and for punishment of actions that are not acceptable.

Thus death in its actual and symbolic manifestations presents a panoply of human concerns and expressions that appear quite early in life. The child's concerns are society's concerns. A society's art forms lend to these concerns focus, explanation, ritual, and legitimacy. As a vehicle for expression, they allow us to prevail over pain, to transcend and partly end it by transforming it into "art."

References

1. Anthony, S. *The child's discovery of death.* New York: Harcourt, 1940.
2. Nagy, M. The child's view of death. In H. Feifel (Ed.), *The meaning of death.* New York: McGraw-Hill, 1959, pp. 79–98.
3. Coburn, J. *Anne and the sand dobbies.* New York: Seabury, 1964.
4. Lee, V. *The magic moth,* New York: Seabury, 1972.
5. Allen, W. *New Yorker,* January 20, 1973, pp. 32–33.
6. Dickinson, E. I never saw a moor. In Williams & Honige (Eds.), *The mentor book of major American poets.* New York: New American Library, 1962.
7. Cohen, B. *Thank you, Jackie Robinson.* New York: Lothrop, 1974.
8. Adler, B. You don't have to do homework in heaven. *Good Housekeeping,* March 1979, p. 46.
9. Bertman, S. *Death education, a primer for all ages.* Unpublished manuscript, Equinox Institute, Boston, Mass.
10. Lee, M. *The rock and the willow.* New York: Lothrop, 1963.
11. Gauguin, P. The spirit of the dead watching. In C. Estienne, *Gauguin.* Cleveland: Skira, 1953. (Painting)
12. Alcott, L. *Little women.* Boston: Little, Brown, 1968.

13. Smith, D. *A taste of blackberries.* New York: Crowell, 1973.
14. Thomas, D. And death shall have no dominion. *Collected poems of Dylan Thomas.* New York: New Directions, 1939.
15. Stolz, M. *By the highway home.* New York: Harper, 1971.
16. Lichtman, W. *Blew and the death of the mag.* Albion, Freestone, 1975.
17. Viorst, J. *The tenth good thing about Barney.* New York: Atheneum, 1971.
18. Lewis, C. S. *A grief observed.* New York: Seabury, 1963.
19. Grünewald, M. *Damnation of lovers.* Strasbourg: Cathedral Museum, 15th century. (Painting)
20. Hoffman, H. *Struwwelpeter.* New York: Warne, 1944.
21. Vogel, I. *My twin sister, Erika.* New York: Harper, 1976.
22. Kudret, C. Feast of the dead. In Adler & Stanford (Eds.), *We are but a moments sunlight.* New York: Pocket Books, 1976.
23. *Harold and Maude.* Los Angeles: Paramount, 1971. (Film)
24. John, E., *Honky chateau* "Think I'm gonna kill myself, suicide rag." Universal City: MCA, 1972. (Music)
25. Gilbert, W., & Sullivan, A. Willow, tit-willow. In *The Mikado.* London: Chappell, 1911, pp. 208-212. (Music)
26. Lichtenstein, R. *Drowning girl.* New York: Museum of Modern Art, 1970. (Painting)
27. Clardy, A. *Dusty was my friend.* Unpublished manuscript.
28. Hopkins, G. Spring and fall to a young child. Gardner & MacKenzie, (Eds.), *Poems of G. M. Hopkins.* New York: Oxford University Press, 1967, pp. 88-89.
29. Donne, J. Devotions. *The complete poetry and selected prose of John Donne and the complete poetry of William Blake.* New York: Random House, 1941.
30. Steinbeck, J. *The red pony.* New York: Viking, 1959.
31. Gilbert, W., & Sullivan, A. Lord High Executioner, In *The Mikado.* London: Chappell, 1911, pp. 267-270.
32. Miller, A. *After the Fall.* New York: Viking, 1964.

Request reprints from Sandra L. Bertman, Humanities in Medicine, University of Massachusetts Medical School, Worcester, MA.

THE PASTORAL COUNSELOR AND THE CHILD
ENCOUNTERING DEATH

EDGAR N. JACKSON

The world of the child is special. When people become adult, they seem to lose touch with the child who lurks within each of them as well as with the child each once was. This makes it difficult to understand children and communicate effectively with them. Young children live in a world where feelings supply most of the life experiences. It is a world that can be both lyrical and frightening, rich in poetic imagery and yet stark in its frightening realities. Trivial events can add delirious joy and excitement to life; yet comparable events can produce painful feelings of fear and abandonment.

It is in this context of a children's world that we have to explore the meaning of their encounters with death. It is a wonderful world of imagination where perceptions tend to create a different brand of reality (1). It is adventurous in the games that are played, where monsters are created at will, and where wonder comes alive in events that may be commonplace for those who have lived a little longer. A child may be defensive but seldom blasé. The child's world has boundaries that are drawn in closely and tightly. What is the impact on this small world of a large experience like the confronting of death? One does not ask this question apart from an interpretation of the powerful emotional drives of young children. Grief and loss stimulate painful emotions in the child, for they are aimed at the security system that is rooted in utter dependence on others (2). Feelings of abandonment are related to fears of death, for the young child cannot make it on his own (3).

This dependence is interrelated with the total emotional life of the child. The child is capable of great grief, but the source

33

of grief may be quite different from that of an adult. The adult knows space and time; the young child does not. Space and time are essential to a concept of death. So the young child obviously experiences acute grief without any concept of death. This may lead adults to fail to understand the intensity of the child's grief. Young children do not fear the death of others, for they cannot conceive it (1, 4-5). Their grief is bound up with their complete dependence for life support and with the fear of the loss of their security. With young children, even the people in their environment are secondary to their security. At early ages they are able to transfer the focus of feelings from one person to another without apparent trauma. Someone to play with, pay attention to, and communicate with a child as well as to meet physical and emotional needs becomes a surrogate who may fill the security needs in place of a parent. But what would be true in this regard for a two-year-old would not be the case for a four-year-old.

So, with young children, emotions are powerfully affected by feelings of insecurity that may be only tangentially related to space, time, and people. Death is not apt to be a part of the reality structure of a young child, but feelings related to separation, abandonment, fear of rejection, and apprehension about threats to security such as loud and violent sounding voices can be as traumatic as feelings about death would be for older children and adults.

The world of the child is unique because of the feelings with which the child furnishes that world. The feelings are so completely integrated into the life structure of the child that they cannot easily be isolated for study. Even the efforts of Jean Piaget, extensive and imaginative as they are, tend to be largely descriptive rather than philosophical in their end results.

LeBoyer (6) provides a meaningful interpretation of the initial stages of human attachment through his description of how the skin becomes the starting point for intense human interaction. Starting prenatally with the skin massage by the amniotic fluid, the body covering is sensitized by this process of gentling. At its best, in the absence of acute spasticity, the passage through the birth canal adds to the message process. Immediately after birth, the varied sensations of the prenatal state continue by placing the infant on the breast, where the rhythms of the heart, the warmth of the skin, and gentle massage can approximate the prenatal sensations. Wisely instituted, this procedure can become the basis for trust and positive organic responses to life outside the privileged climate of the uterus.

Instead of the positive experience of the type LeBoyer encourages, birth may have the opposite results when the newborn is whisked away and placed in a nursery with its unfamiliar bustle, harsh lights, strange noises, and the generalized feelings of separation and abandonment. The neonatal organism may be started in the direction of feeling rejected and distrusting those around. It may further be moved in the direction of active efforts at self-protection by the use of alternatives to love, the overt expressions of hostility that may show up in organic or inorganic behavior. Here we may have the starting point for the sickly, disturbed, or hostile child in the infant who uses the best alternatives available to gain some security and support in an outside world that appears to be largely unconcerned with the interests of the neonate.

Applying Knowledge of the Child's Development

Pastors or other counselors can probably measure their effectiveness by their degree of understanding of the developmental process that defines the emotional growth of the child. With the young child what one does is far more important than what one says. The young child experiences death as abandonment, and so the therapeutic intervention should be directed toward dispelling those feelings. How would that be done? Usually it is best done by applying large doses of tender love and care. This involves holding the child, cuddling and stroking the skin. Any talking should center on the timbre or emotional quality of the sounds, with soft and soothing sounds producing a gentling effect in as many dimensions of sensory response as possible. While it is important to understand where the child is in emotional development, it is even more important to do the things that the child can immediately integrate into basic emotional needs.

If we understand the term *young child* to be those aged from birth to about three, the next stage in development would come from about four to seven years. Here the elements of infancy are past and we have a human being who is using language to supplement a whole variety of other methods of exploration. Children at this age are apt to be curious, quite literal, and actively engaged in exploring verbally and otherwise. Although grouping children by age can be helpful in understanding the general characteristics of a child, it is always wise to keep in mind that each child is unique. Children differ in their rates of development, and they are shaped by the experiences of their lives (3, p. 58–59).

Adults often fail to realize how much they modify language by common usage. Children have not usually developed these refinements and so may show their confusion. If in response to the child's question, "Where has grandpa gone?" an effort is made to speak of a state of pure spirit sometimes referred to as heaven, the child is apt to question further: "Then why did they put his body in a hole in the groud?" When asked if she would like to go to the funeral home to see her grandmother's body for the last time, a young girl responded, "No, I don't want to see Grandma with her head cut off." In her literal use of language, a "body" was that portion of the anatomy from the neck down.

Children during this stage are not only literal but quite body oriented. They are interested in the physical functions and characteristics of their own bodies and the bodies of other people as well. The questions they ask about death are apt to be oriented to this body interest. They may ask questions such as How do you eat when you are dead? or How do you go to the bathroom when you are dead? For them, such questions are completely logical, for they are trying to discover the difference between being dead and alive. For them, it is difficult to know what is lost in the process of dying.

It becomes quite clear for the counselor, then, that the use of abstract language in responding to such direct seeking for information would be self-defeating and possibly damaging. To talk about "going to be with Jesus" may well sound like an evasion to the child. The child needs simple and accurate answers to frame the developing concept of death and its meaning.

I mentioned the damaging answer. Though often given with good intentions, a child's perspective may be so literal that, in acting on it, injury may occur. A four-year-old was brought to a child guidance clinic because of what appeared to be repeated suicidal acts. Exploration of the behavior showed it was quite logical to the child. Her dog had been killed by a car. She was told that her puppy had gone to dog heaven and that if she would be a good girl she would go there too. From the perspective of her grief, the logical answer was to run in front of a car. Several drivers suffered traumatic experiences in trying to avoid hitting the child. How much better it would have been for everyone if the parents had used the child's encounter with death as an educational opportunity. They could as easily have said, "What a sad thing that your puppy had not learned to stay out of the road. I hope this teaches you never to run out into the road without first making sure that there are no cars coming from either direction."

Every death experience for a child can be a learning opportunity. Death is so much a part of the life of a child that it is imperative that it be dealt with in positive ways. Death is the central event of many holidays, for instance, the turkey at Thanksgiving, the hamburger at the picnic, and the fish fry after the day at the brook. If death can be interpreted as a contribution to life, a more positive perspective can be maintained, and the grief can then be understood for what it is—a personal loss. Not all death is bad. It is the death we have difficulty coping with that is painful. So we do not wisely rail against death. Rather, we learn to develop skills in managing the distress that comes with acute personal loss. These skills can begin to develop early in life with proper guidance.

The Pastoral Counselor's Role

The pastor needs to be especially on guard against the unwise use of complex abstractions with younger children. In talking with a young child, it is usually fruitful to listen and ask open-ended questions until it is quite clear what the child is thinking and feeling. Otherwise there may be wasted answers to questions that do not exist. Sometimes the questions a child asks may entrap the person who fails to understand where the line of questioning is going.

Let us take two lines of questioning. The minister is visiting a sick relative, and seven-year-old Johnny asks the pastor, "Can God do anything?" The pastor, who feels called upon to defend God, responds, "Oh, yes, God is all powerful; God can do anything if he wants to." Johnny responds, "I'm glad. Then God can keep my uncle from dying. He's my favorite uncle. We do lots of things together." When the uncle dies, Johnny is left with a dilemma. Either God did not want to save the uncle or really did not care and let Johnny down, or God was not as powerful as he was supposed to be.

There could be another and more useful response to the same question, "Can God do anything?" The pastor could use an open-ended question to find out more of what Johnny wants to know. She or he could say, "Tell me, Johnny, just how do you mean that?" "Well, Uncle Paul is very sick. He might die. I don't want him to die. Could God keep him from dying?" The pastor responds, "I see what you mean. God has great power. It shows all about us in creation. When God made the universe it could only be held together by the laws of creation. Our bodies have laws also. If you fall off the roof, you could be hurt. If you violate the laws of health you can be hurt. The power of God is shown through the laws of the universe he has created. So you would not expect God to violate his own laws, would you?" This line of response would be developed to make Johnny responsible for his own health and welfare. It would affirm the power of God without expecting God to violate his own nature. It would make it easier at some future time for Johnny to learn to cooperate with God's laws rather than violate them. As an authority figure with important teaching functions, the pastor can be important as a helper for children who are trying to learn how to cope with both life and death.

When children become a bit older—8 to 11—their perspectives change. Time and space are more clearly defined, for them and the people who are a part of their lives are more numerous.

Interests change, and this affects their perceptions of death. Instead of a physical interest in death there develops a social concern about death and its implications for life. Because the interrelations of life have become more significant, the impact of death on human relations tends to become more important (4).

This change in relation will show itself in behavior, verbal and otherwise. Instead of curiosity about the physical qualities of death, there will be a more active concern about what happens to people who encounter death. The growing edge of awareness will show itself in the questions asked. The child will be more apt to inquire about what happens to the social fabric of life when death is encountered: "Who will take care of the Johnson children now?" or "Will Jane and Ted have to move away now that their father is dead?"

In contrast to the four- to seven-year-old with a primary interest in the physical meaning of death, the responses will be quite different. Where the four- to seven-year-old needs simple and direct answers to simple questions of information, the more socially interested youngster needs reassurance and an understanding of social processes. The 8- to 11-year-old is apt to bring his own concern about death into the picture. Some of his questions may be exploring the consequences of death for his own life.

The effort to make some sense out of death may show up in questions that may seem unacceptable. When a favorite grandfather died and a feeble great-grandmother lived on, an eight-year-old asked, "Why did Grandpa die and Great-grandma is still alive?" The logic of the question was clear for the eight-year-old even though the child was warned not to talk like that when the great-grandmother could hear. Everyone seemed embarrassed when the same child went to her grandmother and asked, "When are you going to die?" When trying to frame a socially acceptable idea of the relation of life and death, such questions are to be expected. The effort to make sense out of a baffling mystery should be encouraged because the sooner some sense is made, the better for those who will encounter the mystery repeatedly.

Underlying many questions emerging from this age group are security issues. A growing awareness of social dependency carries with it a concern for personal security. When a child asks, "Who will take care of Fred now that his parents were killed?" the implication quite clearly is "Who will take care of me if my parents are killed in an accident?" While it would be unwise to give glib and superficial reassurance, it is essential that the child have a clearer understanding of the broader fabric of family and community life. The reassurance should be honest but optimistic. Parents might say, "I see what you mean, but we expect to be around for a long time; and even if we might not be, there are other people who love you and would take care of you."

I remember an 11-year-old who was being treated at the psychiatric clinic for children that I headed. His father died quite rapidly of a virulent neoplastic involvement. The child had been building a sailboat with his father. When I visited the family, William was not present. When I asked about him, I was told he was out in the garage. So I went out and found him sitting glumly, looking at the unfinished sailboat. When we talked about his feelings it was obvious that he took the death very personally at the point of unfinished business, made specific by the incomplete sailboat. He resented his father's death and felt cheated. It was out of this set of feelings that we began to build a larger view of life and its vagaries. We worked out some plans for finishing the boat, for that was where he was encountering his grief most specifically. We ended our talk with the clarified idea that his father did not die on purpose to create a problem, but that some times in life we have to adjust our programs and plans. The important idea is to understand and adapt to change rather than feeling defeated and bitter. William went back into the house with me and joined the rest of the group.

When we consider the orientation and needs of the adolescent or preadolescent, we are moving into quite different territory. The skill in using language and other abstractions has been developed to the point at which it can be a useful resource. At the same time, the intensity of feelings makes it possible for grief to be a powerful force in life.

Let us look first at the preadolescent. The age boundaries here are not clearly set, for there are considerable variations in how psychophysical development takes place. But usually preadolescence means 11- to 13-year-olds, or those in the junior high level of education. Clinical experience makes it quite clear that this age is a time of recapitulation and consolidation of past experience. It seems that the experiences of the first years of life are restated in a different context. If there has been security and healthy development from birth to three, the years of infancy, there is apt to be a secure and untroubled movement into a larger social orientation of life. If, however, the early years have been fraught with uncertainty and conflict this is apt to be acted out in a larger circle of relationships with hostility and conflict with authority figures. This tends to lay the foundation for emerging ego development in maladaptive forms of social adjustment. Instead of testing the boundaries of social behavior to learn how to conform, there is apt to be an assault on the boundaries to act out hostility. May, in his book *The Meaning of Anxiety* (7), points out the relationship between antisocial behavior and the experience of death or its emotional equivalent early in life.

The preadolescent tends to act out deep feelings in behavior. If the feelings are satisfying, the behavior will tend to be pleasant, socially cooperative, and personally rewarding. If the feelings grow from frustration and resentment, the behavior may be hostile, destructive, and further injuring of the self-esteem, which is already damaged. The encounter with death may show up in extremes of behavior, from, on the one hand, actions unrelated to the event, to, on the other hand, overcompensation in acting out.

Therapeutic intervention will involve talking out the feelings fully, and the ability to talk about feelings may be fully realized at this age. Also, ceremonial acting out will be meaningful, for it usually combines large-muscle activity with conceptualization and abstract language. Much time may be spent in talking about the meaning of life and death with an intensely personal focus. Preadolescents may enter into this talk with difficulty, however, especially with adults. Here, the sharing of thoughts and feelings with a peer group would be more characteristic. This can be a time of emerging idealism, when the heroic and symbolic are enhanced by an active imagination.

The preadolescent is in a time of transition from the dependency of childhood to the more venturesome thinking and acting of adolescence. The combination of the dependent and the independent in thinking and feeling may thus be manifest in ways that, though they appear incongruous, are congruent with the age and state of personal development. Overidentification may show itself in forms of grief that are acted out toward popular figures like Elvis Presley, whose untimely death had a major impact on this age group.

The next stage, adolescence, brings preadolescent behavior to its fuller expression. In positive form it may be life commitment wherein teen-agers decide on the goals for life. Here the heroic may be a statement of faith in the value of life and a desire to make the most of it. A negative attitude toward life may be expressed in the symbolic self-destruction of drug use and the toying with life in such games as Russian roulette and playing chicken with automobiles, where life is risked in acts of bravado. Yet it seems that the underlying statement is one of fear and insecurity. It is as if the game players were saying, "I am not afraid of death, for I make a plaything out of it"; yet the real meaning of their negative behavior may be: "I am so afraid of death that I may be able to control my fear if I reduce my thinking of death to the level of game playing."

The pastoral counselor with teen-agers may find that the emotional commitment is strong and oriented toward the self. Adolescents are apt to think that they are the discoverers of deep and powerful feelings and that no one has ever loved as they love. As love is the other side of the coin of grief, they are highly vulnerable. Because at their stage of development they are self-centered, their love is primarily for themselves and their own feelings, however, and for others only in a secondary way. Thus, they can be doubly distressed. It is a time when they are trying to learn the complicated art of object love, and the learning process is as painful as it is experimental. Though they may shift the focus of love quickly from one person to another, the object tends to be the self. Being in love with love, as in the case of "puppy love," both the idealism and the focus on self enhance the grief when the relationship is broken. Emotional injury at this point may last a life time unless there is wise and skillful intervention. Self-destructive behavior is quite common as a mode of resolving grief among teen-agers.

Cheryl was 16 and attending the junior prom at the time her father died of a heart attack in a motel in a distant city. When she received the news of his death the next day, she was overwhelmed with guilt and grief. That she was having the most wonderful time of her life at the very time her father was dying a lonely death made her experience even more poignant. She locked herself in her room, would speak to no one, and at first ate no food. On the second day of her self-imposed imprisonment, she opened the door to take a tray left for her. On the day of the funeral she was still in her room. When the pastor was informed of her behavior, he came to the house and, through the door, identified himself. He said, "Cheryl, I want to talk with you." After a few moments of silence he heard the key turn in the lock, and he entered the room. He explained the function of the funeral as a tribute to a life that has been lived. He told Cheryl he assumed that she would want to use this opportunity to show her love for her father. She cried, and he accepted her feelings of guilt and grief. She said that no one could feel the way she did, and the pastor affirmed the uniqueness of each person's feelings. After an hour of deep sharing, Cheryl walked out of her room and was reunited with other members of her family. Her behavior was typical of the adolescent in its dramatic action, its self-centered attitude toward a life crisis, and its willingness to respond to an authority figure who was outside of the immediate family.

Pastors have some advantages as counselors because of their easy availability; their in-depth knowledge of families and family members, their strengths and weaknesses; and their ability to move toward people in crises—a privilege not usually granted to any other counselors.

The skills that pastors have acquired as counselors are fortified by the fact that they are able to add a cosmic dimension to the counseling process. They are not afraid to talk about the spiritual aspects of life and the value systems that make it possible for a person to develop inner strength essential to adequate coping skill. Pastors know the importance of attitudes and the place they play in inner stability. Some things are assumed in the pastor's role, so they do not even need to be talked about. Although this may at some point create hazards, it is usually a useful resource.

Counselors of children and the clergy especially have an opportunity to resolve problems that might otherwise plague life for decades. To be effective, they must look at the problem from the child's point of view. This means that they must be clear about the developmental stage of the child so that they are working effectively toward the child's real needs. Also it is important for them to have a working knowledge of the family and social structure within which the child lives and develops feelings. There must be a working knowledge of how others in the family respond to crises and what the emotional learning experience of the child has been.

Some Guidelines for Counseling Children

There are several more specific guidelines for counseling children in the home and family context. These might be shared with other adults so that counselors and family are not working at cross-purposes.

First, children have a right to expect honest answers to their questions. Gorer (8) points out in his study that many adults ignore the questions asked with the implication that the questions are improper or inappropiate. The rest admit that they give answers that they do not believe but cannot think of anything else to say. This is poor treatment of the growing edge of a child's interest in an important subject such as death. Children are so sensitive to emotional content in communication that the built-in lie detector immediately goes to work. Children may lose confidence in the adults to whom their queries are directed. They also are denied the basic information they need for developing a working understanding of life crises. Invariably they will go elsewhere for answers and often find those that are inadequate and threatening. The breakdown in communication also tends to be projected into the future with the feeling that, if there are important answers to be sought, they cannot be found with certain adults, who are obviously threatened.

Second, children have a right to be understood in their own stages of development. Adults tend to be preoccupied with their own thoughts and feelings. It is so important to sharpen up the communication by asking questions like "How do you mean? or Let me be sure I understand; could you be more specific? Then the communication will not break down.

Third, counselors should try to avoid communicating anxiety. When an adult overanswers or underanswers, the anxiety shows through. When a child is trying to grow in understanding, information is important, not disturbing emotion. If anxiety is pervasive the emotion may outweigh the information, and then the emotion may be carried along for a long time. The emotion attached to childhood events continue to plague many adults long after the original problem has been resolved. Children are largely defenseless against the strong emotions of the adults around them, so special care should be taken not to inundate a child. If some adults are disturbed, it then becomes important for other adults to step in and cope with the child's queries with well-balanced emotions.

Fourth, children benefit from large-muscle activity that is related to the crisis. Here the established forms of acting out are beneficial. A child does not have to understand all of the ramifications of a rite, ritual, or ceremony to participate at the level of emotional need. A little girl does not need to know all about human sexuality to be a flowergirl at a wedding. Nor does a child have to understand all about death to participate in a funeral. Ceremonies are made to order for children, for they can participate at their level of comprehension. Adults often err in trying to protect children from funerals. They tend to project their more adult understanding. As a general rule, a child should not be excluded from important family activities, and this would include funerals. If a child does not want to attend, it is already a sign that undue anxiety has been created, and that problem should be faced. If it is not, the anxiety could be cumulative, and the child could be denied the most effective and easily accessible therapeutic intervention that the community provides. Yet children should never be forced to attend or to do things that cause them discomfort. If left alone to do their own exploring, they will find answers to their questions within the range of their own thoughts and feelings.

Fifth, counselors need to remember that children have the capacity for stronger feelings of separation and abandonment than from an understanding of the meaning of death. The growing edge of the child's consciousness is constantly providing opportunities for exploring the nature and qualities of the death experience. It is possible to build a discriminating attitude that knows there are different forms of death. This discrimination makes it possible to enjoy a turkey at Thanksgiving without feeling guilt and at the same time to learn to protect life and health by wise avoidance of the things that could injure life.

Sixth, counselors should remember that every death encounter is an educational opportunity. Wisely managed, it can provide the long-term security to life. Unwisely managed, it can project anxiety and unwise behavior into the future so that it cumulatively impairs life. Pastoral counselors, through counseling, ceremonial activity, and an educational program, are able to provide resources for growth into a mature and discriminative attitude toward life and death.

Conclusion

In times of crisis when emotions run strong, the wise counselor who knows the family and its relationships but is not bound up with its emotions can be a primary therapeutic resource. With children, the counseling opportunity is especially advantageous, for if the early experiences can be handled well, a pattern is set for the wise management of ensuing life events.

The special needs and special opportunities related to counseling children warrant careful study. The methods and the techniques are so different that they are learned only by special efforts. But the benefits in the lives of the children served may well add blessings to life for a whole lifetime.

References

1. Piaget, J. *The child's conception of the world* (C. K. Ogden, Ed.). Totowa, N.J.: Littlefield, Adams, 1965.
2. Bowlby, J. Separation anxiety. *International Journal of Psychoanalysis,* 1960, *41,* 89–113.

3. Rochlin, G. The dread of abandonment: A contribution to the etiology of the loss complex and to depression. In *The psychoanalytic study of the child.* New York: International Universities, 1961, *16,* 451–470.
4. Jackson, E. *Telling a child about death.* New York: Hawthorn, 1965.
5. Jackson, E. *The many faces of grief.* Nashville: Abingdon, 1972.
6. LeBoyer, F. *Birth without violence.* New York: Knopf, 1976.
7. May, R. *The meaning of anxiety.* New York: Ronald, 1950.
8. Gorer, G. *Death, Grief and Mourning.* New York Doubleday, 1965.

Request reprints from Edgar N. Jackson, Washington Road, Corinth, Vermont 05039.

∞∞

HELPING WITH DEATH EDUCATION

∞∞

CHARLES A. CORR

An effective educational program must in part attempt to correct imbalances in our individual and social perceptions of death. Some counterbalances to these perceptions that weigh on the side of a new and more desirable equilibrium are relevant to the aims of this chapter. In the first place, I do not set out here to create new specialists. True expertise is not to be slighted. But my goal is in the main to provide guidelines for ordinary folk who want to be more helpful to children. Second, because education about death and dying in the best sense is properly education about life and living, I am really assisting people to recapture and implement perspectives on life that for many have somehow gone slightly out of focus. Third, this achievement is not beyond the capacities of most people. In general, they will need an opportunity and some direction for examining their own perceptions of death, a certain amount of information, an appreciation of typical concerns of children, a chance to benefit from the viewpoints of others, and practice in elementary interactions skills. Many people with a little time, energy, motivation, and some resources may be able to prepare themselves for this work. Most will benefit from a bit more organized or formal assistance.

The principal divisions of this chapter explore guidelines, preparation, and resources for helping with death education. The first of these subdivisions considers opportunities, responsibilities, and goals for death education with children; the second looks at formal and informal contexts in which to prepare helpers; and the third outlines different types of resources that are available for use by helpers. In addition to its relevance here, this last part of the chapter also lays a foundation for the

section, "Resources," which offers annotated descriptions of
books for adults and for children, and of audiovisual resources
that might be used in helping children. I close with a short
caution about what is, or should be, involved in efforts at
helping the helpers.

Guidelines for Helping

Opportunities

Just as death is a natural part of life, opportunities for
education about death arise in the midst of living. They can be
of many sorts. Some are planned, formal courses of instruction,
but often the most significant are unanticipated, informal occasions that might arise from an encounter with a dead animal on
a hike, a timid question that seems suddenly to come from
nowhere, or the sharing of a child's anxieties at bedtime. Some
of these opportunities center on a request for information;
others seek emotional support; and still others require no more
than a chance for the child to express a concern or explore an
idea. For adults, "death education" is a phrase with many
ramifications, encompassing what we understand as didactic
teaching as well as guiding of experiences, discussion of ideas,
offering of sympathy, and inculcation of values. Because death
education has such broad significance and its occasions are so
widespread, few adults can expect to avoid it altogether. Here
four of the most common types of opportunities for death
education are identified as a way of sensitizing readers to
possibilities and widening the scope of their vision in at least a
preliminary way.

When the phrase "death education" is first mentioned,
perhaps the most likely model to come to mind is a formal
course on death and dying. Such courses are now widespread in
North American high schools, colleges, and universities (1). The
very rapidity of their proliferation since the publication in 1959
of Feifel's pioneering text *The Meaning of Death* (2), and
especially during the 1970s, demonstrates the great interest that
there is in this subject, particularly within the upper years of

ied in such directives, but (as here) this truth is usually
iculated precisely and thus may discourage good workers
they even begin. This underlying truth is that all relation-
are at least two-sided. Hence, the outlook of the adult
is always an operative factor in the relationship. It is
larly important to recognize this when the relationship
ns death, a topic that touches each of us deeply and in
le ways. To believe otherwise is to neglect omnipresent
ns for one's own mortality. One cannot expect to operate
a wholly neutral or disengaged stance when interacting
hildren about death.

is equally true, however, that one cannot operate from a
ed or perfected stance. This is the misstatement or over-
eration in the way in which such advice is typically given
ceived. No one ever comes to terms with death within this
n such a final way that there is nothing left to do. Living
s offers some potential for advancing and deepening one's
ciation of the significance of death. That is the implication
astenbaum's tongue-in-cheek title "We Covered Death
y" (8). Finality is not an achievable goal in dealing with
. What is essential is initiating a process of reflection and
iscovery, not finishing it.

n addition to preparing in an ongoing way in this first
, helpers also need to acquaint themselves with relevant
ent in the field of death, dying, and bereavement. Over the
20 years, the literature and other resources in this field
grown tremendously (3). Few need or will be able to
er the field as a whole, or even the broad subarea of
ren and death. But, again, one can make a beginning, and
improvement in available resources of all sorts is encourag-
In this regard, the adjective "relevant" has two sorts of
ications. First, general knowledge of some topics such as the
rical-cultural situation of children and death in our society,
development of death-related thoughts and feelings during
dhood, and the impact of environment and life experiences,
ecessary in some measure for all adults who seek to interact
children. Such knowledge is available (e.g., 9). Second,
er more specific topics are relevant especially for particular
ations, for instance, an understanding of bereavement patterns

our educational system. Courses of this sort are sometimes taught by a single instructor or from the standpoint of a particular profession or academic discipline. They may have greater richness, however, when conceived as interdisciplinary experiences or when team-taught by people from complementary backgrounds. The diversity of such courses may bewilder those who approach this field for the first time. Nevertheless, a substantial body of literature that describes such courses has become available, and annotated descriptions of that literature in a recent resource guide (3) have greatly facilitated access. Also helpful are an outline of a model syllabus for a comprehensive death and dying course at the college level (4) and discussion of goals and strategies for death education (5–7).

Another manifestation of death education within standard academic settings has occurred in the form of units or aspects of other courses offered within traditional disciplines or subject areas. Thus, one might find a unit on death and dying within a health education course; discussion of biologic aspects of death in a science curriculum; exploration of funeral costs as an example of economic and consumer dynamics; attention to a death-related storybook, novel, or nonfictional work in a section on reading or literature; consideration of conceptual and ethical issues related to definition of death, suicide, or euthanasia in a contemporary issues or honors seminar; or research on epitaphs and burial customs in a social science class. Integration of death education in these ways into the broader curriculum does not necessarily dilute or fragment its integrity. Rather, it follows the principle that topics related to death are to be found throughout the spectrum of living. Also, brief exposures to death-related topics may be less threatening—particularly for younger students—and these exposures may prepare the way for fuller and more explicit treatment at a later level. Finally, while cumbersome formal procedures are often required to gain approval for a full-scale course on death and dying, that may not be the case for less ambitious curricular initiatives or for the implementation of discretionary options within an existing curricular program.

Although programs of formal instruction like these, or variations such as church discussion groups, are valuable in themselves, they do not exhaust opportunities for helping with death education. Education is not confined to the limited time frames of the classroom; and events in life that impinge on the community, the home, the school, or the individual child can have power and potential far exceeding traditional forms of pedagogy. Such events can inspire at least two additional forms of death education. The first has been called "the teachable moment." This is an opportunity created by an event that stimulates cognitive inquiry in a relatively nonthreatening way. It might involve a child who finds a small dead animal in the woods and comes home to ask about the experience, the death in a school of a plant or animal for whom no particular attachment has developed, or a report concerning a public figure, such as a president or some other prominent person whose status is widely recognized yet who is distant. Some of these opportunities may be anticipated, though most will simply arise in the normal course of events without prior warning. Some can be worked into school, home, or other interactions as real-life examples of ongoing discussions. Others inspire such curiosity or have such significance for learning that they warrant interrupting whatever else is going on. Cases of this last sort can be so insistent that adults are rightly said to fail in their duties to children if they gloss over them or refuse to respond appropriately.

A second form of the insistent death-related life event is that which is emotionally disturbing to the child (and perhaps also to the adults) whom it touches. One might call this "a nurturing moment." I am thinking here of occasions when normal people are upset in such a way that they need an opportunity to vent and share feelings and to gain support from familiar people around them. The death of a playmate or peer in school, of a friend in the neighborhood, or a relative or family member can excite strong emotions in a child. Parents and other adults (who may themselves be grieving) must appreciate the child's need for security and support in such moments and must be particularly sensitive so as not to intensify anxiety, confusion, or isolation through word or deed. In these contexts, those who send a child away or who urge others not to talk to the child about the death must learn that this does not erase the reality with which he or she must deal. In fact, such behavior only withdraws the

assistance of a caring community preci... needed. The school that suspends class... student at least recognizes that sometime... business as usual when death intrude... extension of that negative point to com... we also have a positive duty to help c... unfortunate events. We must, in other w... death as an opportunity for growth in c... is to fall back, and death can be a very... learning how to deal constructively with... We neglect that only at the risk of failing... when they most need us.

Responsibilities

Adults who seek to take up opportun... described above should first realize what... endeavor. Four sorts of responsibilities m... incumbent on those who intend or expect t... some kind of death education with childre... description really applies to all of us becau... anything to do with children can really av... ment indefinitely.) The first of these respon... *tion.* We are more likely to be successful an... with interactions that we have anticipated... measure and with those to which we have... thought. Preparation may not guarantee succ... call for a formal or explicit process in... experiences or native endowments already... But for most people in our society it is a... necessary prerequisite. Preparation for helping... tion is mainly of two sorts: (1) initiating reflec... thoughts and feelings about death and (2) a... content in the field of death, dying, and bereav...

It is often said to parents and member... professions that they should not undertake in... to death with children, patients, or other vulne... they have first come to terms with their ow... tudes, and needs in this area. There is an...

for dealing with a child who has experienced a death in the family or some insight into coping techniques for helping a child with a long-term terminal illness.*

In this book, we have attempted to provide a broad and helpful base from which to begin. We do not, however, subscribe to the overenthusiastic blurb that appeared on one earlier book for teachers, claiming that "with no special training, you can teach death education as easily as you teach the basics" (10). (Which educators would find that to be a responsible claim in their own primary fields?) Instead, we urge as full and as rich as exploitation of our subject as may be possible before beginning this task—and continuing thereafter—and I try to show in this chapter how additional self-study and formal preparation might be undertaken.

The second responsibility for helpers is to respond to real needs in children. This may seem obvious, but all too often intergenerational dialogue is hampered when adults do not make a sincere and effective effort to identify and to satisfy the real concerns that are animating children. John Dewey said somewhere that there must be something wrong with schools that bore pupils instead of capitalizing on their native curiosity. Much the same is true of a society that inhibits rather than encourages constructive death education. Responses that do not engage with real needs only frustrate children and discourage them from coming back to such sources in the future. We can become effective responders only by improving our awareness of developmental and environmental factors that relate to childhood and death and by listening in an active way to the concerns of each particular child. Knowledge about developmental and environmental factors in children's death concerns provides a broad framework for interactions with children,† although it never substitutes for careful attention to an individual child. In the general field of death and dying; in programs like hospice, which care for dying people and their families; and in interactions involving children, almost nothing is more important than *active listening*.

---

*These subjects are dealt with more fully in H. Wass and C. A. Corr (eds.), *Childhood and death*, Hemisphere, in press.

†The most recent presentation of such knowledge can be found in ibid., chaps. 1 and 2, and in the following chapter.

Following determination of the real needs of an individual child, the third responsibility for helpers is to communicate effectively. Once adults have heard the child fully and accurately, they must then insure that the child hears them in a similar way. This reception of messages needs to take place at four primary levels: cognitive, affective, behavioral, and valuational. Above all, from a cognitive, or intellectual, standpoint adults must insure that what they say is true. It need not be the whole of the truth as they know it, and it must never be delivered in a thoughtless or brutal fashion. But to be effective communicators, adults must believe in what they say to children. No adult is infallible, and we would probably be better off to acknowledge more often that we do not have an answer or that we have made a mistake. Still, messages that go out to children should not knowingly be based on misinformation, deception, and lies, or be clouded with irrelevant information. Examples of such faulty communications are all too easy to find. Adults who translate death into the language of sleep, who rush out to buy a new guppy to replace a dead fish before their child comes home to find it gone, who hide a death by pretending that the person has moved far away, who claim that someone died because God loved that person and wanted to have her with Him, or who simply give a complex spiritual or theological answer to a simple concrete or biologic question—all are guilty of this sort of faulty communicaton.

At the affective level, one needs to permit children to vent strong feelings and to bring anxiety and guilt out into the open where they can be seen in proper perspective and dealt with accordingly. For this, we need to keep in mind that truth, no matter how bad it is, is almost always less frightening than the demons that will be conjured up in our own psyches. Strong feelings can themselves become a source of trauma when they are merely suppressed and not properly dealt with. Guilt is often unfounded or dependent on unreliable, magical thinking. Moreover, even where truth does not dissipate the underlying reality, sharing a truth can mitigate its emotional overlay. A private hell feeds on itself and increases, whereas a shared anxiety often decreases.

This process is not one-sided; adults can often provide

support merely by sharing their own feelings of sadness, loss, and uncertainty. Even the act of gathering a child into one's lap to offer an explanation that may not be fully understood shows concern and demonstrates that the child need not continue to struggle alone. And every teacher or counselor knows that constituting a group of peers to talk out a problem creates a network of support in which children themselves can be the most effective helpers of their classmates. Adults often hesitate in these tasks because they assume that if they begin such work they will have to have "answers" or appropriate responses for anything that may arise. This is shortsighted because it fails to perceive that children are often their own best helpers and that it is usually quite productive merely to show that we care, are sincere, and are willing to join a common endeavor to resolve the problem.

Within the behavioral arena, adults need to recall that many of the most significant lessons they themselves learned come through bodily behavior and not just words. Children can conclude that death is an undesirable or disreputable topic when adults neglect it or shun it systematically. Worse yet, young people can be taught to misunderstand their own needs as whole persons and members of a community when they are surrounded by adults who take no notice of a death and who refuse to take part in funeral practices. Miseducation of this sort ought to be rejected; instead, we should follow the guidance of Jackson, who has long advocated the value of acting out strong feelings, of using ceremonial ritual to confirm the solidarity and continuity of life, and of permitting children to share in adult experiences (11, 12). A simple illustration of Jackson's viewpoint might be seen in the case of a small child who is permitted to bury a pet fish or turtle that has died and to emulate an adult funeral service. But this advice applies not only after a death. One college student invited several young neighborhood children to help with her "homework" for the university. The help involved no more than visiting a cemetery with her and discussing their reactions. Because the task was presented in a positive and nonthreatening manner, the children were eager to cooperate; and they benefited in many ways from an experience they might otherwise not have had. On-site visits to a funeral home, a mausoleum or crematory, a hospice, or other death-related institutions could have similar results.

A final realm for effective communication is that of values. Because adults are sometimes unclear about their own values in relation to death or are unsure of appropriate ways to impart values, they often hold back from direct engagement with children in this dimension. The false assumption is that fundamental values can be kept apart from everyday interactions with life and death. In fact, basic attitudes and values appear in all of our conduct toward death, even in whether or not we admit that topic into our thoughts and deeds. Thus, it is not only church groups who can engage in the teaching of beliefs concerning death. Parents can impart the values that they prize, and even the public schools can teach about beliefs that bear on the significance of death. The main point is to acknowledge the importance of helping children to acquire a value framework that takes death into account. To help children acquire such a framework, adults must avoid conveying values about which they have no real conviction. Thus, religious stories are often misused as handy "explanations" by adults who have not thought out their own positions. In contast, helpers who are secure in their own values will be able to provide children the freedom and the encouragement they need to learn to cope with death. One cannot "protect" young people from death-related encounters and explorations throughout their childhood years and still expect them to emerge as adults who are adequately equipped to cope with life.

The fourth responsibility that falls on helpers is cooperation. Actually, this responsibility emerges from what has gone before. Thoughts, feelings, behaviors, and values—the salient aspects of what we might broadly term *encounters with death*—will arise throughout life. They cannot be restricted to a specific time or context. One cannot expect that death need only be mentioned in Sunday school or that it can be encapsulated in a particular course or that an "expert" in the field will always be available and appropriate. No one has an exclusive corner on wisdom about death. Children often learn more from their own private experiences and from their peers than they do from adults, but they draw most effectively on those adults with whom they feel close and comfortable, regardless of official labels or roles. We can anticipate the best results when children and their peers are allowed to work together in an ongoing process of death education with parents, teachers, counselors, the clergy, care givers, and all of the other relevant adults and institutions in our society. Our effort in this book is to stimulate such constructive cooperation, to show that it is a feasible project, and to provide both guidelines and resources for its implementation.

Goals

Knott (7) has suggested that death education of all sorts may be understood as involving a triad of overlapping concerns: information sharing, values clarification, and coping behaviors. I think Knott is correct both in identifying these three as basic areas of concern and in noting that they usually interweave in practice. All death education involves a process of sharing information, an attempt to identify values that underlie feelings and actions, and an effort to develop behaviors to cope with the ways in which death impinges on life. A particular program may emphasize one or another of these focuses, but all will be present in some degree, for the implications of death run both deep and broad.

If we apply Knott's three concerns to helping children and set this in the light of our preceding analysis of adult responsibilities, we can restate what has been said in the form of goals for helpers. Perhaps the most fundamental thing that children—and all the rest of us—need to do is to find a way to cope with whatever life presents. Such presentations are of two sorts: those arising from within us, from our own inner needs, and those coming from outside, from encounters with the world. For example, the former might involve a need to be reassured of our own security against a possible threat of loss or separation; the latter might require us to deal with a puzzling or frightening event in the course of our daily affairs. The most basic task for a sound program of death education is to assist children to find effective ways of satisfying such needs—at least insofar as they relate to death. Whatever we have to offer by way of information, feelings, or values will all go for naught if it does not result in or cannot be related to constructive coping.

In fact, however, when we set that goal clearly before us, everything else then falls into place. Functional coping is fostered, initially, by allowing a child to release, share, or explore strong feelings about death. Second, functional coping depends on the acquisition of reliable information and the gaining of relevant experiences. Third, it depends on the testing of our ideas and the exchange of viewpoints or interpretations with others. Fourth, it leads to the identification and the formation of values that can subsequently serve as principles to guide further decisions and actions. All of these aspects, in other words, feed back into and improve our ongoing coping with living.

Another way to view death education has been suggested by the French cultural historian Philippe Ariès (13). Looking back on a time when death was a prominent and recognized feature of life, Ariès offered the following observation:

> Men of that period were profoundly and rapidly socialized. The family did not intervene to delay the socialization of the child. Moreover, socialization did not separate man from nature, with which he could not interfere short of a miracle. (p. 28)

All children undergo a process of socialization as they grow into adulthood and prepare to cope with life in a mature and responsible way. The problem in our society with those aspects of the socialization process that relate to death is that so many of them retard the growth of children and do not prepare them to engage with central dimensions of human existence. We confuse ignorance with innocence, suppression of honest feelings with contentment, segregation with the need to try out behavior patterns, and facile stories with careful value formation. Most of this is little more than misguided protectionism. Adults do not intend harm for their children and many do better than this catalog of thanatological sins would suggest. But too many of us unwittingly are our own and our children's worst enemies. Parenthood does entail safeguarding our children, but that must be accomplished in a thoughtful way and one that looks to the future. We do not help children by avoiding or squelching overt, temporary distress; instead, we should capitalize on it to achieve ultimate mastery and growth. In other words, adults must see their roles in the light of a sensible appreciation of children's needs. Responsible death education—education for life and living—is one of those needs for every child who is preparing to assume his or her rightful roles as a mature person, a member of the social community, and a citizen of the universe.

Preparation for Helping

Formal Programs

A wide variety of programs to prepare adults for helping in death education with children is possible. Programs may range from two-hour lecture-discussions in a course on death and dying and short presentations to lay and professional audiences, through one-day and two-week workshops, to full-scale courses exclusively devoted to the subject of children and death. One might also think of ongoing church discussion groups on this subject or of a series of interrelated presentations sponsored by a civic, educational, or religious organization. We cannot consider all such programs here, but it is helpful at least to suggest that there are many possible options for preparing helpers. I regard the day-long workshop and the full-scale college course as the most basic of all these options because they provide sufficient scope to do a satisfactory job and because most of the other formats can be seen as extracts from or condensations of these two. My emphasis here is on the day-long workshop because it is more common and because the full-scale college course on children and death is not yet a widely recognized model.

Elsehwere (14) I have outlined a number of patterns for day-long workshops on children and death. Every workshop must be geared to the needs of its particular audience, the resources available, and the capacities of its staff. But all have some common threads. The format, is usually four or five 60- to 90-minute sessions with ample time for questions and discussion, short breaks, and meals. Normally, they require little more logistics than a blackboard and a motion-picture or slide projector. But these are largely externals. True communality in such programs can be seen in their essential elements as reflected in a schematic outline and in the description that might be used to announce the workshop. The latter could be phrased in the following way: This workshop is designed to sensitize adults to problems involving children and death in our society; to examine research concerning the formation of death-related concepts and attitudes in childhood and adolescence; and to recommend strategies and resources adults can use to help children understand and deal with death more effectively.

In a four-session workshop, the opening session should be used to introduce the participants, to identify their backgrounds and the issues that concern them, and to begin an exploration of their own early contacts with and present attitudes toward death. The aim is not to complete the last exploration but only to introduce it as a topic for discussion. That reaffirms the operational relevancy of the adult's own death-related encounters and attitudes in all interactions with children, and it opens the way to an investigation of death-related needs in childhood. Another quite compatible way of achieving understanding and legitimization of childhood needs is to approach them through an account of typical death-related experiences and attitudes in our society and of the ways in which these are likely to influence children. Previously (4, 15), I have argued that one can characterize this society's typical experiential pattern as involving limited contact with natural human death, extensive fantasization of death through media presentations, and an increasing proportion of human-caused deaths. That pattern seems to correlate with a rather large share of discomfort, ambivalence, and distancing in our attitudes toward death. The result is a lot of misguided protectionism from adults that attempts to hide death from children through such practices as physical segregation, denial, and evasive or confusing language patterns. If we isolate these behaviors from their normal milieu, their limitations and the defects in their underlying motivations are readily apparent.

The second session of a workshop of this sort properly focuses on what can be said about the formation of death-related concepts and attitudes in childhood and adolescence. Research on this topic of even the earliest or simplest sort demonstrates that normal children do begin to have thoughts and feelings about death at an early age, certainly by the preschool or nursery school years (16). It is important to recognize that learning to deal with death is a part of the child's overall development in learning to deal with life. Hence, it is the development of the child's total psyche that is of concern, not just one or the other aspect; and environmental factors or life experiences are just as relevant as internal processes or capacities. This topic is central to any educational or interaction program that is concerned with children. It need not be belabored; the aim is education for use by ordinary adults, not merely specialists. The aim is satisfied even if the audience gains only a general sense of the relevant patterns and factors that come into question—as long as they also perceive the concomitant moral, which is that we must listen carefully to the concerns of each individual child before we attempt a response or impose our own agenda.

On the basis of this last discussion, the third session of the workshop might lay down some general guidelines for interacting with children. Many of these have already been set forth, for example: Listen and respond to real needs; insure that whatever you say is true; permit release and acting out of strong feelings; provide sympathetic support, acceptance, and reassurance; make good use of community and ceremonial rituals; share value frameworks in which there is real conviction; and work cooperatively in an integrating way, taking advantage of all of the enriching influences in a child's life. General strategies for curricular and teaching programs or for responding to the "teachable moment" could also be considered here. Throughout, it is good to keep in mind that, in many ways, the details of these guidelines and strategies are not so important; what really counts is their overall shape or orientation. The desired outcome is a constructive attitude, not a set of quick tricks or manipulative devices. And the underlying theme is that all of this is well within the grasp of an ordinary, mature adult.

Finally, a fourth session can identify a good resource guide (3) and different types of resources (discussed more fully below). It would also be desirable to give examples of many kinds of resources and to show how each can be used to best advantage. One might even select for detailed evaluation those resources that are especially suitable for a particular audience or in a specific setting. We need no overwhelm participants with bibliography or mediagraphy, but a short list of various types of recommended materials is always useful as something to take home from the workshop. If a fifth or additional session is possible, it might address special concerns of the participants or special cases that are either the most likely to occur or the most difficult to handle.

Self-study Programs

In a new field where historically there have not been many experts, few who now teach or write for adults have themselves been trained in formal programs of death education. More often than not, they have taken advantage of whatever instruction and resources were available; exploited their own existing knowledge, experience, and skills; and taught themselves much of what they now know. As they continue to share and discuss their insights, candor demands recognition that they acquire many ideas, suggestions, and materials from students and others with whom they come in contact. I say this to emphasize the importance of self-study and ongoing informal dialogue. It is quite foolish to think, as many seem to do, that one can only learn something by enrolling in a course or that formal credentials are an exclusive mark of wisdom, especially when the object of that wisdom is a fundamental and enduring aspect of the human condition. Those who enter a program of self-study need to be encouraged and assisted, not denigrated and frustrated by arbitrary barriers.

Because self-study programs are most often individual plans or spontaneous inquiry groups of no more than a very few people, they need not have a very rigid syllabus and they do not lend themselves to much generalization. What distinguishes self-study is not so much its content as its manner of organization, and perhaps also its resources. Those working on their own can march each to her or his own drummer, though they often must make use of instruments and music that are readily at hand. As far as content goes, in the previous section I have outlined some patterns for a day-long workshop in great detail partly to identify topics that could also be applicable to self-study. Obviously, an informal program of personal study could benefit by addressing topics the same as or similar to those taken up in a formal course organized by others. I can illustrate this by rephrasing five goals of the formal workshop as guidelines or objectives for a program of independent study.

The first is to sensitize adults to their own needs and to the needs that children have in dealing with death. Some adults explicitly deny that children have needs related to death; others appear to act on unarticulated but similar assumptions; and still another group is merely unconvinced of the existence of such needs. These adults may or may not acknowledge their own death-related needs, although these needs may be in part the source of their views concerning needs or lack thereof that they attribute to children. Here, the goal is to encourage an un-obscured sensitivity to the reality of death as a significant factor in human life, whether in adulthood or in childhood. Paradox-ically, that objective is often best achieved when death is shrunk from the outsized proportions generated by unfamiliarity and anxiety to its normal role in life. Death education is a process of bringing the elements of life back into harmony, not one of sensationalizing or overemphasizing an object of special interest or special pleading. Of course, those who take up a program of self-study may already be sensitized to death-related needs in themselves and in children. But sensitivity can become dulled, and we need to be alert to the importance of maintaining its keenness.

A second objective for independent study is to realize how death-related needs are influenced by the way in which our society experiences and copes with death, and in particular to appreciate how adult viewpoints and behaviors can influence children's perspectives in favorable and unfavorable ways. This objective carries us from the timeless abstraction of general needs to the concrete idiosyncrasies of a specified historical and cultural context. Death is actually always encountered in a particular context of life, and the nature of that context will inevitably shape the encounter. Further, within any designated society one can identify typical ways in which adults interact with children in regard to death. Because the overall patterns of encounters with death in our society are so distinctive—being quite limited in their realistic qualities and heavily distorted by selectivity and fantasization—we need to understand these patterns and to come to see how they often lead to common adult behaviors that are dysfunctional for children. By exposing inadequacies in need fulfillment, death education prepares the way in this objective for new relationships between adults and children based on more productive coping strategies.

A third goal for our program is to examine recent research and theories on the formation of death-related concepts and attitudes in childhood and adolescence. Even those who deny or are skeptical of death-related needs in early childhood must admit that at *some* point children are capable of considering death and begin to think and have feelings about it. An observant outsider might infer from common adult behavior that this point is not reached until the child has come to adulthood or otherwise left the protective environment of the familial greenhouse to encounter the harsh outside world. But this is patently false, so explicit pronouncements tend to put the watershed at an earlier and often arbitrarily designated age. Thus, in speaking of the young child, Ross says that "there is little need in his spring-green world for an understanding of the dead" (17, p. 250). Unfortunately for this viewpoint, the body of available research demonstrates that children do begin to draw inferences, form concepts, and develop feelings about death at quite an early age (18–20). Inferences may be founded on an inadequate experiential base; concepts may be incomplete; and feelings may be disproportioned or misfocused—but all are real and cannot wisely be dismissed out of hand. Death education should develop a knowledge base for helpers that respects developmental and environmental factors in childhood as well as the uniqueness of the individual child.

A fourth goal for self-study is to learn ways in which helpers should conduct themselves to foster in children a healthy attitude toward death. We need not limit ourselves to identifying flaws or to prohibiting undesirable forms of behavior. There are constructive modes of conduct both in identifying opportunities for death education with children and in responding to such occasions. Conduct with regard to death does not lend itself to cookbook recipes or simplistic formulas, but that need not frustrate conversation or prohibit interactions with children. A positive orientation can be developed that is applicable both to informal education in the home or community and to more formal education in the schools. Death education can aim adults in the right direction without preempting the uniqueness of each encounter with a child or the individual tactics that might suit a special situation.

The final goal for independent study is to learn about resources for use in working with children. Many well-intentioned adults are sympathetic to the needs of children and to contexts of interaction, and they are willing to try to learn about childhood development and a prospectus for their own behavior. But at that point, they often feel abandoned. Lacking knowledge of available materials, they feel as if they have been set adrift on a treacherous sea with only their own wits and words to aid them. Undoubtedly, one can do much with nature itself and a little imagination. Still, unnecessary limitations need not be applauded. Many sorts of resources and many good aids are at hand. Individual adults can select those that are most suitable to their situation if they know where and how to look and what to look for. Awareness of available resources can reinforce constructive behavior by suggesting options in methods and materials, and even in topics, that may not previously have been appreciated. Thus, a comprehensive program of formal or informal death education will see resources as an integral component of the whole, rather than as an optional appendix. In the next section I provide an introduction to relevant sorts of resources, and particular instances follow in the section of the text, "Resources."

Resources for Helping

The one great resource for death education with children that we all share in common is life itself. Our everyday experiences are full of "little deaths," the small separations and losses or beginnings and endings that mark change and growth. These events can teach us all a great deal about death. We need only be sensitive to them and keep in mind the organizing standard of our overriding concern for helping children with death education. Further, there are at least three other primary sorts of resources that can benefit adults and be employed with profit by them for the purposes of death education. These are printed materials, audiovisual items, and organizations in the community. I do not identify individual items here, preferring instead to concentrate on the types of resources available and their potential uses.

There are several sorts of printed materials that can be useful for death education with children. The most obvious are books, which may themselves be intended primarily for adults, for children, or for joint reading. Death education books are beginning to achieve new levels of sophistication. Many early titles in the field were uneven and overconfident. They promised too much and delivered too little. We had much to learn before this subject could be treated with authority. Indeed, there is still room for improvement, but now the literature for adults as described in Chapter 5 includes 44 titles that span fictional or autobiographical first-person encounters with death; studies of conceptual development and coping with dying or bereavement; and compendiums of advice for parents, counselors, and teachers. Adults can now find some discussion of almost any topic related to death education in one of these books.

Recently, there have been published what amount to freestanding bibliographies, books that describe other books in the field of death and dying. Mainly, these bibliographies concern themselves with literature for children and are intended for use by adults. These books demonstrate the rapid development during the past few years of a rather large body of death-related literature for children. Of course, in one form or another, death has long been a part of oral and written traditions for children; but it has recently become more central to plot and character development in many stories. Some of these are avowedly didactic, moralistic, or pedagogical in character. They seek to provide information, to inculcate values, or to teach children something about death. Perhaps the more successful are those in which death in some of its many manifestations is simply part of the tale. These range from the simplest picture books and stories for beginning readers to the most elegant and imaginative works for older children. By reintegrating death with life within their covers, such books teach the most important lesson of all, and they respond to the child's natural spectrum of interests and experiences. Not all are equally well written or suitable to every child, but Wass's descriptions of 155 titles in Chapter 6 gives ample room for selection in theme, treatment, and style.

Some writers (e.g., 21) commend the use of children's literature as "bibliotherapy," a kind of therapeutic or constructive intervention in the lives of children through books. Whatever we think of this concept, it is obvious that books can have an important value for children. All printed materials, but especially imaginative literature of the best kind, can stimulate a child's creative tendencies, enlarge horizons, confirm human solidarity in the face of difficulties, and foster critical assessment. Adults can capitalize on these possibilities by acquainting themselves with the panorama of death-related literature that is now in print and by making some of the best titles available for children. With a little guidance, children will begin to see how they can entertain and eduate themselves through such titles. Of course, it helps if the adults have also looked through the books so that they are prepared for the sorts of questions that a particular story might stimulate.

Some read-along books are specifically designed to be explored by children and adults together. Usually, these tell the simplest stories and are meant for the youngest children. The idea is to create an environment of sharing. To this end, the book is merely an instrument; it is not indispensable and should never become a handicap to free exchange. Although content is important, many children enjoy and profit from the very process of a shared reading or a period of story telling. Many books can be used in this way, particularly those with an interesting story and some attractive illustrations. The only point that may seem new or unusual in all this is my contention that a death-related story can serve as well as many others. But that need not be surprising; for if the essential element is that of sharing, then the object of concern can just as well be a tale of sadness and loss as one of happiness and success. Reading to a child about the death of a pet or the life cycle of a tree may prompt unexpected disclosures that might otherwise have gone unexpressed or unexplored.

Printed resources of a quite different sort are to be found in a few specialized periodicals and a wide range of journal articles. Casual readers often see little more than the popular magazines of the home, a grocery check-out counter, or a physician's waiting room. Even these occasionally print a death-related story, though often it will lack much depth or substance. But helpers should know that nearly every field of special interest has its own supportive periodicals. Many of these that are concerned with children have published during the last 10 or 15 years at least some articles that touch on death education. Interested adults can identify such pieces through the usual indexes to such periodicals or through a good bibliographic guide. A reference librarian can often point out a helpful index or abstracting service for a particular field. Beyond that, within the field of death and dying itself there are three prominent periodicals: *Omega,* an early journal with a slant toward the behavioral sciences; the Canadian journal *Essence;* and *Death Education.* Adults who are interested in death education have much to gain from a quick survey of these sorts of periodical resources.

In addition to printed materials, there are many audiovisuals that can be employed to good effect in death education for children. Films, filmstrips, records, tapes, or cassettes can have particular value for youngsters who may not yet have well-developed reading skills. Audiovisuals can also complement the written word and, in some cases, may exceed its power because of their broad sensory appeal. All too often, adults neglect audiovisual resources because they fear this power when linked to the subject of death and because they are unaware of their accessibility. Certainly, some audiovisuals about death are very powerful and should not be presented to unprepared or unsupported audiences. But that is hardly more than to say that no resource, however good in its own right, should ever be used in a thoughtless or indiscriminate way. A film can be death-related if it does no more than portray a life cycle, and it can be no more threatening than a portrait of a gentle encounter between some children and a dead animal. As for availability, Pacholski's annotated listing of audiovisual materials in Chapter 7 gives 143 titles with descriptions and a topical index. Pacholski rightly reminds us that many of these audiovisuals may also be available through local public, educational, and other resource centers or organizations. Helpers who invest time and energy in searching out such resources can often save money and simultaneously enrich the opportunities that follow for the education of children.

Finally, no list of resources would be complete that did not mention the many community and specialized organizations that are to be found in every local area. Most of these organizations will willingly share their expertise, printed materials, and audiovisuals with interested adults and young people. I have been most grateful to draw on such organizations in my own classes and workshops, whether for children or for adults. Most organizations are in turn pleased to make known their interests and to advertise their goals to members of the community. The very existence of these organizations confirms again the omnipresence of death-related resources in the social and everyday fabric of life all around us.

Helping the Helpers

I close this essay with a short caution about those who would conduct programs of death education for adults to prepare them for helping children. As of this writing, the Forum for Death Education and Counseling is the one national organization in North America that is struggling to develop training programs and criteria for identifying competency among those who teach in the area of death and dying. At the moment, few programs of this sort and no recognized criteria yet exist. This means that almost anyone can announce or conduct a program of death education. That freedom has made possible many valuable initiatives and many constructive programs, but it brings with it a need to scrutinize carefully qualifications in this popular field. Simply to have worked in some aspect of death, dying, or bereavement does not guarantee that one has a sound grasp on the field as a whole or that one is an effective educator. Nevertheless, sufficient time has now passed and sufficient opportunities are now available for writing, publishing, and teaching, that it is not improper to expect a history of accomplishment from most people. Even then, it would be wise to talk with a person at length to explore his or her creativity and flexibility and to insure that the planned educational program will serve the needs for which it is intended.

References

1. Pine, V. R. A socio-historical portrait of death education. *Death Education*, 1977, *1*, 57–84.
2. Feifel, H. (Ed.). *The meaning of death.* New York: McGraw-Hill, 1959.
3. Wass, H., Corr, C. A., Pacholski, R. A., & Sanders, C. M. *Death education: An annotated resource guide.* Washington: Hemisphere, 1980.
4. Corr, C. A. A model syllabus for death and dying courses. *Death Education*, 1978, *1*, 433–457.
5. Leviton, D. Death education. In H. Feifel (Ed.), *New meanings of death.* New York: McGraw-Hill, 1977, pp. 253–272.
6. Leviton, D. The scope of death education. *Death Education*, 1977, *1*, 41–45.
7. Knott, J. E. Death education for all. In H. Wass (Ed.), *Dying: Facing the facts.* Washington: Hemisphere, 1979, pp. 385–403.
8. Kastenbaum, R. We covered death today. *Death Education*, 1977, *1*, 85–92.
9. Wass, H. (Ed.). *Dying: Facing the facts.* Washington: Hemisphere, 1979.
10. Stanford, G., & Perry, D. *Death out of the closet: A curriculum guide to living with dying.* New York: Bantam, 1976.
11. Jackson, E. N. *Telling a child about death.* New York: Hawthorn, 1965.
12. Jackson, E. N. Bereavement and grief. In H. Wass (Ed.), *Dying: Facing the facts.* Washington: Hemisphere, 1979, pp. 256–281.
13. Ariès, P. *Western attitudes toward death: From the Middle Ages to the present* (P. Ranum, Trans.). Baltimore: Johns Hopkins University Press, 1974.
14. Corr, C. A. Workshops on children and death. *Essence*, 1980, *4*, 5–18.
15. Corr, C. Reconstructing the changing face of death. In H. Wass (Ed.), *Dying: Facing the facts.* Washington: Hemisphere, 1979, pp. 5–43.
16. Stillion, J., & Wass, H. Children and death. In H. Wass (Ed.), *Dying: Facing the facts.* Washington: Hemisphere, 1979, 208–235.

17. Ross, E. S. Children's books relating to death: A discussion. In E. A. Grollman (Ed.), *Explaining death to children*. Boston: Beacon, 1967, pp. 249–271.
18. Kastenbaum, R. Death and development through the lifespan. In H. Feifel (Ed.), *New meanings of death*. New York: McGraw-Hill, 1977, pp. 17–45.
19. Kastenbaum, R. *Death, society, and human experience*. St. Louis: Mosby, 1977, pp. 114–134.
20. Lonetto, R. *Children's conceptions of death*. New York: Springer, 1980.
21. Bernstein, J. E. *Books to help children cope with separation and loss*. New York: Bowker, 1977, esp. pp. 20–39.

PARENTS, TEACHERS, AND HEALTH PROFESSIONALS AS HELPERS

HANNELORE WASS

University of Florida, Gainesville

Introduction

This chapter is designed to do three things: (*a*) to provide basic facts and findings drawn from research and clinical observations about death and the child; (*b*) to consider common problems created for the child when he or she comes into contact with death in various contexts and at different levels of intimacy; and (*c*) to offer guidelines and suggestions for helping children cope with these problems.

The chapter is divided into four major sections. The first deals with attitudes and actions considered to be basic requisites for effective helping. The second section concerns death-related thoughts, feelings, and encounters of the typical child, followed in the next section by suggestions for helping the child integrate these experiences and cope with them in a constructive manner. The third section focuses on the special hardships that confront the dying child and offers guidelines for helping that should be useful to health professionals, parents, teachers, and others. The final section deals with the problem of bereavement in childhood by considering three losses through death: of a grandparent, a sibling, or a parent. The section also suggests ways in which helpers can assist the child to adjust to such a loss.

In many places throughout the chapter the reader is referred to additional readings on specific topics that are beyond the scope that a single chapter such as this permits.

Basic Requisites for Effective Helping

Confronting Our Own Death

Some experts insist that one cannot help someone else with
death-related concerns unless one has first come to accept one's
own mortality. That demand is unrealistic. I have known few
people who have fully accepted their own death. Most of us are
nowhere near such reconciliation to our destiny. As effective
helpers we should, however, be *in the process* of personal
confrontation with death. We should from time to time reflect
upon and clarify our concepts, beliefs, and attitudes about
death.

We may not have achieved a well-formulated position or
overcome all of our anxieties, but we should be able to
acknowledge our mortality and not be uncomfortable talking
about the subject. Sometimes the realization that children need
us for reassurance, comfort, or information gives us the emotional strength to overcome our own needs, anxieties, and
ambivalences related to death. At times we find that in trying to
help a child cope with a death-related situation, our anxieties get
the better of us, memories of forgotten pains come crashing into
our minds, and we cease to be helpful to the child at that time.
That is only human. To believe that we now have caused the
child terrible harm may mean that we have taken on too heavy
a burden of responsibility, or that we have too little faith in the
child's resiliency and active participation in the process of
learning to cope. The notion of the perfect helper is a romantic
illusion, but we should do the best we can in assisting the child
in given circumstances.

For readers who are not familiar with exercises designed to
help achieve personal death awareness, I mention a few that,
over the years, I and my students have found valuable. You can
do these exercises alone or with a friend or family member who
is supportive of your interest in helping children with death.
One exercise involves looking back into the past and trying to
remember the first death-related experience you ever had. Who
died? What were the circumstances? How did you feel? What did
you think? What did your parents do and tell you? What did

other adults do? Write down these memories. Other death-related experiences may come to mind. Write them down also. You may relive some of the pain or fears you experienced regarding a death in your childhood. You may discover residues of resentment toward family members for what they did or did not do during those times. Another exercise involves writing your obituary. That requires you to imagine a date and a cause of death, to project who may survive you and what kind of a funeral you will have. You may at first feel that this is a "silly" exercise, but as you write you may also experience other sorts of emotions such as anxiety, anger, sadness, perhaps even peace or joy. A third exercise requires that you suppose you are terminally ill. Now write a farewell letter to a loved one. In another exercise you write down your fears about death. Share what you have written with a friend or family member. Exchange your present thoughts and feelings about death. An exercise to do alone is to suppose again, that you are terminally ill and have a limited time to live. Now write down what you will do in the time left to you. This exercise requires you to consider your values and priorities. While you may feel momentarily depressed when considering your own impending death, you will reflect upon the things that are important to you in your life. You may even make important changes in your plans and goals as a consequence of such reflection.

Perceiving the Child as Worthy and Unique

To be an effective helper implies that we perceive the child as a human being of worth and uniqueness. A child lacks the wisdom, maturity, and life experiences of an adult, but these limitations are not valid criteria for assessing an individual's worth. Adults' possession of these characteristics does not mean superiority. The point made is a subtle one. Adulthood ascribes to us a special status; being a parent, teacher, doctor, or nurse implies a special power and authority that we must exercise with a deep concern for the vulnerability and dependence of the child. The child may look up to us for help but let us not look down when giving it. Our respect for the child's worth as a human being countermands the power we have, which can overwhelm the child. We demonstrate respect for the child's worth and uniqueness in many different ways. When we truly attempt to understand what the child is telling us verbally, through body language, and behavior, we show that he or she is important. In our adult thinking we often find children's thoughts "cute," "precious," "odd," or "funny" and we laugh. Often we share them with relatives or friends, to be laughed at by them in the presence of the child. But what the child shared may have been serious or "a secret" not meant to be passed around. Worse still, a child's thoughts and feelings may offend our sense of what is acceptable and appropriate and we may be quick to correct or admonish. Respect for the child's uniqueness requires that we accept the feelings and thoughts he or she expresses. Negating, belittling, or teasing are powerful messages that we do not consider the child's thoughts and feelings worthy of our serious attention. This kind of respect cannot be faked for two reasons: First, children are far more perceptive than we adults often believe possible. They can distinguish between authentic behavior and role playing. Second, basic attitudes such as respect for the child are communicated not only with words but also spontaneously through our actions and body language that elude our mental censorship.

Knowing and Learning about Child Development and Death

In order to be effective helpers it is important that we learn as much as we can about child development and behavior in general; about dying, death, and bereavement; and about children's death-related thoughts, feelings, and behaviors in particular. I disagree with the idea that so much knowledge is not only unnecessary but may actually prevent us from following our own instincts in being helpful to a particular child. We know that human beings are not born with proper helping instincts; our helping behavior is learned. For example, many parents read books or take courses on parenting, or do both. Others do not, and the way *they* raise their children is not based on any instincts. It most likely resembles the way their parents raised them. This is not necessarily bad as long as one recognizes the source of one's behavior. During the past 50 years we have made important strides in our knowledge of child development and behavior. More recently we have begun studying not only the area of dying, death, and bereavement in general, but also as related to the child specifically. There is no reason to make a case for ignorance. The knowledge we gain is useful as a general frame of reference or basic background. Beyond that we must, of course, consider the child as a unique being and become knowledgeable about each particular child's needs in specific sets of circumstances. Both kinds of knowledge, the general and the specific combined, will make us more informed than either one alone and thus increase our prospect for effectiveness.

Putting Ourselves in the Child's Place

One of the most difficult, yet fundamental, characteristics of effective helpers is their ability to see things and events from the child's perspective. This ability is sometimes called empathy but it is more than that. It involves the capacity to "tune in" to the child's world of thinking, feeling, and being. It involves what Wilhelm Reich has called "listening with a third ear"—being fully sensitive and responsive to the child from his or her point of view and level of maturity. This capacity requires that we remember what it was like for us to be a child, then promptly forget our childhood, and, for a time, forget out adulthood as well. It is difficult to carry out our adult responsibilities as helpers and at the same time to put ourselves in the child's place. Nevertheless, we must be able to alternate in this way. Being in the child's world gives us the insights and understandings we need to interact meaningfully with the child. Adult-child interactions often break down because adults and children are talking *past* each other. We often answer questions our children do not ask and fail to answer those they do. Returning to the adult world enables us to provide the support, reassurance, and clarification the child seeks.

Open and Honest Communication

A child needs to feel psychologically safe and nonthreatened. To accomplish this we need to create an atmosphere of mutual respect and trust. Such an atmosphere of open communication and freedom of expression is essential for effective helping interactions. It encourages children to inquire and to share fears and concerns without the prospect of ridicule or rejection. Without effective communication a child is likely to distrust, and to keep worries and fears locked inside.

We should be honest in our communications. Any subject, especially one as essential and far-reaching as death, deserves honest answers, including admission of ignorance where it exists. Deception, misinformation, and refusal to respond are more harmful to the child than the truth. Not only can these lead to more anxiety-provoking fantasies, but they also weaken the child's trust of the adult and create feelings of loneliness and isolation.

Growing Up in Today's World of Life and Death

Until this century a child growing up in this country was intimately acquainted with death. In 1900 the life expectancy of a United States citizen was a little over 47 years (1). It was common for children to experience the death, not only of grandparents, but also of parents and younger siblings. Until this century most people died at home and children were not only present when the death occurred, they also often helped in the care of the loved one, and, naturally, participated in the funeral ceremonies. Children were included in the funerals of other relatives, friends of the family, and neighbors. Death was an often-heard word in church, in prayers, and in informal conversation. It was the theme of stories in books, including textbooks used in public schools. Death was very much a part of the child's daily life.

Today for the first time in history an individual may be middle-aged before experiencing the death of a family member. This is so because medical and technical progress have increased our average life expectancy to about 76 years (1). Today adults find the subject uncomfortable, difficult, embarrassing, or inappropriate where children are concerned. Many feel that to associate the subjects of children and death is morbid. They note that the terms "children" and "death" are contradictory—one symbolizing life and growth, the other meaning the end and decay. In their view it is best to protect the child from the harsh reality of death. Many adults have convinced themselves that children are not interested in death nor do they have any thoughts about it, which is not true. Children are curious about death when they encounter it; they are concerned about it; they develop notions and concepts about it as well as fears, worries, and anxieties. Questions about birth and death are existential questions that children begin asking at an early age. These questions are a part of a need to make sense of the world as they perceive and experience it, of the events occurring, and of the children's own place in the world. This search for meaning is unique to human beings. It is a sign of healthy, normal development and something to be valued and fostered. Thus it is important that we learn what we can about the child's perceptions, feelings, and responses to death. Fortunately, these subjects have been studied and a decent general knowledge base has been established, although many questions still remain.

The results of research studies and clinical observations of children's death-related thoughts and feelings are summarized in the following sections. For additional study the reader is referred to the section, Resources: Books for Adults, in this volume.

The Development of Concepts of Death

The developmental psychologist Jean Piaget, who devoted his life to the study of cognition, has provided the most comprehensive and widely recognized description of cognitive development from infancy to adulthood. Even though most recent studies (2) indicate that various cognitive abilities occur at earlier ages than Piaget believed, the *stages* of cognitive development he identified have not been successfully challenged. It is reasonable to expect that cognitions of death develop in the same way and follow the same principles as do other cognitions. Indeed, studies conducted in the United States and in Europe over a number of years confirm this (3). Concepts of death develop essentially in four stages. There are, however, as in other aspects of development, individual differences in the *rates* of development, that is, in the ages at which children reach these stages. These differences may be maturational, or they may reflect differences in children's environment or life circumstances, which in turn cause differences in experiences.

First Stage, Infancy. Capacities of perception and perceptual differentiation are developed in this stage. They are precursors of thinking, but there is no actual conceptualization, so infants have no concepts of death. Infants are capable of forming internal images, but these images are of objects found in the infant's immediate world, such as people, food, and toys.

Second Stage, Early Childhood. The child knows he or she is a separate physical entity but the orientation is self-centered, that is, the child can only understand events from the narrow perspective of his or her own experiences. Of seventeen kinds of causality found in the child's reasoning at this stage four are particularly relevant to our discussion (4): animistic, magical, artificialistic, and psycholgoical. *Animistic* thinking refers to the child's belief that the whole world and everything in it is alive. Life is attributed to sun, moon, clouds, rivers, stones, tricycles, and cars. *Magical* causality implies that everyone can make everyone else do things, and that even objects have this kind of power. People and objects can give orders but they must also obey. With this kind of causal thinking anything is possible. There are no surprises. Mountains open when you tell them to, flowers talk, birds tell you secrets, princes turn into frogs and vice-versa. *Artificialistic* thinking is the belief that everything is manufactured for people's convenience. Daylight is turned on so people can see, babies are manufactured much like toys. This kind of reasoning explains why young children frequently assume that dead animals can be fixed up like toys and other objects. *Psychological* causality refers to the child's tendency to perceive a personal motive as the cause of certain events, for example, children believe that bad dreams are sent to them because they have been bad (5). Thus the young child's thinking differs in quality from that of adults. Even though the child knows and speaks the words "dead" or "died," he or she understands death as a reversible event, a temporary restriction, loss of mobility, sleep, or departure. Until the young child comes in direct contact with death, usually with the death of animals such as insects, worms, frogs, birds, etc., death does not exist for that child. Even then death is puzzling. It does not fit with the child's animistic thinking, and the child has no ready explanation for it. Many three- and four-year-olds when asked why things die, respond they do not know. Others offer explanations such as these: "... because they eat too much candy"; "... because they go to jail"; "... because the nurse gives them a pill"; "... because the big bird comes ... "; or "... just because." In our most recent study we asked "what makes things die?" Typical responses from our older four- and five-year-olds were these: "Guns, knives, and stuff"; "they have a car wreck"; "an alligator (tiger, lion) eats them"; "they fall into a meat grinder"; or "they eat a poison pill." About half the children said they didn't know. When asked "What happens after someone has died?"; children at this stage give these kinds of responses: "They put them to bed." (And then?) "He wakes up in the morning." Or, "They fall down and can't get up." (And then?) "The police come and help them up." (And then?) "They eat." In our recent study, young children most often said "They go to the hospital (doctor) and get fixed up." To the question "When will you die?", these children matter-of-factly replied "I don't die," or "Never." When asked to explain further, they responded "because I don't want to," or "I don't have to." Children at this stage who have attended a funeral often believe that the buried dead have feelings, are asleep, want to eat, want some air to breathe, and will come out again (3).

Third Stage, Middle Childhood and Preadolescence. The earlier modes of causal thinking are replaced by logical and naturalistic thinking that is based on the child's objective observation of the concrete physical and mechanical aspects of objects and events, and the laws governing them. Children now know that only plants, animals, and people are alive and that what lives also dies. Death is understood as an *irreversible* event (3). The only possibilities for returning to life are through reincarnation or resurrection, and these are matters of one's beliefs. At this stage children still list external forces such as violence, accidents, or disaster as causes of death but more frequently they describe internal causes such as illness and old age, or give physiological definitions, such as cessation of vital functions or laws of nature. At this stage children are intensely interested in the physiological aspects of death. Regardless of religious affiliation, they are preoccupied with decomposition and decay. When asked what happens when people die, children in our studies frequently responded like this nine-year-old: "They put you in a casket and you get buried in the graveyard. Then you start rotting and you rot and rot until all there is is a bunch of soil and all that soil turns into part of the ground." Only after detailed description of funeral procedures and subsequent decay, almost as an afterthought, do some children say " . . . and your soul goes to Heaven or Hell." In this period children ask questions dealing with the physiology of dying, death, and decomposition, such as "Why does the blood turn blue?" Is it true that a dead body moves one more time before it's buried?" "How long does it take for a person to rot?" "Do people ever get buried alive?"

Children understand that death is irreversible, at the same time they also view it as *capricious* and certainly as something they do not expect to happen to them until they are very old. They hope to be lucky and escape death. As one ten-year-old put it: "When you die they put you in a coffin, then they bury you and you rot. I hope I never die" (3).

Fourth Stage, Adolescence. Children come to the mature understanding that death is not only *irreversible* but also *personal.* Now they are capable of grasping and adopting abstract theological beliefs or other abstract explanations. For example, a 16-year-old wrote: "My interpretation of death is clearly from a Christian's point of view. I believe in eternal life after death without human fault or sign. I believe that all souls will eventually be in Heaven, Heaven being defined as true inner peace within yourself and God" (3). This understanding of personal death in adolescence is closely associated with putting the matter aside and giving it no further thought. Apparently most adolescents do this (4). The response of a 17-year-old is representative of this kind of thinking: "Death for me is a long way down the road of life. Right now I am more concerned about what I am going to do with my life than how I am going to terminate it" (6).

Fears and Anxieties

In psychology a distinction is commonly made between the terms "anxiety" and "fear." Anxiety means an emotional state in which some unknown or vague danger is expected or sensed. This is assumed to prepare us to respond with "fight or flight." Fear, on the other hand, refers to a feeling about a known thing or event of which we are afraid. Children experience many specific fears as they grow, become familiar with their environment and learn about dangers. They learn to fear wild animals, poisonous snakes, and oncoming cars. Anxieties are more difficult to describe. They are more generalized dreads, and the child does not know what or where the danger is. In thanatological studies the terms fear and anxiety are used interchangeably as will be done in this summary.

Infantile Anxieties. Obviously, without the ability to conceptualize death, one does not expect death-related fears to exist. But infants do show anxieties and distress (4). These concern losses and are primarily associated with separation from the nurturing person. They are called separation anxiety or fear of abandonment. They also include fears of being dropped and of being in the dark (7, 8). Well-nurtured infants probably do not experience these anxieties except for short periods of time.

Fears and Anxieties in Early Childhood. Some psychologists with a psychoanalytic orientation believe that young children have many anxieties. In addition to separation anxieties that continue from infancy into early childhood and even later, young children are thought to experience castration anxiety, which involves the dread of physical mutilation of genitals, and other kinds of retaliation for forbidden wishes. These are all thought to be related to children's relationships with their parents in the process of socialization, especially the development of conscience. Some psychologists have suggested that all these anxieties are related to death anxiety and have reported research and clinical observations to support this belief (8-10). Whether this is valid is a matter of interpretation. It is also unclear whether such anxieties are a part of normal development or are indications of pathology. The intensity and pervasiveness of these anxieties are also debatable. Here it becomes important to know the individual child and his or her particular circumstances, including the child's family, to make accurate assessment possible.

Death-related fears and anxieties commonly arise as a direct consequence of immature causal thinking and interpretations of events. Magical thinking has fear-arousing power. For example, a young child may wish a parent or a sibling dead. Should such a parent or sibling actually die later on, the child may believe that his or her wish has caused the death. This can lead not only to intensive guilt but also to fears that such a wicked act will be punished by the child's own destruction. When the child discovers that wishing the loved one back by magic does not work, the feelings of guilt are heightened. Psychological causality is another source of death-related anxiety. For example, some children explain that "people die because they are bad," "God kills them because they've been naughty." Since children do many things that are unacceptable, the belief that death may be the punishment even for minor infractions may cause some children to feel a constant threat. The only consoling aspect is that the young child does not grasp the finality of death.

Another source of death-related fears is the child's interpretation of certain cultural practices. Since young children understand death as a temporary state, they do not understand why people put the dead inside a casket, shut it tight, put it into a deep hole and throw dirt on top of it. One researcher reports children expressing their worries about how dead people are going to get food, how they are able to breathe, and how they will get out when they wake up (11). Remnants of such fears of being trapped sometimes are found in adults. Fortunately, young children often invent ways for the dead to get out by using magic. As one five-year-old boy explained: "They lie in the grave for four days. Then they wake up and say "open up," and the coffin just opens and the earth gets swooshed away and they come straight up." (And then?) "They go home and eat." Even familiarity with dead bodies does not necessarily mean that the young child achieves a better understanding of our funeral practices. An acquaintance, a funeral director from one of the Caribbean islands, told me of overhearing his little boy at play make the following statement into his walkie-talkie in the casket display room: "Now don't move, and don't get up or else my Daddy will get mad at you."

Fears and Anxieties in Middle Childhood. Anxieties related to loss and separation experienced in infancy and early childhood may persist into middle childhood. At this stage, however, since death is understood as an irreversible event and since children's thinking is concerned with physical causality and laws of nature, many fears are focused on bodily mutilation, on being buried alive, and on the physiological processes of death, decomposition, and decay. Children may not admit such fears. But psychologists have pointed out that the recital of limericks and rhymes that deal crassly with these processes, may be understood as attempts to release anxieties about these processes. Such limericks and rhymes have been passed on through the generations, and new ones are added as old ones are discarded. The reader will recall the rhyme with these lines: "The worms crawl out, the worms crawl in, they crawl all over your mouth and chin." Today's "dead baby jokes" apparently fulfill the same function (4).

Another source of considerable anxiety at this stage is the belief that death is capricious and can happen if you are unlucky. It has been suggested that popular superstitions seemingly observed as a joke, e.g., holding one's breath when passing a cemetery, avoiding stepping on the cracks on sidewalks, sometimes have an element of compulsion and are remnants of magical thinking (even adults knock on wood and kick the table leg on which they stubbed a toe).

At this time in the child's life misgivings about what happens after death are common. One 11-year-old girl put it this way: "I think when someone knows they are going to die, they are very scared. I would be. I think after someone dies they just lie there forever and disintegrate. I hope I never die" (12). Now beliefs about immortality and life after death become meaningful and can offer much comfort. Here are some thoughts that children have shared with us: "I believe that after you die, you have another life and you might come back from anything like a cockroach to a royalty." "I'll be buried in a graveyard and go straight up to Heaven." "I think when you die your soul goes into the next baby born." "I get scared and I don't want to die. Whenever I think about it I get all spooked out. I don't know about *you*, but *I* am going to Heaven" (12).

Physiological aspects of death and religious teachings are sometimes difficult to reconcile at this stage. One 12-year-old in our studies wrote "When you die you lie in your grave forever. How could a dead body get to Heaven?" Another child wrote: "I don't think you go to Heaven, and if you did go there, what would you do?" The possibility of "going to Hell" seems to worry many children, and even Heaven is often viewed as a place that imposes a number of restrictions (13).

Adolescents and Death Fears and Anxieties. Adolescents' death anxieties stem primarily from the understanding that death is an irreversible, universal, and inevitable reality. With the comprehension of personal death comes, typically an emotional and cognitive distancing that moves death into the future as previously discussed. This distancing from death removes much of the personal threat and anxiety associated with it. Thus, adolescence is probably a phase in which less death-related fears and anxieties are experienced than at any previous time in the child's life.

Common Kinds of Death in the Child's World

Although it is uncommon for today's children to experience the death of a close family member or peer, death is by no means a total stranger.

Animals and Pets. Early in life children come in direct contact with many kinds of animals. Most children love animals. They watch them and play with them when possible. They see them alive and dead. Very young children are puzzled when they encounter dead animals. They do not understand what causes animals to die. Death does not fit in the young child's world of animistic thinking. Psychologists suggest that keeping animals as pets is beneficial to the growing child for many reasons. One is that it gives the child an opportunity for a direct experience of the life cycle, including dying and death, and the feelings of sadness that follow the death especially when the pet was the child's. Some professionals even believe that experiencing the death of a pet prepares the child to cope better with the death of a close person. Whether and to what degree the keeping of pets helps the child to cope with death depends largely on the parents.

Death and Television. Today's children may not experience death as directly as did children in earlier times. Nevertheless, death is an intimate part of the child's life—on the television screen. Through this medium the most violent and unnatural deaths are brought daily into the living rooms of 98 percent of our homes. The most recent estimate is that three- and four-year-olds spend an average of four hours per day viewing television. This figure increases through the elementary school years, thus suggesting that children spend more time watching television than they spend in school or in interaction with their parents (14). Many studies have reported adverse influences of televised violence on children's aggression. The far-reaching impact of television on family dynamics, life styles, moral development, learning, etc., are current concerns among psychologists and mental health agencies. I believe that persistent exposure and the manner in which death is portrayed have a major impact on the growing child. Three-fourths of the leading characters in action programs on television are involved in violent behavior (15). Children's cartoons contain about six times as many violent episodes per hour as do adult programs. Television gives a highly distorted picture of reality concerning death. For example, in real life, murder accounts for less than one percent of the crimes committed, whereas it is the most frequent crime on television. Not only do children become grossly misinformed, they may also develop unrealistic fears of being murdered. At the same time, continuous exposure to such deadly fare can have the opposite effect: it can lead to psychological numbing, in which the child becomes indifferent both to the act of murder and to the murderer as well. Television deaths are often depicted as quick and painless, thus making them acceptable (4). Natural death is infrequent in television programs. Often death does not happen at all. Cartoon characters, for example, may get tossed into a ravine, stabbed, shot, clubbed, run over, and blown to pieces, yet come out of all this alive and intact. On a "cops and robbers" show characters die violently every night only to reappear on other shows within a week or less (1). Television also has created the Bionic Man and the Bionic Woman who are indestructible—immortals in human form (4).

Death in Children's Literature. Children learn from direct experience and active discovery and by observing people's behavior. They also learn through symbols, such as language. Parents, teachers, and other adults, siblings and peers, live and filmed, all provide information for children and may influence their attitudes through the spoken word. Another major source of learning is the written word, including literary works. This is true for death-related learning as much as for other subjects. Sandra Bertman, in her chapter, skillfully demonstrates the close affinity between artist and child and the writer's uncanny gift for putting into words the various emotions death evokes in us, especially those we may think too horrible to share. In this way children's books are not only excellent teachers that provide the child with valuable knowledge, but they can be therapeutic and comforting as well. Reading about the behavior of others also has been found strikingly potent in changing attitudes (4). With these factors in mind, I have prepared "Books for Children—An Annotated Bibliography, found in the section, Resources, in this volume.

Helping the Growing Child Cope with Death

In the following pages readers will find some guidelines that grow out of research findings and from professional and personal experiences. Writing down a set of guidelines can be risky. Some readers may be seeking specific answers to specific problems that they are presently encountering. These readers will be disappointed because such specificity is not possible without knowing the particular child, the particular situation, and the broader context in which the problem occurs. Other readers may see these guidelines as rigid rules or principles that should apply to all cases. They will be disappointed when they discover that a guideline they followed did not bring forth the desired results. Nevertheless, I believe the risk is worth taking. I would, however, ask the readers to view these guidelines as attempts to provide aids that, together with the illustrative material, will form a kind of gestalt that is suggestive rather than prescriptive, and exemplary rather than exhaustive. I hope that from this the readers will gain some insights that will help in responding effectively to the situations and problems they encounter.

Guidelines for Parents

When to Talk about Death. The best time to talk about death with a child is when the child has had a personal death experience. When a death occurs in the child's circle of significant people, we must typically break the news to the child and thus initiate discussion as we will see later. The subject of death may also be part of a conversation between parents at various times when children are present. That is natural. Children may or may not ask questions then. When they do, we should respond. We should not shut the child out by saying: "You are too young to understand," or "This is grown-up talk, so run along." At all other times, however, we should be guided by the child's own needs. A child usually initiates questions following a death-related event he or she has experienced either directly, such as encountering a dead animal, or indirectly, such as on television, at play, in conversation with playmates, or from conversation by adults the child overheard. The timing of such questions may be inconvenient for us, but, if possible, we should set aside other matters and attend to the child at that time. Actually, the demand on our time may be minimal. When an existential question, such as "where do babies come from?"

comes up, we adults often take a deep breath, then deliver the
dreaded lecture and tell all. But young children usually want a
few quick and simple answers. They do not want to know all
there is to know. If we cannot respond to the child immediately, we should make clear that we are merely postponing, not
evading. Then we should keep our promise. The school-aged
child asks quick questions for information that can often be
handled at the time they come up. In addition, however, the
child now has many troubling concerns; for example, about
being safe from death, about murder, decay, being buried alive,
and about war and terrorism of which there is a daily diet on
the newscast and in the print media. The child also begins to
worry about what happens after death. These kinds of questions
cannot be handled while preparing dinner or after we return
home tired from work. The time for discussing these concerns is
when the parents are relaxed, the television screen is dark, the
stereo not blaring, and there is no party to attend an hour later.
The emotional climate is one of love and mutual respect. It is
the best time for talking about troubling matters.

What Are the Questions? Children differ widely in the way they
approach their parents with questions. Some children ask
straightforwardly; others lead up to the question in a less direct
manner. A child may seek clarification of an experience that was
puzzling and confusing; thus, the question may be primarily
cognitive. A child may also feel uneasy and anxious, thus
seeking not only information but also reassurance and comfort.
Children differ in the depth and breadth of their questions and in
the persistence with which they pursue the subject. A major
factor determining the child's needs is his or her level of
development. With respect to the preschool child, it is not
always clear what the child wants to know. As discussed earlier,
the preschool child typically has an inaccurate concept of death.
The question may, in fact, be triggered by the first encounter he
or she has had with death, that does not fit in the child's
repertoire of knowledge and experience. This gives the parent an
opportunity to learn what the child's perceptions are, what he
or she knows and thinks, and, of course, the circumstances that
led to the question. My suggestion is that we learn how best to

answer by letting children tell us what they think. Readers who have some doubt about this approach should find a young child and bring up the subject. They will be surprised to find that young children do have ideas and thoughts about death. They have a rich inner world of images, thoughts, fantasies, and feelings. I do not think they deliberately keep this world private. The reason they do not spontaneously communicate their thoughts and feelings is that they are self-centered, as we have seen, which involves among other things the belief that everybody thinks and feels as they do, and knows it. Then, too, young children lack the ability to articulate many of their thoughts and feelings with precision.

> Three-year old Kevin was playing with his friend Sheila in the yard when they discovered a lizard that didn't run off. Something was wrong. It just lay there. It looked funny. They poked it, but it didn't move. "It's sick," Kevin offered. "Nah," said Sheila nonchalantly, "it's dead," and with that gave it a kick and ran off. Kevin headed straight to his mother: "Mummy, what is dead?" "What do *you* think, Kevin?" "I don't know, but the lizard didn't run away, maybe it hurt its foot." Mother wants to see the lizard. So they both go and have a look. Mother says: "Kevin, this lizard is dead. It cannot move. It isn't breathing anymore. It's dead." Kevin: "Can't you fix it? Can Daddy fix it?" "But the doctor can fix it."

These are some questions parents can expect from their preschool children: "Who deaded him?" "What made him die?" "Does a tiger die?" "Do alligators die?" "Will Aunt Mary die?" "Will Grandpa die?" "Will Daddy die?" "Will you die?" "Do I have to die?" "How come people die?" "When do they wake up again?" "Why can't they wake up?" "How do dead people get dinner?" "Can dead people still get ice cream?" "Why not?"

School-aged children, as indicated before, understand that death is natural and irreversible. It helps for parents to know the stage of their child's cognitive development concerning death, otherwise they can be put on the spot.

> Seven-year old Ron's cat, Kittie, was run over by a car near his home while he was at school. The parents quickly removed all traces of the accident. After Ron had been home from school for a while he asked: "Where's Kittie?" His parents haltingly and with

considerable discomfort, replied: "Ron, Kittie is in Heaven with God." The boy looked from one parent to the other with a puzzled frown. Then he asked in an astonished tone of voice: "But Mom, Dad, what would God want with a dead cat?"

The preoccupation of older children is with the physiological aspects of death. Their questions are likely to shock us and make us cringe with distaste. Besides, we may not know all the answers. So we often give religious answers to these biological questions. This only frustrates the child.

When my son, Brian, was nine years old he asked the kinds of questions I have long since learned are normal at that stage: "Why do people die with their eyes open?" "Why does the blood turn blue?" "How long does it take for the worms to eat through the body?" Fortunately, at that time a little book titled *Life and Death* (16) had just been published and was our source of information. Another question Brian asked was not so easily answered: "Do people ever get buried alive?" My answer did not reassure. He asked: "But couldn't the doctor make a mistake?" "Are you sure people don't get buried alive?" "But what if it did happen? I mean it could happen, couldn't it?" This question surfaced periodically for about four months. All I could do during that time was to reassure him that it is highly improbable that it would happen today, not to become irritated or impatient, and certainly not to laugh at him. Fortunately, for Brian, *Time* magazine, in one of its issues, carried an article on the subject with a diagram of a contraption rich people in the 19th century bought as a precaution for that possibility. Brian discovered the article before I did and immediately showed me the flaws in this device. Then he disappeared into his room. When he emerged some time later he triumphantly held up a large piece of cardboard. It showed a diagram of a device he had designed using modern technology, such as an alarm system and four amplifiers, that seemed to him effective—and did to me as far as such contraptions go. The problem disappeared as suddenly as it had started.

School-aged children also ask questions about immortality. Some questions are simply inquiries about parents' beliefs. Others seek explanations. Children want to know the "how," such as the mechanics of getting to Heaven. They ask concrete questions and are frustrated with abstract answers they cannot understand. These problems may persist into adolescence. Even adults sometimes have the same problems.

These are some questions parents can expect from their school-aged children: "Is there really, really a Heaven and a Hell?" "How do you know?" "Where is Heaven, I mean it isn't in space, is it, like farther out in space?" "How can the body get from the grave to Heaven?" "Before it rots?" "When does the soul leave the body?" "Does the spirit float around until after the funeral or does it go straight up?" "How does the spirit know the way?" "Could the spirit get trapped in the body?" "If there *was* a Heaven, what would you do there forever?" "What if there is nothing after death?" "Couldn't people get reincarnated after a few weeks, a couple of weeks maybe?"

What to Say. The most important recommendation is to tell the truth. Anything we tell a child about death that is untrue or only partly true, will have to be unlearned by the child. In the process a parent's credibility will suffer. Incorrect answers are unhelpful. Grollman (17) among others, has argued most emphatically for telling the truth. Here are samples of what he suggests parents should tell their preschool child:

> " . . . When you die, you're dead. . . . Dead is dead. . . . The body does not move. It does not breathe. The heart does not beat. The body is still. . . . There is no hurt, no pain, no life" (pp. 9–11).
> " . . . For flowers and for all of us . . . there is a season. . . . There is a time for every living thing to grow and to flourish and then to die" (p. 13).

I cannot think of any way to put it more simply or more gently than Grollman does. Still, there is a problem we need to recognize. Such straightforward, truthful answers to the child's question at this stage of cognitive development probably have no immediate effect even when given repeatedly. As we have seen, the young child's thinking is magical and animistic. Simply telling the child that death is a natural part of the life cycle will not result in a sudden cognitive leap to rational understanding. It is more likely that the child will not understand what we are saying or will not believe us simply because he or she cannot yet fathom such a thing as death. What do we do now? We may bide our time. The child learns by personal discovery. If we are ambitious, we may speed this process up a little. So do we place dead frogs in our children's paths? By all means. Only, dead frogs do not conveniently present themselves to parents for their use. But taking hikes increases the probability of finding a dead animal. So does traveling. On Florida's highways and roadsides, for example, dead armadillos are quite common. A child's personal encounter with a dead animal with parents present to clarify, is a good beginning. Even then it takes a number of such experiences over a period of time before the child can comprehend that aspect of death. Meanwhile, we continue to tell the truth as Grollman suggests, and are not perturbed when the child asks the same or a similar question again and again.

Telling the truth can be very difficult. It is natural to want to shield the child and to avoid the unpleasant subject. But there is no other way. Edgar Jackson (18) reports of the difficulty Gary's parents had had telling him of an untimely death and how they learned to be honest by seeing Gary's anxiety at their evasiveness. Some time later, the following conversation took place between Gary and his mother:

> Mother is baking a cake and some cupcakes. Gary comes into the kitchen.
>
> Gary: Who is this for?
> Mother: It's for the Martin family.
> Gary: Why is it for them?
> Mother: They've had some trouble.
> Gary: What kind of trouble.
> Mother: Mr. Martin died in an accident.
> Gary: Oh. Can I have a cupcake?
>
> Later in the day, Gary suddenly asked: "Was Mr. Martin old enough to be killed?" His mother replied that he was not, that he was too young to die but that accidents sometimes happen and people get sick and die before they get old, that's why we have to be careful and that's why we have doctors to get us well. Gary was satisfied with the answer (pp. 39–40).

On the one hand, death is a natural occurrence. We ought to be able to assist our children in understanding the biological facts of death. But death is also a mystery. This is where our beliefs come in. It is important that we distinguish clearly between beliefs and facts. Our children demand that we respond honestly about our beliefs. If we are confident in our belief in afterlife we should have no problem in sharing that belief. But what if we have doubts, or what if we believe there is no life after death? I think we should share our beliefs truthfully whatever they may be as well as our doubts. Children sense when we are not truthful. They also see our behavior and note the discrepancies between what we say and what we do. To know that we are lying is probably more unsettling to our children than our doubts. It is important, however, to avoid dogmatism, and to emphasize that different people have different beliefs and also that people change their beliefs.

There are many questions children ask to which we do not have answers. For example, children often want to know where Heaven is. It is hazardous to fabricate one that we believe to be at the child's level, such as the mother did who told her little boy that Heaven was "like a huge castle in the sky." Within a minute she found herself trapped in the images and questions her statement elicited in her child: "Oh, boy, does it have a huge drawbridge? And big watchtowers with many soldiers and big cannons and all kinds of guns and lasers? They can shoot down all the planes and the spaceships too."

The best thing is to tell the child when we do not know the answer. We will lose some status and prestige in the eyes of our young children, but sooner or later they will discover that there are many things parents don't know. Besides, children usually create their own ideas and beliefs of what Heaven is like, as we know from research. In one of the studies (11) a six-year-old boy offered the following answer to the question "What happens to people in Heaven?": "If it's a woman, she does the cleaning. If it's a man he'll be an angel . . . he has his own store . . . he is going to bake cakes all year long?" (pp. 14–15). This is what some children said in another study (13): "You can talk to the other angels but you can't play hopscotch because you're supposed to do what Jesus says and angels aren't supposed to play" (pp. 74–75). "You couldn't get out. There is no door and God wouldn't let you out. . . . "They eat whatever God gives them."

Close interactions with our children are important in helping us know about their worries and anxieties. We must encourage

our children to share them with us by creating a warm and
accepting atmosphere and by keeping lines of communications
open. As any psychologist will tell us and as we know from
personal experience, the mere act of talking things out has a
positive effect: it reduces burdens and releases pent-up tensions.
Sometimes, when a deep, secret fear "comes to light" it loses its
blackness and fierceness, and the child may even be able to
laugh about it.

> Susan's parents had moved to a new city. It turned out that Susan
> had to pass a cemetery on her way to and from school each day.
> She was terrified. In summer camp she had heard some gruesome
> ghost stories, and discovered that some of the girls were certain
> that there are ghosts and that they "live" in cemeteries, so passing
> by this cemetery each morning and afternoon was utterly frighten-
> ing. Susan's chest felt tight, she held her breath and tried to run at
> the same time. This went on for a week. Her parents noticed that
> all was not right but thought it was the new school, teacher, and
> classmates. Finally on Saturday of that week Susan shared her
> problem with her parents. They not only reassured her, but her
> mother offered to drive her to school and pick her up after school
> to walk home. So by car as well as foot they passed by the
> cemetery each day. Twice they went inside. They also talked
> about ghosts, graves, bodies, skeletons, and death. Within two
> weeks Susan had overcome her fear and walked by the cemetery
> that was now nothing but an ordinary harmless cemetery.

Pets. Having pets in the family gives the child an opportunity
for close encounters with the cycle of life that includes death.
Of course, families acquire pets because they like them, not to
set up object lessons. Still, having the child experience the death
of a pet and the pain of the loss, can be a valuable experience—
with the help and guidance of a sensitivie parent. A beautiful
example of such help is given in the story "A Child Loses a Pet"
by Ute Carson (19). I highly recommend it to the reader.

I have tried to avoid listing *don'ts.* They offer little help in
what to *do.* Here is one of the exceptions to my rule: When
your child's pet has died, *don't* rush to get another one. By
doing that you first deprive the child of the important experience of grieving. Also, you unwittingly convey to the child that
loved ones can be replaced and that attachments are shallow and

instantly transferable. Fortunately, our children often let us know when we make such a mistake.

Beth and Barry had a lovely puppy named Pippy. They fed him, bathed him, played with him, and went along on any trips to the veterinarian. One day while the children were at their grandparents' house, the dog fell off a second floor balcony. The housekeeper heard the whimpers and called Mother. She took Pippy to the doctor, but it was hopeless. The mother, knowing how much her children had loved their puppy, could not bring herself to tell them what had happened. She and her husband made up a list of possible places they could go to buy a silver-gray poodle puppy that looked exactly like Pippy. One parent went all over town. The other drove 75 miles to the people who had sold them Pippy, but to no avail. In the end they brought home a lovely poodle puppy of just the right age—but it was black. So the parents had to tell the truth. Then with big smiles on their faces, they brought in the new puppy who was sitting in Pippy's basket. They were not prepared for their children's reactions: "I don't want that dumb thing. Get it out of Pippy's basket," Beth screamed. Barry walked toward the basket with a wild look on his face as if ready to smash the intruder against the wall. The rejection of the new puppy was so complete that the parents hurriedly took him away. It was three months before the children wanted another puppy—a brown cocker spaniel.

Television. As we have seen, today's television fare contains much violence and depicts death unrealistically. It is futile to attempt to screen out all that is of potential harm in the child's environment. This does not mean we can do nothing at all. I think parents should carefully screen the television programs their children watch regularly. They might watch such programs with their children for a time and observe the effects the programs have on their children, then engage them in conversations afterward to see what notions and attitudes the children are expressing. It is helpful to counterbalance adverse material by guiding the children toward programs with prosocial models and benign content. At the least, parents can serve a vital role as mediators, especially for young children. They can soften impacts, lessen fears, clarify misconceptions, and correct unrealistic portrayals. Whatever we do as parents, of course, is time consuming. I believe, however, that the time consumed is worth the effort. The television industry has been widely criticized for its violent programming, but this criticism has produced little change. Yet, as individual households we have a great deal of power—we can turn off the programs we find too violent.

Children's Literature. I have already mentioned the value of good children's books on death. Again, parents have an important function as mediators. They know their children and are sensitive to their needs at different stages of development. They can best determine which books are appropriate for their children at given times. They bring the books to their children or the children to the books. For preschool children parents or grandparents make the best readers and provide the best laps to sit on during the reading. Discussions afterwards are valuable in clearing up possible misunderstandings, or in reinforcing valuable ideas and attitudes conveyed in the book. The annotated bibliography of children's books in this volume is designed to assist parents in the selection of books. I would recommend, however, that parents first read the books to form their own opinions concerning their suitability for their children.

Most of the books on death written for young children have as their main theme the death of a pet and how to cope with it. Where a child has lost a pet, it can be very helpful to read or listen to a story that reminds them that other children also lose their pets, and they, too, feel sad or angry for a time, but later on they feel all right again.

Guidelines for Teachers

The best help I can offer teachers is to guide them to the wealth of resources that have been published over the past 15 years. They contain far more information and suggestions than could be given on a few pages in this chapter. A great many articles have been written by teachers at all educational levels, from preschool to college, in which they discuss goals, objectives, and activities they have used and found successful in their classrooms in death-related units, modules, programs, or discussions. For an annotated listing of these articles as well as books, audiovisuals, and other death-related resources, see (20, 21). Some of the available books on death education are also listed in the bibliography for adults in this volume as is an extensive mediagraphy. In addition, the teacher interested in teaching about death will find a journal such as *Death Education* valuable. The reader is also referred to (22), "Teachable Moments Occasioned by Small Deaths," written for primary and elementary school teachers, and "Death Education in the Schools for Older Children" (23), is written primarily for middle- and high-school teachers.

The idea of death education in the schools still meets with doubt and disapproval by many parents, school boards, and even teachers. The argument is that death education is an intimate subject that belongs in the domain of the family. I agree. But it also has a place in the schools, as long as children's and parents' beliefs and values are not infringed upon. I believe with many teachers, psychologists, and parents that not only is death a legitimate subject, but it is also an essential and integral part of any school curriculum that is at all concerned with significant life issues. It is difficult for me to imagine how the subject of death can be avoided at the high-school level. How can teachers keep death out of a course in biology, history, family life, humanities, or current events? How can the subject of death be avoided at the lower educational levels at which much learning is based on the child's immediate experience and where teachable moments present the occasions from which valuable death-related educational experiences emerge naturally? But regardless of how we stand on the question of death education in the schools, death does not wait until the arguments are settled. Teachers, school nurses, counselors, and other personnel who have been in the schools for a time know that death intrudes into the schools and can catch everyone unprepared as in the case that follows:

Mr. Smith was 63 years old when one day shortly after lunch he collapsed in his classroom in front of his fifth grade class. The room was in an uproar. Somebody herded the students into the cafeteria which was now vacated. One of the cooks was asked to keep an eye on them. They were stunned and shocked, and the silence was total. They heard the siren of the ambulance grow louder, stop, start up again and then fade away. Nobody spoke. Finally, the principal came into the cafeteria and told the class that Mr. Smith was on the way to the hospital. He had fainted but he seemed to be all right. The children felt relieved. Back in their classroom, they were given an assignment until it was time for dismissal. Mr. Smith had suffered a massive heart attack and was dead on arrival at the hospital. The next morning a substitute teacher stood at Mr. Smith's desk. When the bell rang he said to the class: "Now open you math books to page 47. Today we will learn how to divide fractions by fractions." Not a word was said about Mr. Smith's death that day or the next day or the next. Mr. Smith seemed to have been erased, and no one was prepared to help the class cope with their shock and grief.

I would recommend that school faculties as a whole meet and discuss what to do in case a classmate, sibling, parent, teacher, or other member of the staff dies. A number of faculties have done that after a death event they knew they had not handled well. Mr. Smith's colleagues even developed a booklet with guidelines for teachers and aides, including procedures and a list of resource persons that can be contacted for assistance.

Mrs. Baker's second grade class was as vivacious as any can be. One Saturday evening Chris, one of the girls in the class, was killed in an automobile accident. Mrs. Baker was told Sunday morning. She was stunned, shocked, shaken, and showed other symptoms of acute grief. Her husband called the principal. She, in turn, called other teachers. Some came over to the Baker's house. Parents called other parents. Monday morning came. Mrs. Baker pulled herself together. She was determined to meet with her children even though others offered to do it. She gathered them close in a circle in the reading corner by the bookshelves, and as she told the children about the accident and Chris' death, the tears came rolling down her cheeks. Soon every child cried. Then Mrs. Baker wiped her tears away, blew her nose and invited her children to tell "how sad" they felt and also to tell something they wanted to remember about Chris. The children did. Some things they told were funny, and everybody laughed. Next, Mrs. Baker wondered if the class might want to go to the funeral. They did. They also wrote condolence letters to the family. After the funeral Mrs. Baker and her second graders organized and led a memorial service for the entire school in the school auditorium. At the end of it the children planted a dogwood tree in the school yard behind the classroom in memory of their dead classmate, Chris.

Helping the Dying Child

Nothing is more taxing and emotionally draining for health professionals than working with a terminally ill child. When the child is suffering from a cancer or another chronic and progressive disease, they have to cope first of all with the fact that no matter how much they wish otherwise, they cannot help the child recover. Thus, the most rewarding aspect of their profession is denied them. Especially in the case of children this brings about guilt, anger, and a sense of helplessness in addition to the anxieties that the proximity of death naturally creates (24, 25). In an emotionally charged atmosphere tensions are high, and hostilities often develop toward other caregivers or the family. In addition to having to overcome these problems, health professionals must interact with their young patients at a level appropriate to their developmental status. Children show behaviors characteristic of their stage of development, but they are also unique personalities. Thus, effective caring requires attention to the individual child and sensitivity to his or her special needs. In addition to providing physical care, health professionals must also provide emotional support. They have to function both as carers and comforters. The latter extends beyond the dying child to include the family. Parents experience even greater guilt, anger, and anxiety than the health care staff. Not only are health professionals called upon to provide emotional help to the parents, but they must strive to achieve their cooperation for most effective care of the child. No wonder that these tasks often overwhelm, and that the problem of staff stress in the care of dying children has been a subject of intensive study and its management a major concern (26).

For an extensive coverage of relevant articles, books, organizations, and audiovisuals, see (20, 21).

Initial Communication with Parents

One of the physician's most dreaded task is that of telling parents of their child's terminal illness. A list of points to be considered by physicians when talking with parents after the initial diagnosis of cancer is given in (1). Among them are the following:

- Recognize the depth of shock and despair the parents must be feeling.
- Explain the basis for the diagnosis and the nature of the type of disease.
- Discuss causes of the problem with emphasis on relieving possible parental guilt.
- Explain the fatal outcome and type of therapy to be undertaken.
- Attempt to gain parental support both in the physical and emotional care of the child.
- Assure parents that medical support will always be available.
- Help parents to anticipate problems involved in the initial telling of others and during the child's illness. Go over possible reactions of siblings (e.g., anger, jealousy, fear, guilt).
- Emphasize any hope possible. If there is hope for remission, dwell on that. If there is not, discuss scientific research going on, if appropriate. If nothing is available, emphasize the support the child will get from the medical staff throughout the illness. Discourage excessive optimism but allow some hope especially in the early stages of the disease.
- Stress the importance of maintaining continuity in raising the child.
- Assess the family's strengths and weaknesses and encourage building on the strengths. It is important to ask each parent how the other will accept the death, thus encouraging empathy and visualizing problems in advance.
- Inform parents of any programs, organizations, community resources, and mutual or self-help groups available.

Helping Parents

There is nothing health professionals or others can do to *remove* the many powerful emotions that threaten to overwhelm parents from the time of the initial diagnosis to the death of their child. We cannot take away the sorrow and the depth of pain and anguish these parents feel. But health caregivers and others can help to *lessen* some of these feelings. *Anger* is one of the dominant emotions parents experience. The unfairness of the situation combined with their helplessness to do anything to change it leads to feelings of frustration that can be destructive. The important question for helping professionals should be: How can parents be helped to express their anger in positive ways? Sometimes, especially in cases of genetically transmitted diseases, one parent will turn his or her anger on the other one, thus adding to the stress of the situation. Siblings and grandparents may have to bear the brunt of displaced parental anger. Other common targets for anger are God, doctors, nurses, and other caregivers, and even inanimate objects such as the hospital bed and machines used in treating the child. If parents turn their explosive anger inward, it can result in depression, suicidal urges, and even psychotic episodes. Parents need to be helped to find appropriate channels for venting anger. Such channels might be ongoing group or individual therapy, joining parent support groups, joining an organization to raise funds for medical research, and physical activities to discharge tension. Another dominant emotion with which parents need help is *guilt*. Since the child's birth the parents have nurtured and protected their child. When they are not able to protect their child from a fatal disease, they may feel irrational guilt of having caused the disease. In addition, if the parent-child relationship has been strained, parents may feel guilt for the negative feelings they have had toward the child. As the illness progresses, guilt may be compounded with parents' recurring wishes for the child to die. Guilt is also exacerbated as the parents become aware of hidden feelings of relief that it is not they who have the fatal illness. Guilt can be tolerated better if the parent can be encouraged to express these feelings openly. The helping professional can then accept the parents' feelings of guilt and join them in attempting to understand those feelings as natural parts of

most intimate relationships. *Anxiety* is another common emotion parents of dying children feel. Parents' anxiety arises from
different sources, prominent among them the inability to help
the child to cope with the situation, the fear of a total breakdown of emotional resources, and feelings of loneliness and
alienation from others (1). One way parental anxieties have been
constructively channeled is through direct and active involvement in the dying child's care as in the model home care
program for dying children developed by Martinson et al. (27).
If the family has strength and resources to care for their dying
child at home, this is, of course, ideal. Kathy and Jay Montgomery (28) give a moving account of how they were able to
provide this care. They write:

> "Seth died with privacy and dignity in the arms of his parents in
> the warmth and security of his home. It was not morbid, as some
> people might think, but beautiful and peaceful. Three years later,
> we continue to grieve for our son. However, the memories of
> those final days remain a source of comfort to us that is
> immeasurable" (p. 125).

Short of home care, the hospital staff may find ways for parents
to participate to some extent in their child's care in the hospital.
In communities where organized support groups are nonexistent
and therapy is not feasible, health professionals can help to raise
community awareness of these needs through the media and
through direct communication with local government and civic
leaders. Availability of published resources in the hospital library
or bibliographies of materials for information is of help to
parents. Any help provided for parents will also benefit the
dying child.

Communication with Children

Whether to tell or not tell terminally ill children of their
condition seems to be settled. Waechter's (23) and Spinetta's
(30) pioneering studies have provided clear answers: Almost all
terminally ill children ages five years and over—some even
younger—are aware of their condition even if caregivers and
parents hide the truth or tell them otherwise. Thus there is

nothing gained by deception. But how is it possible for children to know? One answer comes from health professionals who have worked with dying children for a long time. These carers have observed that suffering a life-threatening illness often accelerates development and makes these children "mature beyond their years." This is shown, for example, in the way they often deliberately play along in the game of pretense to protect their parents who cannot cope with their child's death and even less with the thought that the child knows. There is another related answer to the question. Children, even those very young, *interpret* their experience of the disease and its negative impact on their bodies, the various invasive medical procedures, such as painful injections or blood transfusions, and the anxieties of parents and health care staffs, that are communicated non-verbally. All this adds up to the conclusion of impending personal disaster. These children do not need to have an accurate concept of death's finality to realize that something dreadful is happening to them.

Foley and McCarty (31) have described a typical physician's explanation to a leukemic child of school age:

> You have a serious blood disease, leukemia. Ten years ago, there was no treatment for leukemia and many people died. Now there are a number of drugs which can be used to treat leukemia. There are several types of leukemia and the type you have is the one for which there are the most drugs. Treatment to keep the leukemia cells away will last 3 years. You'll miss at least a month of school, the time needed to get the disease under control. The main problem right now is infection. If you stay free of infection you will be out of the hospital in about 5 days, if an infection occurs, you'll be hospitalized for at least 2 weeks. (pp. 1115–1116)

Allowing children to ask questions after such an explanation and allowing for time to talk even when they have no questions creates the setting of mutual trust necessary in these stressful situations.

Young Children's Needs

The pervasive problem with dying infants is the anxiety created by separation from the nurturing person through hospitalization.

Ideally, a parent should spend most of the child's waking hours with him or her. That is often not possible. Fortunately, at least one member of the hospital staff usually develops a special affection for an infant, in a sense "adopts" the infant and becomes a surrogate parent. Although this is likely to create hostility and jealousy on the part of the parents, it is the best thing for the child. Anxieties related to separation and abandonment continue in the preschool years but now children experience them consciously. As noted earlier, many anxieties and fears in early childhood stem from inaccurate perceptions of events and immature kinds of causal thinking. Terminally ill preschool children are likely to think that by putting them in the hospital, their parents have abandoned them and seek to know why. Similarly, children are trying to discover the reason why they have the dreadful disease, are subjected to such painful medical procedures, and why such terrible things are happening to their bodies. Unfortunately, they commonly attribute a psychological motive to these events: They believe that they are being punished for being bad. Parents, doctors, and nurses are all agressors and punishers. That is why terminally ill young children often frantically appeal to their carers, promising to be good while at the same time raging impotently against them in protest of all the pain they are inflicting, and that very raging and crying by the children is itself another demonstration of their badness to be punished. To make matters worse, young children's self-centered orientation causes them to attribute to the carers and others the same feelings of anger and rage they experience. It seems to be a vicious circle. In addition to the suffering, young children thus actually feel responsible for their disease and all that is happening to them.

> A four-year-old dying boy had made a drawing and had given it to the social worker with this explanation: "This is a little boy. He is very, very sick because he was a bad little boy. He killed a baby bird. This cement truck is coming up and it's going to crush him and dump all the cement on top of him."
>
> A three-year-old girl told another social worker this story: "Once upon a time there was a little girl. She hit her baby brother. They put the little girl on the bed and stuck needles in her. And they bleeded her and then her mummy came and said: 'Poor Jessica'

and cried and cried." (What happened then?) The child, irritated, "That's all, I don't know any more than that."

Not all young children express their thoughts and feelings even when we encourage them to do so, but there are telltale signs in their behaviors.

Young children may not allow themselves to think of their nonexistence until death is close. They may regress into more infantile behavior and become very dependent on nurturing adults as Waechter (32) suggests.

Meeting Young Children's Needs

It is a good idea to explain the cause-effect relationships between hospitalization and disease, disease and its effects, and disease and medical procedures even if the child does not comprehend. Carers should do so at every opportunity and do it in different ways. They should encourage parents to do the same. In addition, the child should be told again and again that he or she is not bad, that the disease is nobody's fault, not the child's, the parents', or the doctor's; that the child is not being punished; that no one wants to hurt the child, but that helping does sometimes hurt. By taking time to tell the child these things we demonstrate that he or she is worthy and that we are on the child's side. A caring tone of voice is soothing and holding or stroking the child's hand while we interact with the child is comforting. Adams (24) suggests that the most helpful thing hospital staff can do is to establish a close personal relationship with the child. Telling stories, making up stories together, reading to the child, playing with the child, listening to music together, and just being there with the child are all ways we demonstrate our care and love. A parent's participation in the care is, of course, ideal, but even frequent visits are of great help. So in large measure, the cognitive distortion caused by the child's immature causal thinking can be counteracted in the affective realm by giving the child love, care, and reassurance. This task is made easier by a simple mental exercise on the part of the caregiver: Just suppose for one minute that you are in the child's place, and imagine how it must feel and what you would need.

It is essential to prepare the child for all medical procedures. It is a mistake for the physician to tell a child: "I'm going to give you a tiny mosquito bite" when in fact preparing to do a spinal tap. This will cause the child to mistrust everyone and to panic every time something needs to be done. Giving the child some choice whenever possible, such as the choice of sites for injections, or permitting the child to assist in some small way with a procedure will minimize the feeling of helplessness, and foster a sense of control. It is important to permit the child to express both pain and anger as a natural thing that is not good or bad. At all times, carers need to remind the child that their task and sole objective is to help the child.

Love, care, empathy, and permission to express pain and anger should not, however, be misinterpreted as an attitude of laissez-faire with respect to the child's behavior. Hospital staff should clearly delineate rules and regulations concerning the child's behavior just as parents in their guilt should not dispense with normal behavioral boundaries. Young children in particular, whether they are sick or well, need the security of limits imposed upon them. They respond to behavioral guidance that is carried out in a constructive manner. This results in positive feedback from the environment, thus helping the child see himself as being good. It also fulfills the dying child's need to have some sense of being "normal" and of being treated so.

Young children who use regression and denial as ways of coping with their situation need the love and care of their parents and of health professionals to reassure them that they will not be left alone to face a calamity they can hardly fathom. No one should try to deprive children of this way of coping. In these cases health professionals are needed most by parents to lend support to them so they, in turn, can find the strength to fulfill their child's desperate need.

School-Aged Children's Needs

Fear of abandonment continues through the school years but is less pronounced than earlier in life. The school-aged child also uses psychological causality, that is, perceives the disease as a punishment, not by parents and caregivers, but by God or some other supernatural power. Adolescents and adults have such perceptions as well. School-aged children are better able to articulate their thoughts and feelings and have more resources for coping with their situations. Their capacities for self-control are growing. At this stage of development children can realistically understand relationships between the disease and its effects on the body, as well as the specific purposes of various medical procedures. Children are intensely interested in what is happening to them and how. Any one who has worked with terminally ill older children knows that they are experts on their diseases. This knowledge is important. Health professionals will find these children eager to cooperate in any procedure and willing to fight their disease with great determination. However, they have many worries. Anxieties about disfigurement and other adverse changes in their bodies are pronounced. Negative body image easily generalizes into negative image of the whole person. During the school years children increasingly become emancipated from the confines of the home. Peers, friends, school, classmates, and organized group activities become important. Thus, having to be away from all these creates a feeling of isolation. This feeling increases with age.

Healthy children now know that death is final and as we have seen, they are preoccupied with the processes of death and decay and with the question of life after death. It should not surprise us that these concerns take on a new dimension for the terminally ill child; they are real and urgent. The fight against the disease and the attempts to master death fears can overwhelm at this stage. Many children openly express their fears. Waechter (32) found a direct relationship between parents' openness to such dialogue and the amount of communication that occurred. She reports on one eight-year-old boy who repeatedly requested that his parents tell him if and when he was going to die so that he could prepare himself (p. 62). Some children's questions such as that by a nine-year-old girl, are indirect: "Mom, will I ever go to high school?" Some children at this stage, as at the previous one, do not seek information, and in fact, request not to be told. Some emphatically declare that they are going to get well. Children give us clear signs that they need denial to cope with their situations. But many more children reach the point when they realize and confront the reality that their tomorrows are numbered. They suffer emotional pain and grief over losing their parents, friends, their future, everything.

Meeting School-Aged Children's Needs

Terminally ill children at any age need love, care, comfort, and the assurance that they will not be left to die alone. Parents and health professionals are needed to provide this reassurance, even though older children may be too embarrassed to admit these needs. Older children appreciate time given freely to discuss in detail with physicians, nurses, and others, their diseases, as well as medical procedures, medications and how they work.

Health professionals can help by contacting the child's teachers, who, in turn, can talk about the sick classmate with the classroom group. Even if only two or three friends and classmates visit and keep the terminally ill child up-to-date on what is going on, this can be of immense help. It keeps the child in contact instead of isolated. Simple gestures such as postcards from classmates are greatly valued. One class videotaped a play the class had put on for parents' night. In another instance children taped entire classes, sports events, and social activities. In some cities children can even participate in all their classes by closed circuit television and can phone in questions. One friend, a nurse, recently told me how her small pediatric ward had managed to accommodate a surprise party given by a young patient's class of 34 children! In many large medical centers "hospital" teachers regularly work with school-aged children and adolescents. Such intellectual activities can be of great therapeutic value. They give children a sense of keeping up with their peers; they lead to mastery of new skills and are thus rewarding; they offer needed diversion, and most of all, such teaching programs demonstrate that the child is a valued member of the school and worthy of such special efforts. No professional helper and no program, no matter how well designed, however, can wholly replace the parents' love. At this stage it is important that parents are able to communicate openly with their children. In matters of belief, it is the parents who have most to say.

Doctors, nurses, social workers, teachers are reluctant to impose their values and beliefs on children. And parents generally want it so. But if parents are not available for open talk, one of the others will be questioned; in most instances this will be less helpful. Ideally, there will be close communication between parents and the hospital staff on matters of religion. Where beliefs coincide, the child will greatly benefit.

Even deep religiosity does not prevent the school-aged child from having to suffer the pain of grief over the impending loss. School-aged children need to feel safe to express emotions of rage, anger, disappointment, and resentment over the unfairness of their situation. It helps immensely when parents can find the strength to be with their children at these times, to share this pain openly no matter how difficult it is. Such sharing of grief helps the child, and it may also help the parents. It is then that the child most needs parents' reaffirmation of their love. Health carers need also let the child know that they are available to listen and to stand by at these times of special hurt.

Adolescents' Needs

Terminally ill adolescents have not been studied as intensively as have younger children. Nevertheless, clinical evidence concerning this group is accumulating. Adolescents share the same fears of abandonment as do younger age groups. They need the same love and reassurance, but unlike younger children they are more aware of the immensity of their impending loss. They have a more highly developed sense of time and are hungry for a life that stretches far ahead into an exciting future. Thus, their anger and bitterness over their impending death are much stronger. They, too, see their demise as punishment, but they consider it as more cruel and undeserved. Terminally ill adolescents are understandably envious of their peers. Their peers are developing their identities as young adults, they are playing close attention to their maturing bodies; they are relating at various levels to the opposite sex as well as to friends of the same sex, and they are in the final period of breaking their emotional bondage to their parents. While all this is happening to healthy adolescents, dying adolescents are about to lose everything—their dreams, hopes, aspirations; a world to be explored, experienced and conquered; a life to be lived. Instead of being able to take pride in their physical development, they find themselves trapped in disfigured bodies they despise. They are deprived of romantic and sexual involvements, and at a time when self-assertion and independence from authority relationships become dominant needs, their forced dependency on adults as a constant in their daily lives is the final insult. No wonder that dying adolescents are bitter and enraged, that they lose self-esteem and self-assurance, and in a desperate attempt to prove their independence, often alienate themselves from those they need the most!

Meeting Adolescents' Needs

Helping terminally ill adolescents is a great challenge for health professionals. To be the target of rage, resentment, and rejection when one offers affection, friendship, and support is difficult, even for those specially trained and those with infinitely patient personalities. Therefore, hospital staff should share the task. They should not give up on such patients no matter how defiant they are. Health professionals understand how adolescents feel, and in fact, have their own rage to cope with in the face of their impotence in healing their young patients. I think adolescents, even in their rage, realize and appreciate the helping hand that is offered. Those adolescents who control their anger and withdraw into silent depression tend equally to reject support but need it just as much. Parents, however, are the main target for adolescents' anger. Health professionals can help indirectly by telling parents that such behavior is not abnormal, and by urging them not to retaliate. There is nothing worse than a dying adolescent and the family locked in an explosive or silent deathbed battle. Fortunately, adolescents often "adopt" one person from the health care team as their confidante and accept from that person all the love and comfort they need. Waechter (32) observed that in the terminal phase most adolescents *do* come to accept loving relationships with parents and other family members. Many parents have reported that their adolescent children demonstrate amazing emotional strength toward the end and a quiet acceptance of their fate such that they even comfort their parents at the time when parents are in deep despair.

Helping the Bereaved Child

Many studies over the past decades have been devoted to discovering how people in contemporary society cope with bereavement. Most have focused on adults. For informative and thoughtful discussions of the subject of bereavement and grief in general, the reader is referred to Jackson (33, 34). For professional and lay readers alike, Worden (35) offers a valuable source of information. These readings provide a broad basis for understanding the special dynamics involved in childhood bereavement. In addition, the reader will find resources such as books, articles, organizations, and audiovisuals listed in (20, 21). Childhood bereavement has received less research attention than is needed. Hopefully, new studies will focus on this important area. Meanwhile we have the findings and reports of a number of dedicated researchers and practitioners in the helping professions that enable us to derive guidelines for helping.

A frequently asked question is: "Should parents let children attend the funeral?" My answer is always "Yes"—with one qualification: if children want to attend. A child should not be forced to be present at a funeral. In the case of children who have no idea what is involved, a parent should describe in detail what happens at the funeral, and be sure to add that "grownups will be crying because they are all very sad." Parents may also suggest that the child may go but not stay. Parents frequently decide to send the children away "until it's all over." Children get in the way when funeral preparations have to be made, and the atmosphere of gloom in the house is so depressing. Why not spare the child? Most often it turns out to be a mistake, and it cannot be undone. Many young people have told me they sometimes still get angry at their parents for having kept them away from the funeral of a beloved grandparent. They feel that they were cheated. It is unfair to toss the child out of the family unit at a time of crisis. By doing that we are depriving this child of being part of an important step in the family's grieving process. The presence of children when a death has occurred also helps the adults. For what better way to be reminded of the continuity of generations and the cycle of life than through the presence of our young!

Children experience many kinds of losses. Even growing up is a form of loss. A basic source of comfort, security, and pleasure is lost through weaning, toilet training, and other aspects of socialization away from dependency on the nurturing adult (1). Children lose relationships: playmates or friends break up their association, a favorite uncle or aunt moves to a different place, etc. Children also experience losses of objects: favorite toys break, a special blanket finally gets tossed away, a favorite outfit is outgrown, etc. None of these losses, however, can be likened to the loss of a loved one through death, because the loss caused by death is total. It often is a devastating experience, and overcoming it may take a long time.

To help a bereaved child it is first necessary that we consider what that person's relationship was to the child. At the same time we must consider the child's developmental stage. Then we should be aware how other forces affect the child at the time of death and after. One major force is the family. As a member of a family unit, the child also experiences the impact of the loss on the other members of the family. When a child's grandparent has died, the parents have lost a parent; when a sibling has died, the parents have lost a child; and when a child's parent has died, the surviving parent has lost a spouse.

In the next pages, we will consider needs of children who have lost a grandparent, a sibling, or a parent through death.

When a Grandparent Dies

When grandparents live in the household or when interactions with the family are frequent or intensive, it is likely that relationships with grandchildren are close. There is often a special affinity between grandchildren and grandparents. In most cases, both live outside the mainstream of productive society and in a sense are disenfranchised. One has everything to gain and the other nothing to lose. Grandparents do not carry the responsibility of raising the child and so are not sources of frustration or targets for rebellion. This can allow for a carefree and mutually enhancing relationship. When such a relationship is severed through the grandparent's death, the child's loss is profound.

Infants are probably least affected by a grandparent's death because they may not yet be able to differentiate grandparents from other adults, but principally because they do not lose the primary nurturing person.

The *preschool child* will have great difficulty understanding where the grandparent went, and why he or she is not coming back. It is most important that parents tell the truth as Grollman (17) has suggested, and that they repeat telling the truth with patience. This is not easy. The preschool child is at the stage where answers such as "Grandpa has gone on a long trip," or "he is asleep," make sense and satisfy his or her curiosity—for a while. Eventually people come back from trips and wake up from sleep, so parents have merely postponed the problem. How we answer the child's questions, beyond the facts of biological death, depends upon our beliefs.

It is important that we keep the preschool child's immature understanding of death in mind in interpreting his or her reaction. Misjudging the child's behavior can create more difficulties for the child than already exist.

> When Michael came home from nursery school his mother met him by the door, hugged him close to her and said: "Michael, I have very sad news to tell you." Michael wanted to know what. "Your Grandpa died." Michael broke out of the embrace: "Oh yeah? Can I go swimming at Greg's house? His mom said it's O.K." Michael's mother was appalled. With tears running down her cheeks she managed to reply: "How can you be so selfish? Your Grandpa just died and all you want is to swim. What a cold-hearted boy you are!" Michael is confused, astonished, and angry: "I want to go swimming at Greg's house," he cried.

Michael is a sensitive child who loves his grandpa. They often fish and hike together. When Michael's mother tells him of the death Michael does not know the term, nor does he want to know. He has swimming on his mind. Not until weeks later did Michael learn what Grandpa's dying meant: that he could no

longer take him hiking, or fishing, and that he would no longer
get presents from his grandpa.

A beautiful example of the responses and actions of sensitive
and knowledgeable parents can be found in (36). See also the
Books for Children: An Annotated Bibliography in this volume.

Older children and adolescents often experience a deep sense
of loss when a grandparent has died but find that the parent
most affected by this loss will bear his or her grief in stoic
silence. Sometimes a parent finds it easier to grieve alone.
Whatever the reason, children then are also forced to remain
silent. Studies have shown, however, that it is important for
grieving persons to express their feelings and their thoughts,
especially with loved ones. This is particularly true for children.
On the other hand, children are resilient. They have many
exciting things to learn in the process of growing up. When they
feel secure in the love of their parents, they generally overcome
their sadness over a grandparent's death long before their parents
do.

When a Sibling Dies

How the death of a child affects surviving siblings is one of the
topics in childhood bereavement that needs much additional
research to help us gain deeper insights into its dynamics and to
guide us to be more effective as helpers for these children.
Nonetheless, several research studies have provided some basic
data and reports of clinical case studies are accumulating. For a
recent and extensive discussion of this topic the reader is
referred to (37), which reviews the existing studies, provides a
number of clinical case illustrations, and proposes research
questions that need to be answered so that we can differentiate
healthy or normal from pathological grief reactions of surviving
siblings.

At present the information we have is primarily about
disturbed emotional and behavioral reactions to sibling death,
such as suicidal behavior, depression, hysterical pains, and death
phobias. This is so because most of the research and clinical
studies are based on children who were treated for these
reactions. From these reports we know what can go wrong and

the conditions that produce these results. Thus we know what should not happen. This identification of danger areas is an important beginning.

It is generally believed that death after a long illness is somewhat easier for parents to cope with than a sudden death, because it gives them time before the death occurs to begin the process of adaptation which is termed "anticipatory grief." For the surviving child, this may actually exacerbate the problem. The healthy child may have felt neglected and rejected for many weeks or months during the sibling's illness when the parents' time and energies were spent on the dying child. Thus the surviving young child probably has built up a great deal of resentment against the sick sibling and the parents, and may actually be glad at the news of the death.

> When five-year-old Stephan was told that his little brother died, he exclaimed: "Goodie! Can I have Nicky's Teddy and his tricycle? Will you now take me to Disney World? And lots of shows, and play checkers, and can I have a story every night?"

Parents and others should understand the cause for such expressions. It would be a mistake to punish this child. Unfortunately, children like Stephan will find that after the sibling's death their parents will not do any of the things they demand to make up for the lost attention and feel reassured of their parent's love. Their parents' grief and sorrow probably so overwhelms and depletes them that there is little strength left to attend to the living child. Although convinced that loving and caring for the living child is needed and may actually ease their pain, parents still may be too emotionally and physically exhausted to give appropriate attention to the suriving child for a considerable length of time. There are no easy solutions to this problem. One way to help is for a relative, friend, or even neighbor to "adopt" the surviving child, to be a surrogate parent until the actual parents can cope better. This may take weeks or months.

The surviving child often feels a great deal of guilt. Sometimes, as we have seen, the child may feel he or she brought about the sibling's death through magic power. Then the child may feel great anxiety about being punished for this terrible thing. Another source of anxiety is the young child's belief that he or she will get the same disease and have the same fate. The helper should discuss these feelings with the child and reassure the child in every way possible.

Older siblings who understand the finality of death, experience much the same pain of loss and can identify with their parents in this respect. At the same time, however, they feel anger and jealousy for the special privileges given the sick child and the parents' continued unavailability after the death much as do younger children. Older siblings' guilt is a direct consequence of these feelings. Guilt and remorse also arise from memories of fights, teasing, and other negative interactions children had with their sibling. They may be haunted by the memory of having told him to "drop dead" or "get lost." The fear of catching their sibling's disease can be very strong at this stage also and is often reinforced by parents' overly protective attitude and behavior regarding health.

Much of the difficulty that surviving siblings experience is caused directly by parents' pathological grief reactions. So whenever we help parents cope with their grief, we also help their living children. One pathological grief reaction of parents that affects siblings in major ways has been studied by several researchers. It is termed "replacement." Replacement refers to the grieving parents' use of another child to take symbolically the place of the one who died. Replacement children have to endure a sad life in their childhood years. They carry a heavy burden of duty trying to live up to expectations that are often unrealistic and certainly unfair. Replacement children feel a deep sense of guilt for not being able to please their parents, and a constant anxiety that their parents may reject and abandon them at any moment. One of the most dramatic cases of replacement I have heard of is that reported in (38).

> Jim was born ten months after his sister Mildred died at the age of nine. He recalls: "As far back as I can remember there was some sort of disappointment with me—a male—what with all attempts on my parents' part to dress me, adore me, and look upon me as a girl. . . . Practically all comparisons were in terms of Mildred. Expectations of her soon became expectations of me. It really wasn't my life at all. . . . My whole childhood was wrapped under a wrap of sorrow. . . . Actually, Mother had never worked through

her grief over Mildred's death. . . . I remember vividly one morning when I opened a drawer to find something wrapped in newspaper—and my mother's horror at my unwrapping a pair of Mildred's shoes she had bought for her shortly before her death. I was made to feel thoroughly guilty over even touching something that was Mildred's . . .My stuttering was diagnosed as a manifestation of tension and stress . . . even today under stress I block—the curse of unfinished mourning seems to hang over me yet today . . . "

When a Parent Dies

The death of a child's parent is a tragedy that imposes special hardships on the child. Furman (39, 40) has done the groundbreaking work in this area. She points out that the primary nature of the child's dependency on a parent leaves the child with an overpowering sense of despair, helplessness, abandonment, and threat that adults often find difficult to recognize. Adjusting to this loss is an awesome task. The child is not equipped psychologically to cope alone with a crisis of such proportions. Even with the best possible help, it is a rough road to recovery, and no amount of help can spare the child pain, suffering, and sadness. In fact, these are important components of the grieving process. Their absence is a sign that the child has not begun to grieve.

When a parent dies, increases in the child's needs are manifold. Among the most essential needs at this time are continued love, comfort, and support from family and others and reassurance of continued care. In addition, the child needs the security of a familiar environment, as much as that is possible. Often the death of a parent involves moving from a familiar home and neighborhood to a strange place with unfamiliar people, a new school, and new teachers; all these create additional stresses and bring with them additional losses.

Physiological Responses. Children show acute physiological responses to the death of a parent similar to those of adults to the death of someone close. Wessel (41) observed that children may suffer digestive problems such as vomiting, diarrhea, or constipation. Younger children especially may temporarily lose bladder and sphincter control. Younger and older children may lose appetite, complain of an empty feeling in the abdomen, suffer from dizziness, tightness in the chest or throat, or insomnia. A child may exhibit one or more of these symptoms but not all. It should be remembered that these responses are acute, that is they occur primarily in the first few days, but occasionally extend over weeks following the death. A child may also develop an illness. For example, gastrointestinal symptoms during the early part of bereavement may reflect an early phase of malabsorption, peptic ulcer, or ileitis. Diabetic and thyroid conditions have also been observed. Wessel advises that the family consult with the pediatrician regarding any such symptoms for they are real and uncomfortable, some of them embarrassing, and, most importantly, they are frigthening to the child. It is immensely reassuring to the child when these symptoms are taken seriously and treated immediately. Often bereaved children, particularly the young, constantly dread illness and even a minor problem such as a sore throat can cause them to panic because they are terrified that they may be dying also. An empathic pediatrician can be of significant help to the child. The pediatrician is an authoritative source of information about what is happening to the child physiologically, and how common these symptoms are for children who have such a sad experience. This can be reassuring to a bewildered and frightened child.

Psychological Responses. The death of a parent is a shattering event for a child, evoking a host of emotions. It stuns, shocks, bewilders, overwhelms, and frightens a child. The child feels abandoned, desolate, helpless, and hurt, in addition to experiencing strong emotions of anger and guilt. Not all children, however, experience all these feelings with the same intensity. A critical factor determining the bereaved child's emotional response is his or her developmental status. *Infants* perceive a parent's death as a separation and loss and respond with anxiety, anger, and apathy. Spitz (42) described a syndrome he called "hospitalism" in which young orphaned children from infancy through preschool age reacted to separation from their mother first with anger, then with a kind of quiet, resigned despair.

Some of the children actually refused nutrition, turned their faces to the wall, and died. But we now know that infants and young children will overcome the loss of the primary nurturing person if another will take over the functions of care and provide a quality of love and nurture similar to that the child has lost (7). *Preschool children* consciously experience feelings of abandonment and threats to their own lives. Magical thinking may create enormous guilt and fears of punishment by death. What child has not been frustrated and angry and wished a parent would die? When the parent actually dies the young child often believes that he or she caused the parent's death by willing it. Psychological causality may lead the child to believe that the parent died because the child was naughty. The child hopes and expects that the parent will come back since death is understood as a reversible event. Eventually the child will progress from immature causal thinking to the more mature thinking of physical causation but this process takes time. Meanwhile the child may become severely troubled. It is important for adults to recognize that these responses are normal and highly probable even if the child does not express them.

As with the loss of a child, the parent who has lost a spouse is commonly so overwhelmed with his or her loss and pain that there are no inner resources left to devote to the needs of the child in the early period of bereavement. This is a difficult problem and, I suggest again, that a relative or friend "adopt" the child until the surviving parent is able to cope. A complete network of support is necessary for the family but for the child there should be a special helper who can enter into a continuing, intimate relationship with him or her and who is available whenever needed.

The preschool child needs repeated explanations about the parent's death, and patient answers to his or her questions. This means that there should be repeated discussions with the child over a period of weeks or months. In these discussions the helper should stress such points as the following:

- Daddy didn't die on purpose. He couldn't help it. Dying is something you can't help.
- It isn't anybody's fault that Daddy died. It's not the doctor's fault or Mommy's fault. It isn't your fault.

- Daddy was sad that he had to die. But he couldn't do anything about it.
- Daddy wasn't angry with you.
- Daddy loved you very much.
- Daddy can never come back to us. We miss him terribly. We are very, very sad. We will be sad for a long, long time. We will always remember Daddy. We will think and talk about the trips we took and all the good things that happened when he lived. We will talk about Daddy a lot. You tell me when you want to talk about Daddy. You can ask any questions you want.
- Mommy will take care of you. You will be doing many of the things you did when Daddy was alive.
- It's all right to cry. You can cry any time you feel sad.
- It's all right to feel angry.
- It's all right to laugh and play and have fun. Daddy would like that. He wanted you to have fun.

In this way the child comes to learn of our caring, patience, understanding, and support. There is, of course, no manual that tells us the right things to say at the right time and in the right way, but adults who are attuned to a child's needs usually do the right things.

Older children and adolescents may still feel a deep sense of abandonment but they now know that there is nothing voluntary about the death (except when the parent commited suicide). Feelings of overwhelming sadness and loneliness are common. In addition, the older child or adolescent often feels extremely angry—with the parent for dying when he or she was needed, with the surviving parent who might have been able to prevent the death, sometimes with that parent for being alive instead of the one who has died. Anger is also turned on other children who have not lost a parent. If the family is religious, the child is often angry at God for letting it happen (or for "killing" the parent). Older children and adolescents often feel diminished, less valued by their peers, and have lower self-esteem. Frequently they feel embarrassed and ashamed.

Older children and adolescents do not require explanations about the cause of their parent's death but they nevertheless need a special friend and helper with whom to share their feelings and pain. Ideally, parent and child will be able to share their grief as much as possible. A parent should not hide grief from the child. It should be helpful when both parent and child hug and hold each other in their common sorrow. Both loved the person who died. Both feel deep pain. I see no harm in the surviving parent and child crying together. It tells the child that crying is all right and that the parent feels miserable, too.

Behavioral Responses. Many bereaved children behave in ways that are certain to get attention. They become uncooperative, aggressive, hostile, or destructive. When we observe such behavior we may not know quite what to do and how to help but at least most of us recognize "the cry for help" and see what we can do or where to get assistance. If the behavior is misunderstood, children's problems are compounded because they may receive punishment instead of empathy and therapeutic aid. Other children do not "act out," instead, they withdraw. They literally withdraw from others and crawl into a remote part of the house or a favorite secret hiding place. They also withdraw figuratively by keeping their fears and thoughts to themselves. Withdrawal is a more dangerous coping mechanism than "acting out" because it is more easily overlooked, and these children may receive no help at all.

Teachers should be informed when a parent has died because *school-aged children* may exhibit aggression and withdrawal in school. Almost always a child's academic achievement falls far below his or her typical performance. A child may be unable to concentrate. On the other hand, a child may behave quite normally concealing inner turmoil and pain, and participate in school activities as if nothing happened. These children are self-conscious and would be deeply embarrassed if their situation were publicly discussed. The teacher should expect a child to show symptoms of deep distress, such as periods of uncontrollable sobbing, disorientation, and inability to function in daily classroom routines. It would be important for teachers, school counselors, or other service personnel to help the child individually, to allow the child to leave the classroom for a time to spare embarrassment and shame the child may feel. Teachers can be of help to a bereaved child in many ways.

> Danny had been in kindergarten when his father was killed in an automobile accident. One day, almost a year later, he suddenly jumped out of his seat in the middle of a reading lesson and ran sobbing to the teacher who gathered him in her arms and asked: "What do you need, Danny?" With a look of anguish and sadness, the little boy said: "I forgot what my Daddy looked like." The teacher nodded gravely and agreed: "That's a sad thing to happen but I think we can do something about that." She then proposed that she get one of the helpers to take him home to get a photo of his dad and bring it back to school. Danny said he wanted that very much. A telephone call to Danny's aunt who was taking care of the baby brother prepared her. When Danny returned later on he smiled at the teacher. "Can I see the picture?" the teacher asked. "Oh," said Danny, "I left it at home 'cause I know what he looks like again."

One of the students in my death course wrote down the following childhood memory:

> I was twelve when my father died. I remember the empty feeling, the sadness, and the anger but I also felt something else. I am ashamed to confess it even now—I was embarrassed. I didn't want my classmates to know about my father's death. That would have made me a freak. So I told them my father was a navy commander. That would explain his absence.

Another student wrote:

> When my dad died I felt like I wasn't part of the gang any-more. . . . The kids used to talk about their dads and what all they could do. Well, mine was dead. A dead father is nothing to brag about.

Ten-year-old Eric explained why he would not tell his classmates of his father's death this way: "They would feel sorry for me and I couldn't stand that." In another session he spoke of his fear that they might not ask him to play baseball or race bikes, "and I don't want to be left out."

Teachers can help a bereaved student by identifying class-mates and friends who may become a support group. Sometimes several bereaved children are in the same school. A school may invite these children to share their problem in group sessions. Teachers and counselors may also help classmates who are awkward in their attempts to interact with their bereaved friend. The school library should have books on death and grief available and these could be offered to the child. But teachers cannot be expected to solve the grieving child's problems. They can only assist in lessening them and in avoiding a compounding of the problems.

Children who are seemingly indifferent about the death of a parent are often sadly misunderstood. One should be careful about interpreting such absence of overt sorrow and grief. It may all be kept inside, as mentioned in connection with withdrawal. It may also be a denial on the part of the child that protects him or her against having to deal with the loss at that time. With the help of understanding and patient adults, such children will eventually begin to talk about their feelings (39).

There is no magic formula for helping the bereaved child, nor are there any shortcuts. I have stressed the difficulties a bereaved child experiences. But we should remember that children have a remarkable resiliency to overcome painful experiences, even the death of a parent. There is no definite answer to the question of the length of the child's grieving. It may take several months, a year, two years, or longer. There are clear signs indicating when the child has made a full readjustment. The grieving process is essentially completed when the memory of the dead parent no longer pains and saddens the child except intermittently. Tears no longer flow at the memory of the parent's death. The child has fully resumed all activities, plays happily, or works with full ability to concentrate. There may be periods of reliving the events and regrieving the loss that can last for many years, but when the child can "do a cartwheel on her daddy's grave," a skill he loved to watch her do, then we know that she can go forward with her living and growing (43).

References

1. Stillion, J., & Wass, H. Children and death. In H. Wass (ed.), *Dying: Facing the facts*. Washington: Hemisphere, 1979, 208–232.

2. What do babies know? *Time*, August 15, 1983, 52–59.
3. Wass, H. Concepts of death: A developmental perspective. In H. Wass & C. A. Corr (eds.), *Childhood and death*. Washington: Hemisphere, 1984, 3–23.
4. Wass, H., & Cason, L. Death anxiety and fears in childhood. In H. Wass & C. A. Corr (eds.), *Childhood and death*. Washington: Hemisphere, 1984, 25–45.
5. Piaget, J. *The child's conceptions of the world*. C. K. Ogden (ed.), Totowa, N.J.: Littlefield, Adams, 1965.
6. Wass, H., & Scott, M. Middle school students' death concepts and concerns. *Middle School Journal*, 1978, *9*, 10–12.
7. Bowlby, J. *Attachment and loss, Vol. III, Loss, sadness and depression*. New York: Basic, 1980.
8. Rochlin, G. The dread of abandonment: A contribution to the etiology of the loss complex and to depression. In *The psychoanalytic study of the child*. New York: International University Press, XVI, 1961, 451–470.
9. Zilboorg, G. The sense of immortality. *Psychoanalytic Quarterly*, 1938, *7*, 171–199.
10. Wahl, C. W. The fear of death. In H. Feifel (ed.), *The meaning of death*. New York: McGraw-Hill, 1959, 16–29.
11. Nagy, M. The child's theories concerning death. *Journal of Genetic Psychology*, 1948, *73*, 3–27.
12. Wass, H., & Shaak, J. Helping children understand death through literature. *Childhood Education*, 1976, *53*, 80–85.
13. Gartley, W., & Bernasconi, M. The concept of death in children. *Journal of Genetic Psychology*, 1967, *110*, 71–85.
14. Singer, D. G. A time to reexamine the role of television in our lives. *American Psychologist*, 1983, *38*, 815–816.
15. Gerbner, G. Violence in television drama: Trends and symbolic functions. In G. A. Comstock & E. A. Rubinstein (eds.), *Television and social behavior, Vol. I. Media content and control*. Washington, D.C.: Government Printing Office, 1972, 28–187.
16. Zim, H., & Bleeker, S. *Life and death*. New York: Morrow, 1970.
17. Grollman, E. A. *Talking about death*. Boston: Beacon, 1970.
18. Jackson, E. *Telling a child about death*. New York: Hawthorn, 1965.
19. Carson, U. A child loses a pet. *Death Education*, 1980, *3*, 399–404.
20. Wass, H., Corr, C. A., Pacholski, R. A., & Sanders, C. M. *Death education: An annotated resource guide*. Washington: Hemisphere, 1980.
21. Wass, H., Corr, C. A., Pacholski, R. A., & Forfar, C. S. *Death education: An annotated resource guide*, II. Washington: Hemisphere, in press.
22. Carson, U. Teachable moments occasioned by "small deaths." In H. Wass & C. A. Corr (eds.), *Childhood and death*. Washington: Hemisphere, 1984, 315–343.

23. Crase, D. R., & Crase, D. Death education in the schools. In H. Wass & C. A. Corr (eds.), *Childhood and death.* Washington: Hemisphere, 1984, 345-363.

24. Adams, D. W. Helping the dying child: Practical approaches for nonphysicians. In H. Wass & C. A. Corr (eds.), *Childhood and death.* Washington: Hemisphere, 1984, 95-112.

25. Schowalter, J. E. The reactions of caregivers in dealing with fatally ill children and their families. In O. J. Z. Sahler (ed.), *The child and death.* St. Louis: Mosby, 1978, 123-138.

26. Vachon, M. L. S., & Pakes, E. Staff stress in the care of the critically ill and dying child. In H. Wass & C. A. Corr (eds.), *Childhood and death.* Washington: Hemisphere, 1984, 151-181.

27. Martinson, I. M., Armstrong, G. D., Geis, D. P., Anglim, M. A., Gronseth, E. C., MacInnis, H., Kersey, J. H., & Nesbit, M. E. Home care for children dying of cancer. *Pediatrics,* July 1978, 106-113.

28. Carlson, P., Simacek, M., Henry, W. F., Martinson, I. M., Montgomery, J., & Montgomery, K. Helping parents cope: A model home-care program for the dying child. In H. Wass & C. A. Corr (eds.), *Childhood and death.* Washington: Hemisphere, 1984, 113-127.

29. Waechter, E. H. Children's awareness of fatal illness. *American Journal of Nursing,* 1971, *71,* 1168-1172.

30. Spinetta, J. J., Rigler, D., & Karon, M. Anxiety in the dying child. *Pediatrics,* 1973, *52,* 841.

31. Foley, G. V., & McCarthy, A. M. The child with leukemia in a special hematology clinic. *American Journal of Nursing,* 1976, *76,* 1115-1119.

32. Waechter, E. H. Dying children: Patterns of coping. In H. Wass & C. A. Corr (eds.), *Childhood and death.* Washington: Hemisphere, 1984, 51-68.

33. Jackson, E. N. *The many faces of grief.* Nashville: Abingdon, 1972.

34. Jackson, E. N. Bereavement and grief. In H. Wass (ed.), *Dying: Facing the facts.* Washington: Hemisphere, 1979, 256-281.

35. Worden, J. W. *Grief counseling and grief therapy—A handbook for the mental health practitioner.* New York: Springer, 1982.

36. Fassler, J. *My grandpa died today.* New York: Human Sciences, 1971.

37. Coleman, F. W., & Coleman, W. S. Helping siblings and other peers cope with dying. In H. Wass & C. A. Corr (eds.), *Childhood and death.* Washington: Hemisphere, 1984, 129-150.

38. Irving, J. Playing my dead sister's surrogate. *Death Education,* in press.

39. Furman, E. *A parent dies.* New Haven: Yale University Press, 1974.

40. Furman, E. Children's pattern in mourning the death of a loved one. In H. Wass & C. A. Corr (eds.), *Childhood and death.* Washington: Hemisphere, 1984, 185-203.

41. Wessel, M. A. Helping families: Thoughts of a pediatrician. In H. Wass & C. A. Corr (eds.), *Childhood and death.* Washington: Hemisphere, 1984, 205-217.

42. Spitz, R. A. Hospitalism: An inquiry into the genesis of psychiatric

conditions of early childhood. *The Psychoanalytic Study of the Child,*
Volume I. New York: International University Press, 1945.

43. LeShan, E. *Learning to say good-by.* New York: Macmillan, 1976.

RESOURCES

BOOKS FOR ADULTS:
AN ANNOTATED BIBLIOGRAPHY

CHARLES A. CORR

The bibliography that follows describes 44 books for adults that are in some way related to helping children cope with death. This listing is restricted to book-length entries, as distinct from journal or periodical articles, because the former are judged more likely to be of substantial and enduring value. Readers should be aware of the journal literature, however, and those with special interests might wish to explore its potential. That can most easily be undertaken by consulting the annotated descriptions of literature concerning death education and the references to death-related bibliographies in the resource guide prepared by Wass and her colleagues and described in this bibliography.

The present bibliography is intended to be both selective and representative. That is, the titles listed here have been chosen from among the available book-length literature either because they most deserve to be recommended to readers or because they have achieved some prominence and require comment. At the same time, these choices are also designed to reflect examples of each principal type of work and to include major topical areas within the field, such as analyses of various types of loss; first-person accounts, either biographical or fictional; and treatments of developmental, educational, counseling, and bibliographic considerations. In view of this breadth, I hope that those who examine this bibliography will be able to get a quick sense of the range and depth of books available for helping children cope with death.

Each entry in the bibliography contains a short description of the contents of the book in question. Few people will need or be able to read all of the books mentioned here. Nevertheless, by skimming over these descriptions, readers can save time and determine for themselves which titles to seek out for more leisurely exploration in the light of particular interests. Where it seems helpful, annotations include information about an author's background or a brief evaluation of a book's special strengths or weaknesses.

Some books can be read with profit both by older children or adolescents and by adults. Others are designed to be read together by young children and adults. In such cases, the same title may appear both here and in Chapter 6. Where that occurs, the annotations will naturally be similar, although one may emphasize the book's value for adults while the other relates it to children.

Agee, J. *A death in the family.* New York: Grosset & Dunlap, 1967; Bantam, 1969. This Pulitzer Prize-winning novel describes the sudden and unexpected death of Jay Follet and the impact of that event on his family. The scenes in which six-year-old Rufus and his younger sister Catherine attempt to make sense out of what has happened are rich with insight into the ways in which children often misunderstand and are misunderstood by the adults around them. The scene is Tennessee early in this century, but the themes are timeless. Every adult can benefit from Agee's masterful evocation of the children's perspective in which we see clearly the problems that they have in dealing with their feelings and in framing questions to resolve their confusion.

Anthony, S. *The discovery of death in childhood and after.* New York: Basic, 1972. This book is described by its publisher as "an enlarged and thoroughly revised version" of the book published in 1940 under the title *The child's discovery of death: A study in child psychology.* The original book was based on research conducted in England between 1937 and 1939, but it has long been out of print and difficult to obtain. In general, it favored a developmental theory of death-related concepts but insisted that they are closely associated with other ideas and factors and that the idea of death occurs very readily in the fantasies of normal children.

The author sees the revised version as "repeating and adding to earlier observations, relating them to later researches in kindred fields, placing the whole in the sort of setting such a subject deserves" (p. 12). In other words, the revised version is more accessible, more up to date, and more concerned with a broad cultural perspective. A classic text that shows influences from Freud and Piaget and that is of some importance for specialists.

Berg, D. W., & Daugherty, G. G. *The individual, society and death: An anthology of readings.* DeKalb, Ill.: Perspectives on Death, 1972. This is an example of the scissors-and-paste approach to anthologizing snippets from many diverse sources. The text is part of a package for high school students, which also includes the *Student Activity Book* and *Teacher's Resource Book.* Perhaps the earliest entry of its type in the field, this private publication is just the sort of approach to death education that we need now to put behind us.

Bernstein, J. E. *Books to help children cope with separation and loss.* New York: Bowker, 1977. As the title indicates, the scope of this bibliographic resource is much broader than the field of death, dying, and bereavement. Part I deals with the use of books to help children and with the concept of bibliotherapy; Part II provides an annotated bibliography of 438 books for children that address themes of separation (new siblings, schools, neighborhoods, etc.), loss (death, divorce, or marital separation; desertion; serious illness; war; and displacement), and security (who will take care of me?—foster care, stepparents, adoption, and homelessness); and Part III adds unannotated selected lists of readings for adults on separation and loss and on bibliotherapy. There are indexes by author, title, subject, interest level, and reading level. This is a rich and unparalleled resource. The section on death alone fills almost 50 pages and offers paragraph-length descriptions and evaluations of 112 titles.

Bernstein, J. E. *Loss and how to cope with it.* New York: Seabury, 1977. This book is primarily addressed to older children and adolescents, but it can also be read with profit by adults. The author's purpose is to help readers achieve a better understanding of the impact of loss and of the normality of responses that may at first seem unusual. In addition to practical guidance, there is information on books, films, and organizational resources that are relevant to this subject.

Bluebond-Langner, M. *The private worlds of dying children.* Princeton, N.J.: Princeton University Press, 1978. What distinguishes this book is the effort by its author to examine the distinctive worlds of dying children from the viewpoint of a cultural anthropologist. The children in question ranged in age from three to nine years old. They all had leukemia and were observed during the author's research in the pediatric ward of a large teaching hospital. Many adults believe that small children are unaware of their condition; previous research and this study contradict such wishful thinking. Hence, the key issues here are: How do these children come to know that they are dying when no one tells them (a process of socialization), and how or why do they choose to conceal this awareness from adults (a reflection of the social order that they have accepted)? These issues are exemplified in a playlet that dramatizes the world of a composite dying child, which is then subjected to careful theoretical analysis. The author's conclusions challenge common viewpoints and the methodologies of many earlier studies; her book can be read with profit by most adults but is indispensable for those who work with or seek to understand dying children. A short appendix discusses problems involved in doing this sort of field work.

Claypool, J. *Tracks of a fellow struggler: How to handle grief.* Waco, Tex.: Word, 1974. John Claypool is a Baptist minister who experienced the death of his eight-year-old daughter, Laura Lue. This short book consists of four sermons in which Claypool shared his experiences with his congregations. The sermons were preached on the occasion of the diagnosis of acute leukemia, nine months later at the end of the first remission, four weeks after Laura Lue died, and one year afterward. The perspective is that of biblical Christianity, but it is also very personal and human. The book conveys suffering, strong feelings, and questioning, together with a sense of survival, healing, and growth.

Fargues, M. *The child and the mystery of death* (Sister Ger-
trude, S. P., Trans.). Glen Rock, N.J.: Paulist, 1966. Marie
Fargues is a prominent figure in the French Catholic cate-
chetical movement. In this slim paperback English version of
her book, she combines religious and psychological perspectives to guide the pastoral teaching of children about death.
The book is divided into three principal parts representing,
respectively, the points of view of observers, families, and
pedagogy. Each of these sections conclude with 15 study-
club questions for discussion.

Fassler, J. *Helping children cope* (W. B. Hogan, Illus.). New
York: Free Press, 1978. A reference guide by an author and
student of children's literature. The book addresses stress
that might be brought about by death, separation experiences, hospitalization and illness, lifestyle changes, and
events or situations. In each case the author joins a brief
discussion of professional viewpoints on the topic to an
analysis of selected books (mainly for four- to eight-year-
olds) that might help children deal with stress. For example,
the 25-page section on death provides a narrative account of
strong and weak points in some 30 books ranging from
stories about change or death in nature, pets, and humans to
informational books and books about the death of a child.
Thoughtful, but far more limited than the Bernstein volume.

Furman, E. (Ed.). *A child's parent dies: Studies in childhood
bereavement.* New Haven, Conn.: Yale University Press,
1974. The classic volume on bereavement in childhood from
a psychoanalytic viewpoint. The editor provides here, on
behalf of her colleagues, an introductory account of the
study on which this book is based, theoretical insights on
helping bereaved children, grief and mourning, the process of
mourning, individual circumstances, differences between children and adults in mourning, effects of parental death on
the child's personality development, and observations on
depression and apathy, and a 64-page review of literature
that relates this work to other studies. Meanwhile, nine
lengthy examples by individual therapists appear throughout
the text. Indispensable for professionals.

Gordon, A. K., & Klass, D. *They need to know: How to teach
children about death.* Englewood Cliffs, N.J.: Prentice-Hall,

1979. Intended primarily for parents and teachers, this book marks an important advance over earlier, less sophisticated works on death education for children. Part I offers a background sketch of the interaction between children, adults, and death in our society, and general guidelines for parents and teachers. Part II outlines a program for death education including four overall goals, suggested curricula with specific resources and activities by grade and goal, and consumer information regarding medical and funeral services. Nine appendixes reproduce documents like a living will, natural death legislation, and a patient's bill of rights that are useful in this kind of education. Readers will particularly benefit from the pedagogical schema provided by Gordon and Klass, which they can now supplement from our more extensive list of resources.

Green, B. R., & Irish, D. P. *Death education: Preparation for living.* Cambridge, Mass.: Schenkman, 1971. This slim paperback of less than 150 pages is based on a symposium held at Hamline University, St. Paul, Minnesota, in February 1970. Three invited speakers included: Herman Feifel, who surveys the meaning of death in American society; John Brantner, who reflects on implications of death for the self; and Daniel Leviton, who discusses the role of the schools in providing death education. Following the texts of these three major addresses is an essay by Donald P. Irish, who argues from a sociological viewpoint that death education at various levels can properly be seen as preparation for living. Finally, there are excerpts from 12 discussion groups at the symposium and a selected bibliography. Now 10 years old, but still of interest and value.

Grollman, E. A. (Ed.), *Explaining death to children.* Boston: Beacon, 1967. Grollman is a well-known rabbi, counselor, and writer in the field of separation and loss, and his book is a pioneering effort to help adults deal with children and death. Now dated and limited in several ways, *Explaining death to children* still contains some interesting chapters: Robert Fulton on death in our society, Gregory Rochlin on strong feelings that very young children seem to have about death, Robert Kastenbaum on the development of children's understanding of death, and an unusual piece by Claiborne Jones on biologic aspects of death. There are also chapters on Protestant, Catholic, and Jewish perspectives on death, and an early essay on children's literature. The author of this last piece maintains that for the young child up to about age eight "there is little need in his spring-green world for an understanding of the dead" (p. 250), a contention with which many experts disagree.

Grollman, E. A. *Talking about death: A dialogue between parent and child* (G. Héau, Illus.). Boston: Beacon, 1976. This book is described as "a new edition with a Parent's Guide and recommended resources" of the 1970 book by the same title. It begins with a 25-page section of text and pictures that is meant to be read along with young children. The parent's guide then responds to typical questions, statements, or situations that might come up in connection with this joint reading experience. Here the author stresses the need to combine straightforward honesty with sensitive support. Two concluding sections describe recommended individuals, organizations, books, and audiovisuals from which additional information and assistance can be obtained. This is probably the best-known resource in the field for parents of young children.

Gunther, J. *Death be not proud: A memoir.* New York: Harper, 1949. Johnny Gunther died in 1947 at the age of 17; this book is his father's story of Johnny's fight for life in the 14 months before his death. *Death be not proud* is very well known for many reasons: It is an early example of its type; its author is a prominent writer; and it has recently been made into a film for television. The story is one of a gallant and brilliant young man, a malignant brain tumor, frantic efforts at orthodox and heterodox treatment, tension with phsycians, and both good and bad times before death. A concluding section contains some of Johnny's letters, extracts from his diary, and a haunting afterword by his mother.

Gyulay, J. E. *The dying child.* New York: McGraw-Hill, 1978. This book is aimed primarily at members of the health care team; its author is a pediatric nurse. Four central parts discuss: concerns of the child—young children, older children, and special children, such as those who are physically or emotionally handicapped, mentally retarded, adopted, from one-parent families, of foreign descent, twins, or an only child; problems affecting the grievers—parents, siblings, and significant others (taken very broadly); phases of illness and death, from diagnosis through remission, relapse, the terminal state, or sudden loss, to the postdeath period; and guidelines for nursing care of dying children. No references within the text, but an extensive bibliography at the end. Commendable for its broad scope. Otherwise not particularly new but useful as a blend of existing knowledge and common-sense insights.

Hughes, P. R. *Dying is different.* Mahomet, Ill.: Mech Mentor Education, 1978. The author has designed this book to promote discussion of death between adults and preschool through second-grade children. The 18 children's pages use drawings, strong colors, and poems to present a graduated succession of living and dead states in flowers, ants, fish, a cat, and a grandmother, followed by vivid thematic depictions of the inevitability of death, its justification, remembering, acceptance, grief, funerals, cemeteries, and the importance of love during life. An introduction, facing pages for adults, and some concluding remarks suggest questions and guidelines for parents and teachers. The book can be read alone either by children or by adults, but it is perhaps best used jointly as a basis for sharing. Available in both a large instructional edition designed to stand upright by itself and a smaller personal edition in standard book form.

Irish, J. A. *A boy thirteen: Reflections on death.* Philadelphia: Westminster, 1975. In 1973 the Irish family (parents and two sons; a third, younger son had died in 1969 of a congenital heart defect) was accompanying a student group in Europe when their 13-year-old son suddenly died of acute meningitis. The boy's father—a teacher of philosophy and theology—wrote this short essay, as he says, in an effort "to articulate my own response to Lee's incomprehensible death" (p. 18). It explores anger at the unacceptability of death, aloneness and the abandonment of death, and freedom in the opportunity to love and thereby to overcome ending and separation.

Jackson, E. N. *Telling a child about death.* New York: Hawthorn, 1965. From a Protestant minister and counselor who has written extensively on grief, stress, funerals, and children, 83 pages of practical advice. Jackson's basic premise is that "the emotional crises of life can be used to teach wise response to deprivation and loss" (p. 23). Thus, *both* children and adults can benefit from sharing ideas and feelings that are related to death.

Klagsbrun, F. *Too young to die: Youth and suicide.* Boston: Houghton Mifflin, 1976; New York: Pocket Books, 1977. This is the first book about suicide among adolescents and college students that was written to be read by young people as well as by their parents, counselors, and teachers. Its three parts deal, respectively, with: the realities of suicide among the young, that is, statistics, common myths, suicide as a communication, the role of depression or psychosis, and uncounted or "chronic" suicides; practical guidelines—What can you do?—for dealing both with crisis situations and with survivors; and social aspects, that is, sociological or psychological causes, cultural attitudes, and prevention techniques. Appendixes document the sharp rise in suicide rates among the 15- to 24-year-old age group over the 20-year period from 1954 to 1974 and list many suicide prevention or crisis intervention agencies in the United States. There is also an eight-page bibliography. A good introduction for adults to an increasingly important subject.

Kotzwinkle, W. *Swimmer in the secret sea.* New York: Avon, 1975. This is a deeply moving account of a young couple's joyful preparation for the birth of their child (the figure in the title), sudden complications during the birth process, unsuccessful attempts of the medical personnel to bring their stillborn son back to life, and their decision to build a simple pine box and bury their baby in the woods. Descriptions are grimly realistic, and the language is taut and powerful. The reader is not protected from the shock and pain experienced by the parents. Some readers may even be appalled at times by the stark and unmitigated reality of the descriptions. For example, when the parents receive their dead baby in a green plastic garbage bag after having consented to an autopsy and open the bag, they find that the little boy had not been sewed together again. Despite such almost unspeakable experiences, the young couple comes to accept the death of their son. The message is one of triumph of love and faith. This short story is a must.

Langone, J. *Death is a noun: A view of the end of life.* Boston: Little, Brown, 1972; New York: Dell, 1975. John Langone is a medical journalist who surveys here many prominent social issues concerning death. Using research reports, historical analyses, and human interest stories, he deals with basic attitudes toward death, with euthanasia, abortion, capital punishment, murder, suicide, the problem of determining the presence of death, grief, and the mystery of death. Langone writes clearly and simply for young readers, but his book can also serve as the simplest introduction to the field of death and dying for adults.

Langone, J. *Vital signs: The way we die in America.* Boston: Little, Brown, 1974. This book is a kind of documentary drama, "a work of assembly," as the author terms it. Focusing on dying, Langone skillfully weaves together a variety of materials: classical quotations, scientific data, legal case material, news reports, and interviews conducted with doctors, nurses, clergy, and dying people and their families. The themes are communication and caring, those giving and those receiving. As he informs, Langone also calls us to greater empathy for the needs of dying people. Another good place for mature young readers and adults to begin their inquiry.

LeShan, E. *Learning to say good-by: When a parent dies* (P. ·Giovanopoulos, Illus.). New York: Macmillan, 1978. Eda LeShan is a well-known writer and family counselor who speaks here to children in a simple, straightforward manner about the problems they face when losing a parent and how to overcome them. The main thrust throughout this helpful and comforting book is the acceptance of the griever as a person who is suffering much pain and disorientation but who is healthy and will be capable of coping by expressing and sharing her or his feelings in open communication with interested and caring adults. The book is well written, and examples are used liberally to illustrate a situation or clarify a point. An informative, nonthreatening, supportive book that can be quite useful for sympathetic and concerned adults.

Lonetto, R. *Children's conceptions of death.* New York: Springer, 1980. This is the most detailed, recent effort to understand the development of children's views of death. The investigation is framed in the context of our general knowledge of childhood development and in the light of previous research on death-related concepts. But the special feature of this book is its extensive interviews with Canadian children as reflected in the reproduction of many of their comments and drawings. This research suggests three general phases in the development of children's concepts of death from ages 3 through 12. A concluding chapter briefly considers special problems of dying children, childhood bereavement, and explaining death to a child.

Lund, E. *Eric.* Philadelphia: Lippincott, 1974. In 1967 just before he was about to go off to college, Doris Lund's 17-year-old son was found to have acute lymphocytic leukemia. This book is about the 4 1/2 years that followed until his death. During that time, Eric went in and out of remission as he endured the twin hardships of disease and chemotherapy. Always he fought hungrily to experience life, insisting on running his own risks and living his own life. Eric obliged his parents to give him the freedom to be himself, a difficult task under normal circumstances and one made ever more demanding under the shadow of life-threatening illness. *Eric* combines candor, courage, wit, and sadness in a compelling way without ever descending into sentimentality and self-pity.

Mills, G. C., Reisler, R., Robinson, A. E., & Vermilye, G. *Discussing death: A guide to death education.* Homewood, Ill.: ETC, 1976. This curriculum guide for educators is divided into four age levels: 5-6 years, 7-9 years, 10-12, years, and 13-18 years. Within each level, it describes curricular concepts and a series of learning opportunities (e.g., life cycles or grief expression) and suggests specific objectives, activities, and resources or strategies for teachers. Flawed, oversimplified, and now superceded by better and more reliable guides.

Reed, E. L. *Helping children with the mystery of death.* Nasvhille, Tenn.: Abingdon, 1970. Offered as "a book of religious substance," about half of the space in this volume is given to resources for adults and children, such as biblical and poetic excerpts, stories, suggested activities, and prayers. The text shares this concern for Christian education.

Roach, N. *The last day of April.* New York: American Cancer Society, 1974. This little 40-page booklet tells a mother's story of the time between her 2 1/2-year-old daughter's diagnosis of leukemia and Erin's death 4 1/2 years later. The twin principles that guided these parents came to them early, after two months of grief and self-pity: "We had to stop feeling sorry for ourselves," and "hard as it would be to lose her someday, it would be easier knowing we had done all we could for her." A powerful tale sharing simple lessons learned at great price.

Rudolph, M. *Should the children know? Encounters with death in the lives of children.* New York: Schocken, 1978. When 4 1/2-year-old Rachel died suddenly at home, the author called an urgent parents' meeting to ask what she should tell the children in her nursery school class. Although the parents were unsure what to do, it became evident that the children wanted to be told the truth about their classmate (whether they understood it fully or not), and they wanted to be given an opportunity to share the thoughts and feelings engendered by this event. In this book, the author argues for such honesty and sharing and suggests ways to help preschool children deal with death through books, caring for plants and animals, and direct experience with human death.

Sahler, O. J. (Ed.). *The child and death.* St. Louis: Mosby, 1978. Growing out of a 1977 symposium at the University of Rochester Medical Center, this book consists of 23 papers by professionals on the following general subjects: families and the death or fatal illness of a child, with some principles for helping; viewpoints and problems of those who care for dying or chronically ill children; survivors—of death or suicide, whether they be children, parents, or grand-parents, and how some might be helped by bereavement parents' groups; and ethical or educational considerations, including issues for the clergy, the right to information and freedom of choice for dying minors, a program for death education at the high school level, and an annotated biblio-graphy categorized by a modified Kübler-Ross schema. The book opens with a short preface and introduction by the editor and a chapter on the development of the child's concept of death; it closes with two short personal state-ments by the mother and sister of a child who died at three months of age. Many good chapters for professionals, with some fuzziness in conception and unevenness in execution.

Smith, A. A. *Rachel.* Wilton, Conn.: Morehouse-Barlow, 1974. The author is an Episcopal priest who experienced the sudden and unexpected death of one of his daughters when she was 10 years old. In this 55-page booklet, he describes the impact of that event on himself and his family in order to share with others in similar situations a sense of normalcy in the midst of the abnormal. Short lists of things for surviving parents to do or not to do and gentle advice for outsiders manage to be practical and helpful without becom-ing preachy. The concluding paragraph summarizes an orien-tation for everyone:

> Death is not a private affair. Except for rare instances, every death affects many people in varying ways. The entire community is, or should be, involved in helping those affected most to resume a normal life. This should never take the form of trying to erase the memories or the hurt, rather it should enable those hurt most to accept death as a normal, inevitable, and necessary part of our humanity. (p. 55)

Stanford, G., & Perry, D. *Death out of the closet: A cirriculum guide to living with dying.* New York: Bantam, 1976. This fairly early book in the field is addressed mainly to teachers and counselors. It offers a rationale for death education at the secondary school level and suggestions regarding problems (with principals, parents, students, or lack of prior training) that such programs are likely to encounter. Beyond that, the authors propose topics, materials, and strategies for introducing different aspects of death education in various curricular contexts. The last chapter of the book (occupying nearly half of its 200-odd pages) provides questions for study or discussion and synopses of 19 books (mainly by the same publisher) that seem to be popular or particularly suited for young people. There are some good things here but also fairly obvious defects and limitations. Critical users can benefit from Stanford and Perry, but most will appreciate the greater sophistication and expertise of Gordon and Klass.

Sternberg, F., & Sternberg, B. *If I die and when I do: Exploring death with young people.* Englewood Cliffs, N.J.: Prentice-Hall, 1980. Based on the experiences of a junior high school social studies teacher who accidentally stumbled into teaching a nine-week death and dying class, the bulk of this book is the work of children themselves. The narrative text describes the organization of the course and lays out a skeleton structure of key topics, such as sharing experiences about death; exploring beliefs; dealing with fears, humor, old age; and facing our own deaths. But the most lengthy and interesting parts of the book are the many interspersed statements, poems, and drawings by the students.

Talking to children about death (U.S. Department of Health, Education, and Welfare Publication No. (ADM)79-838), Washington, 1979. Single free copies are available by writing to: Public Inquiries, National Institute of Mental Health, 5600 Fishers Lane, Rockville, MD 20857. This short pamphlet from the federal government surveys issues of death-related communications with children and recommends sensible approaches to common problems or situations. The briefest introduction that could be recommended.

Ulin, R. O. *Death and dying education.* Washington: National Education Association, 1977. Ulin argues the appropriateness in the schools of death education that is designed "to expose young people in an unthreatening way to some of the facts about death, aging, and dying in our society, to introduce them to a variety of perspectives from other cultures and from artists, philosophers, sociologists, psychologists, poets, and novelists, and most importantly, to help them sort out their own thinking on the subject" (p. 40). He also discusses preparations and qualifications for teachers in the field and includes an outline of a high school course on death and dying. There is a short bibliography and list of audiovisual resources. One can find better curriculum and resource guides, but the detailed rationale for death education and the sponsorship of this book make it useful.

Vogel, L. J. *Helping a child understand death.* Philadelphia: Fortress, 1975. Linda Jane Vogel teaches Christian education at a college in Iowa. This thin paperback book is intended to offer guidance for those who share her religious convictions. It is based on her personal experiences and some not-very-sophisticated reading in the field of death and dying. Elementary but quite readable.

Wass, H. (Ed.). *Dying: Facing the facts.* Washington: Hemisphere, 1979. This is one of the best and most recent comprehensive basic texts on death and dying. It is used in many college classrooms and can be read with profit by professional people and other interested parties. Nearly all of the material in this book has been newly written by experts in their respective fields. Topics covered include: death in our society, physiology and psychosocial aspects of dying, dying in institutions, hospice programs, the elderly, funeral practices, bereavement and grief, the law, defining death, euthanasia, and death education. A chapter on children and death should be of special interest to the readers of this volume. It provides a concise review of research and clinical studies dealing with children's death concepts, anxieties, and grief reactions and offers suggestions for parents and professionals on how to help effectively. Provides a broad basic background.

Wass, H., & Corr, C. A. (Eds.). *Childhood and death.* Washington: Hemisphere, in press. This will be a valuable reference work for medical personnel, counseling practitioners, clergy, teachers, and parents as well as a major textbook for the student in the health and helping professions. All chapters in this book present newly written material by experts in the respective specializations. Some of the topics have not been discussed in any book before. Topics covered include: patterns of coping in dying children; the pediatrician's role; how other care givers can help; helping parents, siblings, and health professionals cope with a dying child; children's patterns of mourning; stillbirth, neonatal death, sudden infant death syndrome and how to help survivors grieve; suicide in childhood; the development of death concepts and anxieties; and death education in home and school. Highly recommended.

Wass, H., Corr, C. A., Pacholski, R. A., & Sanders, C. M. *Death education: An annotated resource guide.* Washington: Hemisphere, 1980. A comprehensive, annotated resource guide intended primarily for those who teach in this area, but many sections will be valuable for others. Coverage includes: printed resources—books and articles describing death education for all levels and audiences, selected text and reference books, bibliographies, periodicals, and literature on research and assessment of death attitudes; audiovisual resources—films, videotapes, filmstrips, slides, audio tapes, and cassettes, together with distributors; organizational resources; community resources; and an appendix with last-minute entries. An indispensable reference tool.

Watts, R. G. *Straight talk about death with young people.* Philadelphia: Westminster, 1975. Based on discussion groups with junior high school students, this short paperback by a Presbyterian minister is intended to illustrate the kinds of issues and approaches that interest such students. The central topics are learning about death, dying, grief, funerals, and beliefs about life after death. Useful in the context from which it originated.

White, J. D. *Talking with a child* (J. Orlando, Illus.). New York: Macmillan, 1976. This book "is intended to help adults to have a pleasant, positive time sharing language" (p. x) with children. A bright and interesting account of a wide range of elements in successful interactions with children. The chapter on death (pp. 229-252) might be read on its own by those who do not have time for anything longer.

Wolf, A. W. M. *Helping your child to understand death.* New York: Child Study, 1958; rev. ed., 1973. A very successful book of advice and counsel by a child development specialist writing for parents and other concerned adults. The text of approximately 60 pages consists of some prefatory material, a short three-page introduction to the setting and aims of the book, two long chapters addressed respectively to issues posed by children and those raised by parents, and a brief conclusion on our religious and cultural heritages in regard to death. The twin central chapters are organized around typical questions or statements used as focuses for analysis and discussion. The advice that emerges takes shape as a sensible and constructive program for familial and other interactions with children about death.

Zeligs, R. *Children's experience with death.* Springfield, Ill.: Thomas, 1974. Written by a child psychologist, this book attempts a very broad reach in both scope and audience. For the latter, it intends to be useful for readers ranging from high school students and parents to professionals such as clergy persons, nurses, social workers, and physicians. For the former, it discusses developmental concepts and fears of death, sick and dying children, the handicapped child, suicide, parental death, and religion. Simply written for those who seek a broad overview, but there are better books now available on most of these subjects.

BOOKS FOR CHILDREN
AN ANNOTATED BIBLIOGRAPHY

HANNELORE WASS

In the 18th and 19th centuries, children's books were written primarily by clergymen or their wives or daughters. "Death," "hell," and "judgment" were part of almost all stories and were often portrayed in a frightening manner to teach the child moral behavior. At the end of the 19th century religious leaders departed from the grim stance of traditional dogma to a liberal position in which "hell" and "damnation" were replaced by the comforting concept that death means "going to Heaven" and "God's call to come home to eternal bliss." Then, too, with the development of public education late in the 19th century, the role of the church in the education of children diminished. Correspondingly, there was less emphasis on death in children's books. Decreasing infant mortality further reinforced this trend, and death almost disappeared from children's literature except from books of rhymes, fairy tales, and the McGuffey Readers series published as children's reading texts from 1836 to 1936 and used primarily in the schools of the midwest.

The 20th century is in many ways the "century of the child" in which individuals and society beyond the bounds of churches and synagogues are concerned with the development of values and the use of constructive and benign means to help children grow into maturity. Among the many demonstrations of these concerns is an extensive literature specifically written for children and adolescents by writers who are sensitive to the needs of the young and who possess deep insights into their world of perceptions, thoughts, and feelings. In most of the books written by such writers early in this century and in many recent volumes, the subject of death is embedded in the main theme and not specifically emphasized. Many of these books are outstanding. They depict death as a significant part of life within a variety of themes. Examples of classics of this kind are M. K. Rawling's *The Yearling,* E. B. White's *Charlotte's Web,* and P. S. Buck's *The Big Wave.* Among the recent books of this kind are M. L'Engle's *A Ring of Endless Light,* B. Miles's *The Trouble with Thirteen,* and P. R. Naylor's *To Walk the Sky Path.*

In recent years a new death awareness in our society has stimulated a desire to cope more effectively with dying and death and to help others do so. Probably inspired by this Zeitgeist, a new genre of gifted writers has chosen death as the main theme of their stories, both fictional and nonfictional. J. Fassler's *My Grandpa Died Today,* P. R. Hughes's *Dying is Different,* D. B. Smith's *A Taste of Blackberries,* A. Slote's *Hang Tough, Paul Mather,* H. Zim's and S. Bleeker's *Life and Death* are but a few of the many moving and inspiring books available today. All books that deal well with death can be helpful, but those that *center* on the subject require special sensitivity and can be particularly informative and therapeutic, not only for children but for adults as well.

This bibliography was begun modestly with a listing of 25 books first published in *Childhood Education* and in the chapter "Children and Death" in H. Wass (Ed.),*Dying: Facing the facts,* Washington, Hemisphere, 1979, and has grown to a total of 160 titles. The selection of books was guided by my judgment that the portrayal of dying, death, and grief in a book is sensitive and realistic, low-keyed rather than sensational or melodramatic, honest and straightforward rather than vague or evasive, and believable rather than exotic, all in the general context of hope and the strength of the human spirit. I have attempted to provide a good balance of books for various age groups, but there are relatively few books available for the very young child, and this is reflected in the bibliography. Obviously, I missed some oustanding books because they did not come to my attention or, in some cases, were simply not obtainable. I do think, however, that the titles listed below are representative of the field.

Aaron, C. *Catch Calico!* New York: Dutton, 1979. Fiction. Age 12 and over. Fourteen-year-old Louis goes with his grandfather to the mountain cabin to catch Calico, a semiwild cat who has lived near the cabin for 10 years, is getting old and blind, and is not likely to survive the harsh mountain winter that is fast approaching. Grandfather explains that it will be better to shoot Calico than to leave her to die slowly and in misery. But Calico scratches and bites Grandfather, who soon afterward gets very sick. Being the son of a doctor, Grandfather realizes that Calico is rabid, but he cannot get his shots in time. The story tells about how Louis copes with his grandfather's worsening condition and his eventual death, how Louis learns to gather the courage to shoot Calico himself, and how he mourns both losses. A highly readable story of love, pain, courage, and strength of spirit.

Abbot, S. *The old dog.* (G. Mocniak, illus.). New York: Coward, 1972. Fiction. Ages 8-10. Ben's old dog dies in her sleep one night and leaves her young owner lonely and bereft when he realizes that his pet is not only asleep but will never again play and run with him and lick his hands and face. The technique of shadow illustrations to depict Ben's memories is very effective. Whereas silhouettes are used to portray memories, orange is used to portray current reality. A shortcoming of this story is that Ben's parents do not allow him time to grieve his dead pet. His father brings home a new puppy the same evening, implying that loved ones are interchangeable. Otherwise good.

Agee, J. *A death in the family.* New York: Avon, 1938. Fiction. Age 14 and over. This Pulitzer Prize-winning novel is a classic. It vividly portrays the wide range of emotions that are evoked in the members of a family by the death of one of them. This is a powerful saga of human strengths and weaknesses in the face of tragedy. The author has great depth of insight into the complex world and emotions of a growing child and his or her attempt to make sense out of the events in which he or she participates and to understand those who love and care for him or her.

Alcott, L. M. *Little women.* Boston: Little, Brown, 1968. Fiction. Ages 9-13. This popular piece of fiction provides a wholesome introduction to, and a vicarious experience of, the inevitability of death and the grief it causes. Beth, one of the four March sisters, dies surrounded by her loving family. This closely knit Civil War-era New England family grieve for their beloved Beth, but the young reader is left with the impression that the grieving is made easier by the sharing and the strength of the family bond. A very skillful portrayal of the pain of mourning and the continuity of life and interpersonal relationships.

Anckarsvärd, K. *Springtime for Eva* (A. Macmillan, Trans., from Swedish). New York: Harcourt, 1959. Fiction. Age 12 and over. This novel sensitively explores a young girl's attitude toward death and her relationships with family and friends. Eva tries and succeeds in putting the death of her friend in perspective, in accepting the fact that life must go on. This healthy understanding of death is contrasted to Lena's morbid brooding, for Lena chooses to dwell on death so that she can elicit sympathy for herself.

Angell, J. *Ronnie and Rosey.* Scarsdale, N.Y.: Bradbury, 1977. Fiction. Ages 12-14. After 13-year-old Ronnie Rachman and her parents move to Uniondale and a new junior high school on Long Island, it takes some time for her to meet and make new friends. Just when she has formed a threesome with Evelyn Racanelli and Robert Rose, Ronnie's father is killed in an automobile accident. Ronnie and her mother deal with their grief first by clinging to each other and later by withdrawing, each into herself. They attempt to cope with their pain by repressing thoughts and feelings about their dead father and husband. Their growing estrangement is compounded as Ronnie and Robert begin meeting each other secretly without their parents' permission in order to share each other's company. Ronnie and her mother have different needs during this difficult time, which they only realize after a major confrontation. Finally, they both see that they must allow each other independence in order to go forward together.

Armstrong, W. *Sounder.* New York: Harper, 1969. Fiction. Age 11 and over. After stealing a ham to feed his family, a black sharecropper is taken away to jail. In the process, Sounder, the family dog, is shot at and runs off. The sharecropper's son is happy when Sounder comes hobbling back home.

When the father is transferred to a labor camp, the boy sets out to search for his father. A kind schoolmaster takes him into his home, where he does chores and attends school. During one of the boy's visits home, he finds his father has returned but is ill and dies. A gripping story of hardship, stoic suffering in the face of death, resilience, and self-reliance.

Arundel, H. *The blanket word.* Nashville, Tenn.: Nelson, 1973. Fiction. Age 15 and over. The blanket word is *love*, which for Janette Meredith, the brilliant 19-year-old student, means family responsibility. Jan is the youngest of four children. Her two sisters and her brother are all married, have families, and are all dutiful family people. Jan does not care for her family, and she is honest about it. But news that her mother is dying of cancer produces in Jan an emotional turmoil for which she is unprepared. On the train returning home she is filled with guilt and self-reproach for having missed vacations at home, for not having called, having failed to write letters, and not having done thoughtful things for her mother. Her feelings turn to rage when she discovers that her sisters and brother had failed to tell her of her mother's illness until her mother was in the final difficult and painful phase of dying. Jan hates Mrs. Williams, the nurse, who reports that her mother is making "splendid progress." This hypocrisy—in fact, any kind of hypocrisy—is appalling to Jan. This includes some of the conventions of the funeral arrangements. Eventually, back in college, Jan discovers her admiration for her brother Jim, who with quiet efficiency and deep care has taken responsibility and has helped the family during her mother's final day and following her death. Jan learns that she loves her brother and is ready to help when he needs her. This well-written, thought-provoking book sensitively portrays young people's idealism and self-doubts. Its most striking feature is the insistence on honesty in matters of filial and familial love even in the face of death.

Asinoff, E. *Craig and Joan: Two lives for peace.* New York: Viking, 1971. Nonfiction. Age 14 and over. Two teen-agers, Craig and Joan, products of a conservative upbringing, form a suicide pact and commit suicide to protest the Vietnam

War. The author's interviews of Craig's and Joan's relatives and friends form the major portion of the book. Why do two well-liked adolescents elect to die to speak out against war? Is altruistic suicide an "appropriate" and defensible means of protest? Are there better alternatives? This book forces the reader to confront basic issues of war, destruction, self-destruction, and idealism. It is recommended as reading to be followed by group discussion or dialogue with parents.

Babbitt, N. *The eyes of the Amaryllis.* New York: Farrar, 1977. Fiction. Ages 9–11. In 1880, thirty years after the sinking of the brig *Amaryllis,* Geneva Reade still waits in her ocean-side house for a message from her dead husband, the ship's captain. When Geneva's granddaughter, Jenny, comes for a visit, she too is drawn into the twice-daily searches at high tide for the communication. She meets a strange person on the beach who is said to be the man who had carved the figurehead for the *Amaryllis* and later attempted suicide on the spot where the ship had sunk. One day the sea gives up a sign—the figurehead—but the man urges Geneva and Jenny to give it back; when they refuse, the sea rises in a fierce hurricane and reclaims the figurehead. An adventure of the sea, rich in fantasy and imagination.

Bartoli, J. *Nonna.* New York: Harvey House, 1975. Fiction. Preschool to 7. This story is about a young boy who learns to accept the death of his grandmother Nonna. At first he refuses to believe that Nonna is gone and he can no longer get cookies and gifts from her and that she will never play with him again. Eventually new people move into Nonna's house and life goes on. But the memories of the boy's grandmother are cherished. The story portrays the need for patience and the need for understanding that young children may respond to the death of a loved one in very specific and concrete ways.

Bauer, M. D. *Shelter from the wind.* New York: Seabury, 1976. Fiction. Ages 10–14. Twelve-year-old Stacy resents her stepmother, Barbara, especially since Barbara is pregnant. So one day in a blind rage, Stacy runs away from home. After long, hot hours of walking in the desert, Stacy comes upon two German shepherds who guide her to the little stone house where an old woman, Ella, lives as a recluse. Through helping take care of a litter of puppies, having to see one sick puppy mercifully killed by Ella, and through absorbing Ella's philosophy of life, Stacy comes to grips with her own problems and decides to return home and try to get along with Barbara. The plot is loosely woven, but the story is well told.

Bawden, N. M. K. *Squib*. Philadelphia: Lippincott, 1971. Fiction. Ages 11-13. Twelve-year-old Kate Pollack has difficulty facing the reality of death. Her father has drowned after saving Kate and unsuccessfully trying to save her little brother, Rupert. Later, playing with her friends in the park, Kate sees a strange, frail, shy little boy called Squib and soon convinces herself that he is her little brother, who had somehow survived. The children discover that Squib is mistreated by his guardian and report this to their families. Squib is then removed legally from the care of his guardian. Kate is now forced to accept her young brother's death and Squib's true identity.

Bernstein, J. E. *Loss and how to cope with it*. New York: Seabury, 1977. Nonfiction. Age 12 and over. In this book the author addresses older children and adolescents and discusses in a straightforward manner the responses of people to the death of a loved one, stressing that many reactions that are apparently bizarre are actually normal and common. The author relates personal stories that serve effectively to make a point or convey a concept. Along the way, much practical advice is offered to the reader. The book includes a list of other books on death and dying as well as some films and organizational resources. Valuable not only for children and youth, but for adults as well.

Bernstein, J. E., & Gullo, S. V. *When people die* (R. Hausherr, Photographer). New York: Dutton, 1977. Nonfiction. Ages 6-10. This sensitive, beautifully written book explains honestly and at the same time reassuringly how people feel and act when a loved one dies and gently leads the reader through the grieving process, including shock and denial; physical distress; and feelings of emptiness, anger, and isolation. The authors do not shy away from dealing with the biologic and physiological aspects of death, decomposition, and body disposal. This book answers many questions children ask about death. The stunningly beautiful photographs by the young Swiss photographer add greatly to the value of the book. Particularly striking and poignant are the photos of the newborn infant who has just entered the world and whose wrinkled face expresses need for care, followed a page later by the beautiful face of an old woman (actually Mrs. Michaelson, a retired principal) whose wrinkles tell of the joys and sorrows of a long life well-lived and of wisdom and serenity achieved. A must.

Bluenose, P., & Carpenter, W. S. *Two knots on a counting rope* (J. Smith, Illus.). New York: Holt, 1964. Fiction. Ages 6–9. This simply told story centers around a young Navajo Indian boy's respect and love for his grandfather, who teaches him many things. Among them, he teaches the boy how to count, using knots in a rope. The rope and its knots are symbolic of a person's life. After the last knot, one dies. Life and death are connected. Death is a natural part of the life cycle.

Borack, B. *Someone small* (A. Lobel, Illus.). New York: Harper, 1969. Fiction. Preschool to age 7. This story describes a young girl's gradual acceptance of her new sister and her love for her pet bird, Fluffy. One day Fluffy dies. The girls wrap him in a handkerchief, kiss him good-by, put him in a box, say a prayer, and bury him, thus going through a full funeral ritual. The colored pictures are essential to the story, for they portray feelings not specifically mentioned in the text.

Bradbury, B. *Where's Jim now?* Boston: Houghton Mifflin, 1978. Fiction. Ages 12–16. The difficulties experienced by a woman, Beth, and her 15-year-old son, David, after the death of her husband are complicated by the sudden reappearance of a troubled older son, Jim, from the father's first marriage. Beth and David try to take in the older boy, but the relationship never quite works out and Jim is eventually killed by a prison buddy. Divorce and death often have tragic consequences for those left behind. This story is starkly realistic.

Bradley, B. *Endings: A book about death.* Reading, Mass.: Addison-Wesley, 1979. Nonfiction. Ages 12–14. This book for young people ranges across the field of death and dying in order to provoke discussion and reflection. The author is a professional writer, not a content expert. Nevertheless, his information is up-to-date, and individual discussions are clear, even though it is sometimes difficult to follow the order of the chapters and their internal subdivisions. The text makes good use of model cases and literary references to illustrate points.

Brooks, J. *Uncle Mike's boy.* New York: Harper, 1973. Fiction. Age 9 and over. Pudge is a lonely boy whose only friend, his younger sister, has died as a result of a car accident, which Pudge himself survived. His parents offer no comfort because they cannot deal with their own problems. Fortunately, the boy's Uncle Mike, who himself has suffered the loss of two loved ones, offers Pudge support and friendship. With Uncle Mike's help, Pudge regains his self-confidence and is able to cope with his grief and the guilt he feels over his sister's death and his own survival. With his uncle's help, he is also able to cope with his mother's remarriage and his father's mental breakdown. A story of a grim reality, unsentimental but believable. Sometimes it is not the parents but a relative who provides the nurture needed to cope with hardships.

Brown, M. W. *The dead bird.* Reading, Mass.: Addison-Wesley, 1965. Fiction. Preschool to age 8. A group of children find a dead bird in the park. They observe what "dead" is like by touching and looking. Then they decide to have a funeral and bury the bird before resuming their play. Each day the children return to the bird's grave, put fresh flowers on it, and sing to the bird. They continue this ritual of mourning "until they forg[e]t." The final illustration depicts the children as they play ball, with the bird's grave in the background. The author's insight and understanding of young children is evident. The story is straightforward, practical, detailed, and matter-of-fact, yet tender and caring. Valuable.

Buck, P. S. *The big wave.* New York: Scholastic, 1960. Fiction. Ages 9–11. Pearl Buck's classic tale of Jiya, the fisherman's son, whose family is killed by a tidal wave and who then goes to live with his friend Kino, the farmer's son, and his understanding family. Although a wealthy gentleman offers to adopt Jiya, he decides to remain poor along with Kino's loving kin. With his new family's help and encouragement, Jiya is able to grieve the loss of his own family, which helps him to face the unknown and years later makes it possible for him to choose to move back to the seaside with his bride, Kino's sister. Powerful.

Burchard, P. *Bimby* (P. Burchard, Illus.). New York: Coward, 1968. Fiction. Ages 8–12. This story is set just before the Civil War. It centers around Bimby, a young slave on St. Simon Island, Georgia, and one-armed Jesse, his old friend, who is a wagon driver. Both are slaves of "Massa" Pierce Butler. One day, as everybody is busy preparing for a big party, Jesse takes Bimby in his dugout canoe and tells him about the rumor that Butler is planning to sell his slaves to the highest bidders and move north. This would mean Bimby would be separated from his mother. Jesse helps the boy realize the hopelessness of being a slave and how important it is to be in charge of oneself. When Jesse gets crushed by his master's wagon, Bimby rows his canoe south—toward freedom or death—pursued by his master's barge. The run for freedom is Bimby's way of paying his last respects to his dead friend Jesse. Although the names of the characters are ficticious, the story is based on historical records, including the auction of the slaves in 1859, and anthropologists are currently conducting archeological investigations of the Butler plantation to further authenticate the record. This story tells vividly about a dark side of United States history and the terrors of being enslaved. At the same time it introduces the reader to a meaning of life and death in a context that is unfamiliar to young North American readers today. A deeply touching story that speaks eloquently about the courage of the human spirit.

Byars, B. *Good-bye, Chicken Little*. New York: Harper, 1979. Fiction. Ages 8–12. Ever since his father was killed in an accident in a coal mine, Jimmie is possessed by a terrible fear. As a kind of self-punishment, he calls himself

"Chicken." Then one day, in Jimmie's presence, his uncle Pete drowns. This tragedy adds a deep sense of guilt to the fear Jimmie has been trying to cope with—a heavy burden for young Jimmie to carry. Fortunately, the offbeat family clan all get together, and their rough and roguish ways cheer Jimmie. His pride to be one of the "Little clan" helps him regain his self-confidence and assuage his guilt. At this time, also, an old friendship that seemed lost is renewed. The story is in many ways very funny, providing a good counterbalance to the stark reality of the two deaths and their impact on the boy. Sensitive and comforting. The author makes a good case for the need for and effectiveness of the family as an emotional support group.

Callen, L. *The deadly mandrake* (L. Johnson, Illus.). Boston: Little, Brown, 1978. Fiction. Ages 9-14. This is a suspenseful story about evil forces presumably emanating from a mandrake, a canelike plant the roots of which spread to resemble arms, legs, and a head. The plant has been used in primitive societies for casting spells. Among a number of unusual happenings in Four Corners, Jeremy Nix, who uproots the plant, gets sick and dies. Aside from the mystery that keeps the reader glued to the book, the story gives a detailed account of early death customs in this country that include the building of the coffin, preparing the body, the procession from the home, the burial, and the participation by the entire community in the funeral rite. This description is interesting and valuable.

Carrick, C. *The accident*. New York: Seabury, 1976. Fiction. Ages 5-8. When a child's beloved pet dies, sorrow is often accompanied by anger and guilt, especially when the pet dies in an accident. That is what happens to Christopher's dog, Bodger. Bodger is killed by a pickup truck near their summer cottage as they are on their way to join Christopher's parents. The little boy has a hard time believing that his father cannot "fix" Bodger and make him well again. Christopher is furious with the truck driver even though the driver is very compassionate. Most of all, Christopher feels guilty and blames himself for the death of his pet. Why had he not taken a different road? Could he have prevented the accident by calling Bodger? His father should not have buried Bodger without him, but Christopher is comforted when they canoe down the creek together and choose a suitable stone for Bodger's grave. Enfolded in his father's arms, Christopher is able to cry. A touching, realistic story with good illustrations.

Cleaver, V., & Cleaver, B. *Where the lilies bloom.* Philadelphia: Lippincott, 1969. Fiction. Age 12 and over. Mary Call Luther, age 14, lives in the mountains of North Carolina with her sharecropper father, two sisters, and a younger brother. Father knows he is dying and pleads with Mary Call to promise she will bury him secretly and keep the family together. When he dies, Mary Call carries through her promise and so prevents the Welfare Department from separating the children. Mary Call's courage and determination get the family through the harsh winter. Fortunately, Mary's older sister, who is 18, decides to get married to Kiser Pease, who helps the family stay together. A fine story. Well written.

Cleaver, V., & Cleaver, B. *Grover.* Philadelphia: Lippincott, 1970. Fiction. Age 9 and over. This sensitive story is about 10-year-old Grover who has to learn to cope in his own groping ways with the changes that the suicide of his ailing mother brings about. Grover's father is too grief-stricken to be of any help to his son. Both Grover and his father, along with the reader, are confronted with the question: Does a person have the duty to endure life no matter how hard the suffering and pain? Grover finds out that there is no simple formula for overcoming grief. It takes much time; one needs friends and maturity, particularly when a suicide is involved. A valuable book for young and older readers.

Cleaver, V., & Cleaver, B. *A little destiny.* New York: Lothrop, 1979. Fiction. Age 12 and over. Set in a small Georgia community at the turn of the century, the story is about 14-year-old Lucy who is determined to find her father's killer and to bring wealth to her poverty-stricken family. Somewhat melodramatic. Lucy, the main character, is not quite believable. The novel is not on a par with the author's other oustanding books, *Grover* and *Where the lilies bloom,* but better than many books on the market for children in their early teens.

Coburn, J. *Anne and the sand dobbies.* New York: Seabury, 1967. Fiction. Ages 8-12. Danny tells of his encounters with death in this gentle and deeply religious book. He tells about his sister Anne, who dies in her sleep of a respiratory infection, and about Bonnie, his dog, who runs away and is found frozen to death. With the help of a neighbor and imaginary characters, the sand dobbies, Danny learns to understand the essence of spiritual life, the presence of God, and that Anne resides in a place of love called heaven. A very comforting book. Most valuable for children raised in the Christian faith.

Coerr, E. *Sadako and the thousand paper cranes* (R. Himler, paintings). New York: Putnam's 1977. Nonfiction. Ages 12-14. Sadako Sasaki died on October 25, 1955, as a result of leukemia caused by the atomic bombing of Hiroshima 10 years earlier. This book tells about the last year of her life, the time following the diagnosis of her illness. In Japan, the crane is a symbol of longevity, and there is an old legend that the gods will give health to a sick person who makes 1,000 paper cranes. Before her death, Sadako folded 644 paper cranes. Afterward her classmates finished the remaining 356. Later they also collected and published her letters (on which this book is based), and eventually a monument was erected to her memory in Hiroshima's Peace Park. This is a gentle and touching story of death in another culture.

Coffin, M. *Death in early America.* New York: Nelson, 1976. Nonfiction. Age 12 and over. This is a reference work that describes artifacts such as tombstones, caskets, and mourning paraphernalia and explains how they are reflections of their culture and times. Interesting.

Cohen, B. *Thank you, Jackie Robinson.* New York: Lothrop, 1974. Fiction. Ages 8-11. This is a well-written story of the slowly developing and deepening friendship between 12-year-old Sam Greene and the elderly black cook, Davy. Both Sam and Davy are interested in sports, and both have the same hero, whose career they follow together: the black baseball player, Jackie Robinson. When Davy dies from a heart attack, Sam mourns the death of his friend. Because his friendship had been strong, the pain of loss is intense for Sam. The reader becomes deeply involved in Sam's pain and grief.

Colman, H. *Sometimes I don't love my mother.* New York: Morrow, 1977. Fiction. Age 12 and over. Following her father's heart attack and sudden death, 17-year-old Dallas finds herself having to cope both with her own grief and with her mother's clinging dependence. To help her mother, Dallas sets aside plans to go away to college but is then caught up in resentment, anger, and the ensuing feelings of guilt. The publisher's note says that in 1957 the author "turned to writing books for teenage girls." This is very much a book for teen-age girls.

Cooney, B. *Cock Robin.* New York: Scribner's, 1965. Fiction. Ages 6–9. This story of a robin, his happy marriage and sudden death caused by an accident, is written in poetic form. It won the 1959 Caldecott Medal. The story is accompanied by beautiful drawings. The death of Cock Robin and his funeral are described realistically and movingly. An appealing book.

Corley, E. A. *Tell me about death. Tell me about funerals.* Santa Clara, Calif.: Grammatical Sciences, 1973. Nonfiction. Ages 8–12. The author, a funeral director and embalmer, explains to a girl whose grandfather has died what happens in funerals. The book deals with the function of a funeral home, the embalming process, caskets, hearses, various types of burials, even the possibility of planning one's own funeral. Such detailed information is what children in this age range often request and seldom get. Amid all this factual information are words of comfort given by the parents. Even some humor is injected, as when the girl is confused about the role of "polar bears" [pallbearers] in a funeral. Valuable.

Cormier, R. *The chocolate war.* New York: Pantheon, 1974. Fiction. Age 12 and over. Jerry Renault's mother has recently died from cancer; his father seems to be sleep-walking through life and shift work as a pharmacist. Then, when Jerry enters a New England Catholic Prep school, he becomes involved with a secret student organization and finds himself under pressure from them and from the school's sadistic assistant headmaster to take part in a fund-raising drive. Can he refuse to sell the candy? "Do I dare disturb the universe?" Jerry's self-assertion has unanticipated and chilling consequences. Like its successors, *I am the cheese* and *After the first death,* this carefully-crafted story explores the dark and complex sides of human behavior.

Cunningham, J. *Burnish me bright.* New York: Pantheon, 1970. Fiction. Ages 10-14. This is a moving story about a mute orphan boy and his short apprenticeship to a dying old man who once was the world's greatest mime. It is set in a small village in the south of France. The story has two main themes. One is that adjusting to being different and handicapped is difficult and requires great strength and courage. The second theme is death. Both are handled with unembellished directness and poignancy. Beautifully written.

Cunningham, J. *Wings of the morning* (K. Peake, Photographer). Los Angeles: Golden Gate Junior Books, 1971. Fiction. Ages 8-12. The photographer's young daughter encounters a "sleeping" bird that is actually dead. This is the girl's first experience with death. The explanations and comfort offered are subtle and symbolic. The young reader is not clearly confronted with death as distinct from sleep. With adult help, however, this clarification can be achieved. Otherwise this book is beautiful with exceptionally good photographs and poetic language. A sensitive story.

Cunningham, J. *Tuppenny.* New York: Dutton, 1978. Fiction. Ages 12-14. A mysterious young girl named Tuppenny comes to a small town where there is much guilt and hatred. The minister's daughter is dead, supposedly a suicide; the older daughter of the factory owner has run away; and the couple who own the café have put their retarded child in an institution. After helping the latter two families to achieve some self-understanding and reconciliation, Tuppenny exposes the evil in the minister. A disconcerting story from the well-known author of *Dear rat* and *Drop dead,* etc.

De Bruyn, M. G. *The beaver who wouldn't die.* Chicago: Follett, 1975. Fiction. Ages 6-9. Cyrus, a beaver who lives in the north woods, is granted through magic his wish never to die.

As he keeps on growing and becomes larger and larger, and particularly as he sees his peers and even his children and grandchildren die, he feels out of place and out of time, gets very lonely and depressed, and wishes he could die. Fortunately, his wish to die is granted, and he happily joins his loved ones in a warm pool, where he hopes to stay forever. A very creative story with colorful and interesting illustrations. The story has an important message about the naturalness of the life cycle. Very well written.

De Paola, T. *Nana Upstairs and Nana Downstairs*. New York: Putnam's, 1973. Fiction. Preschool to 7. This low-key and simply written story depicts with great ease and care the loving relationships four-year-old Tommy has with his great-grandmother (Nana Upstairs) who is 94 years old and bedridden and his grandmother (Nana Downstairs). When Nana Upstairs dies, Tommy is very sad. His mother explains what it means to be dead in a way that is straightforward and honest: "Nana Upstairs won't be here anymore and won't come back except in your memory." Later Tommy's grandmother gets sick and moves upstairs, and then she dies, too. But Tommy's belief that both Nanas are upstairs—in heaven—is comforting when he is confronted with the inevitability of death. The pictures vividly portray feelings and serve well to underscore the story.

Dexter, P. *The emancipation of Joe Tepper*. Nashville: Nelson, 1976. Fiction. Age 12 and over. Joe Tepper has had more than his share of problems for a 15-year-old. He has no father; his mother drinks heavily; and Joe has been on his own for a long time. The family is in financial straits. The money Joe makes on his paper route is just enough to pay for the rent. Then Joe's mother is killed in an accident. Joe is shocked, angry, and distraught. Even though his mother had not been "good" by normal standards, Joe loved her very much, and he misses her and deeply grieves her death. But Joe will not let the social worker take him to a foster home. He will not give up his paper route and his part-time job at the bowling alley. The story tells of Joe's courage, independence, and strong sense of responsibility in the face of hardships and grief. A suspenseful, realistic, and moving story.

Dixon, P. *A time to love—a time to mourn* (Originally published as *May I cross your golden river?*). New York: Scholastic, 1975. Fiction. Age 14 and over. At 18, Jordon Phillips discovers he is slowly dying of the same muscular disorder that killed the famous Yankee baseball player Lou Gehrig. The book vividly describes Jordon's and his family's reaction of shock, anguish, and pain. The reader is not spared details of the pain and the progressive weakness that Jordon experiences, but the reader is also permitted to share Jordon's innermost thoughts and feelings and his interactions with his family and friends. The loving, caring support of his family helps Jordon to prepare himself and them for his death. This is a moving book by a gifted and sensitive writer that depicts masterfully a painful reality but also portrays the power of love to help overcome fears and anxiety and cope with death at an early age.

Dixon, P. *Skipper.* New York: Atheneum, 1979. Fiction. Age 12 and over. A sequel to *May I cross your golden river?* After his brother's death, 14-year-old Skipper sets off from Colorado in search of the father he has never known. The boy never finds this elusive and irresponsible parent, but he does discover four generations of his family in Llangollen, a small North Carolina town. There are tensions in Llangollen, and Skipper's encounters are not all without difficulties (including the death of his great-grandfather); but in the end, he finds a way to go forward with his own life.

Dobrin, A. *Scat!* New York: Four Winds, 1971. Fiction. Ages 6–9. This story deals with a child's emotions and attempts to cope with the loss through death of his beloved grandmother. The boy Scat loves music. He also remembers at the right moment his grandmother's advice: "Listen to what your heart says . . . not your head." He leaves the funeral services, goes to a quiet spot near his grandmother's grave, takes his harmonica out of his pocket and begins to play. This special personal memorial allows him to express his sadness and gives him comfort. A very touching story.

Farley, C. *The garden is doing fine.* New York: Atheneum, 1975. Fiction. Ages 6–8. This book describes the impact of parental death on a young child. Corrie's father is dying of cancer. Corrie and her mother refuse to accept this. Corrie recalls former happier times and is outraged at the injustice of her father's suffering. She prays for him and thinks of him often, but another part of her is also aware of boys, games, and school activities. Finally, when she can no longer deny the imminence of her father's death, she is consoled by the realization that his kindness and love will always be remembered and will live on through her memory.

Fassler, J. *My grandpa died today* (S. Kranz, Illus.). New York: Human Sciences, 1971. Fiction. Preschool to 8. This beautifully written story is about a little boy David who, in narrative form, tells about his beloved grandfather's death and how he feels about it, how those around him feel, what they do, and particularly how caring and understanding they are toward David. David's grandfather had taught him many things and had shared his thoughts about life and death. One day he had said: "David, I am getting very old now. And surely I cannot live forever . . . but I am not afraid to die . . . because I know that you are not afraid to live." With this memory, David is better able to cope with his grief and can get on with life. An essential part of this warm and comforting story are the exceptional illustrations that vividly depict in simple strokes the emotions of love, sadness, shock, the gentleness of comfort, and, yes, the joy of life. A must.

Feagles, A. M. *The year the dreams came back*. New York: Atheneum, 1973. Fiction. Ages 10-12. Nell hardly knew her mother. Yet she is guilt-ridden over her mother's suicide and possessed by fear. When her father decides to remarry, Nelly's barely repressed feelings come to the surface and threaten to overwhelm her. Happily, her relationship with a young man intensifies, and a new girl friend gives support; surprisingly quickly Nell's depression turns into happiness. The characters are well developed. The author lightens much of the gloom and despair by a light touch in style and a realistic, natural dialogue.

Fisher, L. E. *The death of Evening Star: The diary of a young New England whaler*. New York: Doubleday, 1972. Fiction. Ages 10-14. Jeremiah Poole is 14 when his father, a preacher, dies and leaves his family penniless. Jeremiah is indentured as a cabin boy to a whaling ship, *Evening Star.*

The book tells of the hardship Jeremiah endures on the high seas, of rough men he encounters, and of the excitement and skill of catching a whale. While in port, Jeremiah runs a high fever and is hustled off the ship to stay with an elderly couple. For a while he is supected of having the plague. The *Evening Star* runs into a storm and goes down with all hands. All this happens in 1841; then, 100 years later, Jeremiah's diary-log wrapped in oilskin mysteriously shows up and is handed to the narrator by an old lighthouse keeper. This is an exciting and engrossing story of high adventure at sea, where death is always close by and accepted stoically. An important focus in this book is the struggle between good and evil forces in men. Most impressive and artistic are the black-and-white drawings by the author, who has illustrated more than 200 children's books.

Fitzhugh, L., & Scoppettone, S. *Bang bang you're dead* (L. Fitzhugh, Illus.). New York: Harper, 1969. Fiction. Preschool to 7. This little book is about James, Timothy, Stanley, and Bert, who dress in their Indian outfits, soldier suits, and cowboy boots to play their games of "Bang Bang You're Dead" almost daily. They fire their make-believe bullets and throw their make-believe rocks and "take a hill" near their homes. The end of the battle for the hill ends with all four little boys lying "dead" on the ground, and then they troop off for a snack. One day there are four frowning strangers on the hill and an argument begins about whose hill it is and who can play there. A war is declared. At 3 p.m. the next day, the war begins. This time the hitting is real, and real blood flows, and everyone gets hurt. That is when the boys decide that having a war is not fun. "Bang, bang, you're dead" happily is not true. The authors portray very effectively how a group of young children discover the seriousness of war and the unreality of make-believe death. The drawings are very well done. They underscore the message and add a richness and vividness that make this little book even more attractive.

Forrai, M. S. *A look at death.* Minneapolis: Lerner, 1978. Nonfiction. Ages 8–10. The photographs are by Forrai, but the text is by Anders. The book is part of the Lerner

Awareness Series (the foreword is by Robert C. Slater, Professor/Director of the Department of Mortuary Science at the University of Minnesota) aimed at making children aware of dying, death, and our death customs. This, the author-photographer is ambitiously trying to accomplish in 16 black-and-white photographs. Some of the photographs are excellent, but others are ambiguous or misleading. The text that accompanies each photograph is very well written; it makes this little book worth reading.

Gardam, J. *The summer after the funeral.* New York: Macmillan, 1973. Fiction. Age 11 and over. The three children are sent off to grieve alone after the death of their father, while the mother does *her* grieving separately. The story poignantly depicts the impact of a parent's death on a teen-ager. Described are all the feelings of anger, denial, frustration, loneliness, and eventually acceptance after an extraordinary summer following the father's death. The various responses to grief are handled perceptively and sensitively. Through all the sadness, the message is hopeful and life affirming.

Glaser, D. *The diary of Trilby Frost.* New York: Holiday House, 1976. Fiction. Age 14 and over. Trilby Frost is 13 when her father gives her a diary in which to write her experiences and feelings. At first, Trilby's entries are sporadic. Trilby only writes when something awful happens, and—unfortunately—Trilby finds much to write. First her father dies, leaving Trilby and her family bereft and in financial need. A boarder is taken in to supplement the meager family income; but that turns into tragedy as he makes Katherine, Trilby's older sister, pregnant, then moves away. Before he does, however, Caleb, Trilby's little brother, is killed trying to ride the boarder's horse. Caleb's death is very difficult for Trilby. She confides to her diary the guilt she feels about the many times she was annoyed with him, about how often she wished him away or dead. She also is angry with God for taking away both her father and brother. Then Katherine miscarried at six months of pregnancy, and this death is quite confusing to Trilby. After all, everybody was unhappy about this unwanted pregnancy, most of all the young mother. Yet now she is grieving. Through all these harrowing experiences, Trilby is able to share her feelings not only with an unresponsive diary but with a flesh-and-blood friend Saul, a half-breed Indian who lives on a neighboring farm. Trilby and Saul are childhood friends and turn to each other for understanding. But even this friend is torn away from her as Saul dies as a result of a wagon accident and is buried on his 17th birthday. There is almost too much to bear for one growing girl in this story, set at the turn of this century. Yet, the story is hopeful in that Trilby is able to cope with her losses and become more mature in the process.

Greenberg, J. *A season in-between.* New York: Farrar, 1979. Fiction. Age 12 and over. Carrie Singer is in between many things. She is a seventh grader growing into young adulthood and her first relationship with a boy friend; she is also one of the few Jewish students at an expensive private school for girls in St. Louis. More important, she is between the diagnosis of her father's cancer in spring and his death that summer; she is further constrained by her own mourning and the needs of her mother, who is now trying to continue to operate the family shoe factory. Carrie is resilient enough to survive these pressures and to begin to see the wisdom of the old rabbinical tale about turning scratches on a jewel into a beautiful design.

Greene, C. C. *Beat the turtle drum.* New York: Viking, 1976. Fiction. Ages 9-13. This beautifully crafted story is about Joss and her older sister Kate. Both love horses, and with enough money saved they rent a horse for one week. Kate, who narrates the story, describes it as the happiest week of their lives until Joss falls from a tree and breaks her neck. Joss's death stuns and paralyzes the family. Mother lies in bed sedated with tranquilizers; Father stays drunk; and 13-year-old Kate is left alone in her pain and grief until her older cousin Mona, the wife of the man who rented the horses, provides comfort. The story ends at the height of grief, but Kate's ability to express her feelings in poetry suggests that she will be able to cope. A realistic and sensitive story.

Grimes, N. *Growin'* (C. Lilly, Illus.). New York: Dial, 1977. Fiction. Ages 12-14. Pump—short for Pumpkin, Yolanda

Jackson's nickname—is a young black girl whose world seems
to collapse when her father dies in an automobile accident.
He had always been the one who had seemed to understand
her and her poetry. After his death, Pump's mother moves
them to a new neighborhood, where Pump strikes up an
unlikely friendship with Jim Jim, the class bully. Their
adventures help Pump through a hard, lonely time until she
accidentally discovers that her mother had also tried to write
poetry as a young girl. Lack of success condemned Pump's
mother to a career as a typist, but the shared interest brings
them together again. Unusual for the author's insights into
the life and feelings of a black girl and for the eight
drawings that highlight key events in the text.

Grollman, E. A. *Talking about death: A dialogue between parent
and child.* (G. Héau, Illus.). Boston: Beacon, 1976. Nonfiction. Preschool to 6. This is a new edition of the author's
1970 book by the same title. In this new edition the
"Parents' Guide" is expanded to include various ways of
using the book, of helping parents themselves come to
acknowledge death and grief. This book is for children to
read or to have read to them. The author discusses death in
an honest, simple, straightforward manner. He insists that
the reader understands that dead is *dead.* There is no
flinching from the facts, no silence in response to the child's
questions. At the same time, the book is warm, loving,
sensitive, and tender. Gisela Héau's incredibly beautiful illustrations underscore the text and create a hopeful mood.
This is one of the best nonfiction books about death for
young children on the market. A must for parents with small
children.

Grollman, E. A. *Living when a loved one has died.* Boston:
Beacon, 1977. Nonfiction. Age 14 and over. Although the
intent of the well-known author and rabbi was to write this
book for bereaved adults, it is equally suited for mature
adolescents and youths. The book skillfully blends new
scientific information about the grieving process with the
compassion and gentleness of a friend, counselor, or pastor,
making this book particularly helpful to those who have just
experienced the death of a loved one. The language is simple

and direct, in keeping with the author's other book, *Talking about death*. Some unusually good black-and-white photographs add to the impact of the book.

Gunther, J. *Death be not proud: A memoir*. New York: Harper, 1949. Nonfiction. Age 14 and over. This first-person narrative gives a moving account of the author's son's 15-month fight with a brain tumor. Johnny is 15 years old when the diagnosis is made. His determination and courage are inspiring. His dream is to go to Harvard University, and his brilliance and willpower help him to keep up with his studies. His need for hope and for living each day fully are vividly shown. He continues to do laboratory experiments while confined to bed and studies diligently to prepare for the college board examinations even at the time when his tumor is progressing relentlessly. The reader is confronted with the difficulty the parents have in acknowledging that their son is dying and their efforts to keep the truth from him. But it is Johnny who protects his parents. Interspersed in the narrative are letters and notes written by Johnny that are deeply touching and make the reader want to laugh and cry. Johnny's strength of spirit is an inspiration.

Hamilton-Paterson, J., & Andrews, C. *Mummies: Death and life in ancient Egypt*. New York: Penguin, 1979. Nonfiction. Age 12 and over. Embalming or mummification practices in ancient Egypt occurred over a period lasting some 2,700 years. Although the most prominent forms of these practices applied mainly to a small minority of the population— members of the royal or upper class and later some middle-class people, but never to the large body of ordinary people—they still excite widespread interest and curiosity today. Despite some confusing theology and technical detail, together with an obviously British tone and vocabulary, that interest will be well satisfied in this thorough and informative study. Fascinating reading for adults and adolescents alike!

Harnden, R. P. *The high pasture*. Boston: Houghton Mifflin, 1964. Fiction. Age 12 and over. Thirteen-year-old Tim is sent away from home to spend the summer with his great-aunt Kate on her ranch because his mother is ill in the hospital. When Aunt Kate's old dog dies early in the summer, Tim becomes apprehensive and anxious. Tim's anxiety must be blamed on his family's failure to inform him of the nature and seriousness of his mother's illness. In talking to his father, Tim learns that his mother is going to die but that the parents wanted to protect him because they love him. This story describes well what parents ought *not* to do in such a situation. Fortunately, there is much mutual sharing of grief, and Tim is surprisingly tolerant, given the circumstances. Written for children but profitable reading for adults, particularly parents.

Harris, A. *Why did he die?* Minneapolis: Lerner, 1965. Non-fiction. Preschool to 6. A mother explains death to her young son Scott, whose friend Jim has lost his grandfather. This mother is open and honest in her attempt to answer her child's questions. She likens death to the leaves falling in autumn but with new ones to come in the spring. Another way she explains death is by using as an example a worn-out motor. The whole story is in poetic form and has beautiful illustrations to match. The emphasis is on the concept that, though loved ones die, their memories will not. Warm, frank, and hopeful. A good example of how death can be handled with a child of kindergarten age.

Härtling, I. *Oma* (A. Bell, Trans., from German; J. Ash, Illus.). New York: Harper, 1977. Fiction. Ages 8–12. The orphaned five-year-old Kalle is sent to live with Oma (German for grandma) in Munich. During the following years Kalle and Oma have to deal with a number of people—welfare workers, teachers, other old people. The story is ably crafted to show how child and grandparent learn to adjust to one another and become fond of one another after many episodes of anger, frustration, mistrust, and misunderstanding. The narration is natural, simple, and flows well. The author captures the difference in patterns and styles of communication between the young and the old. The reader receives additional insights about Oma's personality through her first-person comments that are set off at the end of each of the 15 brief chapters of the book. Throughout, an apparent message to the reader is "You're as young as you feel" (perhaps this book should be recommended for adults as well as children). The black-and-white drawings effectively underscore the light and comic events. Excellent.

Hughes, P. R. *Dying is different.* Mahomet, Ill.: Mech Mentor Educational, 1978. Nonfiction. Preschool to 8. This beautiful book by a gifted writer, artist, and psychologist is intended to promote discussion of death between adults and very young children. The 18 children's pages use drawings, strong colors, and poems to present a graduated succession of living and dead states in flowers, ants, fish, a cat, and a grandmother, followed by vivid thematic depictions of the inevitability of death, its justification, remembering, acceptance, grief, funerals, cemeteries, and the importance of love during life. An introduction and concluding remarks for parents and teachers suggest questions and guidelines for discussion. A very helpful resource for adult-child interactions, one that adults can read alone or share with children. Available in both a large instructional edition designed to stand upright by itself and a smaller personal edition in standard book format.

Hunter, J. *A sound of chariots.* New York: Harper, 1972. Fiction. Age 12 and over. Bridie McShane experiences a happy childhood in Scotland that comes to a sudden halt: Her father dies. Bridie had been her father's favorite child, and she had loved her father immensely. She is grief stricken. From her father's death on, her life is marred by the pain and sorrow of her loss. Her thoughts become morbid as she gropes to adjust. Eventually she discovers that she loves poetry, and she begins to write and express her thoughts and feelings and thereby learns to cope. Although this story is lacking in action and adventure (the title is misleading), it conveys convincingly a problem seldom discussed in other stories with a similar theme: the problem of delayed or prolonged grief.

Hunter, M. *The third eye.* New York: Harper, 1979. Fiction. Ages 12-14. According to the Ballinford doom, for hundreds of years no first-born son has lived to inherit the Scottish title Earl of Ballinford. In 1935, a young girl, Janet (Jinty) Morrison, is asked to give testimony in an inquiry into the

death of the old earl, which occurred on the day his only
son reached the age of 21. Was the death a tragic accident,
or did the earl die by his own hand to break the curse? Told
as a flashback over a three-year period, this well-executed
novel introduces the Morrison family: a quiet father, a
strong-willed mother who is determined that her girls will get
what she herself has missed in life, two rebellious older
sisters, and Jinty. Jinty gains the earl's friendship by her
honesty and intuitive sense of inward feelings (her "third
eye"), traits that also appear in her artwork in school and in
the way she helps a blind boy to "see" through tactile
analogues before his death. A story of adventure and fore-
boding in which Jinty's wisdom helps her troubled family
and village.

Huntsberry, W. E. *The big hang-up.* New York: Lothrop, 1970.
Fiction. Age 12 and over. High school seniors Corey, Rick,
and Jim are triple-dating for an important fall dance. The
night of the dance, Rick drives his mother's new Lincoln.
Later in the evening they drink beer, and Corey, feeling
high, urges Rick to see how fast the new car can go. They
have an accident and one of the girls dies. Blaming himself
for the accident, Corey is sick with grief and guilt. When he
returns to school he learns that Rick is blamed for the
accident and drops out of school. Corey slowly comes to the
painful realization that he must bear his guilt, for people are
responsible for their own behavior. A starkly realistic story.
The reader is left with the suggestion that Corey finally is
able to cope with the tragic event, recognizing that no
amount of guilt and self-blame is going to bring back the
girl. A hard lesson learned, and Corey will become a
responsible adult.

Hyde, M. O., & Forsyth, E. H. *Suicide: The hidden epidemic.*
New York: Watts, 1978. Nonfiction. Age 12 and over. A
significant recent increase in the incidence of suicide among
young people makes this an important subject for them to
study and understand. This book, written by an experienced
children's writer and a child psychiatrist who have collab-
orated on two previous books, offers factual and theoretical
information as well as practical advice. The writing style is

clear, and the presentation is aided by numerous subheadings within each chapter. The book concludes with a list of crisis intervention centers in the United States and two pages of suggestions for further reading. An authoritative study for young people that can also be read with profit by adults.

Jones, M. A. *Tell me about heaven* (M. Cooper, Illus.). Chicago: Rand McNally, 1956. Nonfiction. Ages 6–8. This book is exceptionally good in helping children understand death and what happens afterward. It is based on the Christian belief system. The author's insight into children's thoughts and concerns is impressive. Many parents of small children are probably confronted with similar questions: Is heaven above the sky? Will dogs go to heaven? What is heaven like? Can we come back from heaven? What do people do in heaven? The answers provided to the questions are appropriate for chidren with a Christian background without being contrary to scientific fact. The writing is beautifully simple and appealing. This book would be helpful to parents who have difficulty dealing with such questions.

Kantrowitz, M. *When Violet died.* New York: Parents' Magazine Press, 1973. Fiction. Preschool to 8. When Amy's and Eva's pet bird Violet dies, the children plan a funeral and a memorial. They invite other children to participate in the ceremony, which includes singing, recital of poetry, and serving punch. The children behave very much as adults do when a death occurs, but their grief is quickly resolved when they discover that Blanche, their cat, is pregnant. The children excitedly await the birth of the kittens. Kantrowitz very skillfully shows the comfort that is derived from the knowledge that life is a continuous process. The story also shows that funerals do not *have* to be all sad. Written with warmth, compassion, and insight into children's thoughts and feelings.

Kaplan, B. *The empty chair.* New York: Harper, 1978. Fiction. Ages 6–9. This is a story of Jewish family life, with Becky Levine as the central character. Although Becky's life with her brother Saul and Mama and Papa is basically good, she secretly yearns for the luxuries her friends can afford and she cannot. One day Mama announces that she is pregnant, and the family is sparked by the joy of anticipation. Unfortunately, both Mama and the baby die during childbirth. The story skillfully and touchingly depicts the emptiness in the hearts of the surviving family members and the well-intentioned actions of relatives and friends. Eventually Papa remarries, and Becky has to learn to accept the new mother.

Kerr, J. *A small person far away.* New York: Coward, 1979. Fiction. Age 12 and over. Judith Kerr's three autobiographic novels follow Anna and her family after they leave Germany just before Hitler's election in 1933. They flee because they are ethnic Jews and Papa is a prominent anti-Nazi writer and intellectual. *When Hitler stole Pink Rabbit* (1972) covers a two-year period during which 9-year-old Anna, her 12-year-old brother, and their parents move from Berlin, first to Switzerland and then to Paris. *The other way round* (1975) follows teen-age Anna as she develops her artistic abilities in London during the war. Throughout both of these books, Anna's young perspective is fresh and unique; loss and deprivation lead her to hard work and well-earned growth. In *A small person far away,* Anna, who is now in her early thirties, newly married to a successful television writer, and beginning her own writing career in London, is called back to Berlin in the middle of the Hungarian and Suez crises in 1956, where her now-widowed mother has attempted suicide. During the six days of her visit, a welter of thoughts and feelings tumble about in Anna's mind—dominated always by the warmth of her memories of gentle Papa and the intensity of her image of Mama. Eventually, Mama recovers and seems to be on the way to resuming life with her friend Konrad, and Anna returns to England to discover that she is pregnant. Judith Kerr has a marvelous ability for deft characterization and evocative description. All three of these books are splendid reading for younger and older readers alike; perhaps the last deals most intimately with themes of life and death.

Kidd, R. *That's what friends are for.* Nashville: Nelson, 1978. Fiction. Ages 12–14. Two boys meet and become close friends in seventh grade in a California junior high school. A year later one of them falls ill. Scott is not told the truth about his condition, but Gary accidentally learns that his friend is dying of leukemia. Gary is bewildered by these events and by the atmosphere of secretiveness. He is especially shaken by his own inability to help his friend—he even stays away from the hospital during the last two weeks before Scott's death—or to find solace at the funeral. Gary shares his story and feelings in this book: "I have to tell someone."

Klagsbrun, F. *Too young to die: Youth and suicide.* Boston: Houghton Mifflin, 1976; New York: Pocket Books, 1977. Nonfiction. Age 14 and over. This is the first book about suicide among adolescents and college students that was written to be read by young people as well as by their parents, counselors, and teachers. Its three parts deal, respectively, with the realities of suicide among the young—statistics, common myths, suicide as communication, the role of depression or psychosis, and uncounted or "chronic" suicides; practical guidelines—"What can you do?—for dealing both with crisis situations and with survivors; and social aspects—sociologic or psychological causes, cultural attitudes, and prevention techniques. Appendixes document the rise in suicide rates among the 15- to 24-year-old age group over the 20-year period from 1954 to 1974 and list many suicide prevention or crisis intervention agencies in the United States. There is also an eight-page bibliography. An excellent resource on a subject that deserves more attention. Valuable for adult reading.

Klein, N. *Sunshine.* New York: Avon, 1974. Nonfiction. Age 16 and over. Kate Hayden is the 19-year-old mother of Jill, who is six months old. Kate has a rare form of bone cancer. After having divorced Jill's father, she finds Sam. They love each other deeply, and they get married. As the cancer progresses, Kate decides to refrain from taking medication, thus shortening her life. Sam does not understand. He accuses her of committing suicide. Kate states her case: Off the drugs she will die more quickly, but she will be capable of feeling and loving. She has much love to give to Sam and Jill. Kate's doctor supports her decision and gives her the tape recorder whose tapes form the basis for the book (and the film). This is a story of love, loneliness, and a need to die with dignity. It is tender and gripping but also painful and starkly realistic.

Klein, S. *The final mystery.* New York: Doubleday, 1974. Nonfiction. Ages 8-13. The author explores the meanings of death for people living in different times and regions and having different religions. The discussion is unique in its emphasis on ways in which people have attempted to fight death through the generations. Studies of people's feelings about death, especially fear, are described as well as burial and funeral customs. Through all of this, the author is able to show that death, like some other events, remains a mystery.

Krementz, J. *How it feels when a parent dies.* New York: Knopf, 1982. Nonfiction. Ages 9 and over. In this unique book a gifted writer has set down the thoughts and feelings of 18 children, aged 7-16, who lost a parent. Reading these accounts of anguish, confusion, anger, and guilt is a painful experience but the reality of losing a parent in childhood *is* shattering. The author believes that these shared experiences may help and comfort young readers who have themselves lost a parent through death. Certainly, it will help such readers realize that their reactions to their loss are normal and appropriate. Jill Krementz' sensitive photographs of the children add to the book's impact.

Landau, E. *Death: Everyone's heritage.* New York: Messner, 1976. Nonfiction. Age 14 and over. The author, a children's librarian, uses a variety of anecdotes to illustrate issues concerning medical death: euthanasia, terminal care, suicide, cryonics, funerals, cemeteries, and the grief of survivors. With the help of new stories, cross-cultural data, and interviews, the author carefully presents both sides of each issue. This book is informative and thought provoking. The author shows sympathetic insight into the dynamics of suicidal people and the pain of despair.

Langone, J. *Death is a noun: A view of the end of life.* Boston: Little, Brown, 1972; New York: Dell, 1975. Nonfiction. Age 12 and over. This simply and clearly written book presents a broad survey of important aspects and issues concerning death. Using research reports, historical analyses, and human interest stories, the author deals with basic attitudes toward death, euthanasia, abortion, capital punishment, murder, suicide, problems of determining medical death, grief, and the quest for immortality. In addition, various philosophical and religious beliefs about life after death are discussed, such as animism, theism, deism, atheism, Christianity, Judaism, Hinduism, Buddhism, and Islam. Highly instructive. Should have wide appeal not only for young readers but for adults as well. A good companion to Langone's book *Vital signs: The way we die in America.*

Langone, J. *Vital signs: The way we die in America.* Boston: Little, Brown, 1974. Nonfiction. Age 16 and over. In this documentary the author skillfully weaves together a variety of materials: classical quotations, scientific data, legal case material, news reports, and interviews with doctors, nurses, clergy, and dying people and their families. In doing this he reaveals startling facts about the way people die today. The reader is immediately involved in the current dilemma about the definition of death, in the depersonalization of contemporary dying, and in the universal desire for dignity. This book is instructive and humanistic in its plea for greater empathy for the needs of the dying. Indignant and compassionate. A valuable book for mature young readers as well as adults.

Lee, M. S. *Fog.* New York: Seabury, 1972. Fiction. Age 12 and over. This book deals with the grief and sense of loss that Luke experiences at the death of his father, as well as another kind of grief, hurt, and anger he feels when he and his girl friend decide to stop seeing each other. The reader is also drawn into the boy's struggle over his choice of a career and his feelings of guilt about the clubhouse fire. The language is contemporary and attractive. The characters portrayed are vivid and believable.

Lee, R. *The magic moth.* New York: Seabury, 1972. Fiction. Ages 8–11. Ten-year-old Maryanne is the middle child in a family of five, and she has a heart defect. Everything possible has been done, including heart surgery, but now the family is told that Maryanne cannot be cured. The story tells of the love, courage, strength, and support of the Foss family and the problems that had to be overcome in helping

each other cope with Maryanne's impending untimely death.
A moth bursts from its cocoon as Maryanne dies, and seeds
sprout just after her funeral, symbolizing that "life never
ends—it just changes," a belief that offers much comfort to
both young and old readers. This is a touching story told in
a straightforward and unsentimental manner.

L'Engle, M. *Meet the Austins.* New York: Vanguard, 1960.
Fiction. Ages 9–12. Vicki Austin is 12 years old, a happy
member of a happy family including her older brother
John, younger sister Suzy, and little brother Rob. Mother is
preparing a gala dinner for Uncle Douglas, who has arrived
for a visit. The phone rings, but that is a frequent event at
the Austin's as Father is a doctor. But this call is different.
It brings the bad news that Uncle Hal has been killed in a
plane crash. He was the pilot. Also killed was his copilot,
which left his 8-year-old daughter Maggie an orphan. The
Austin's take Maggie into their home until her eccentric
grandfather can decide what to do with her. The story
describes with great sensitivity how Vicki tries to cope with
the loss of her favorite uncle and with the deep resentment
she feels toward Maggie, who appears to be a spoiled and
selfish child but who actually has never had the security and
warmth of a family. Eventually, Maggie is accepted to the
degree that the Austins hope Maggie's grandfather will let
her stay with them, which he finally decides to do. All
through the story, one is impressed with the love, insight,
and patience of Vicki's parents and with their effectiveness
in helping the children to be tolerant of each other and to
care. A very readable book by a well-known writer.

L'Engle, M. *A ring of endless light.* New York: Farrar, 1980.
Fiction. Age 12 and over. During the summer when she is
almost 16, Vicky Austin finds herself with three young men
on her hands: Leo, who lives on the island where they are
visiting, seeks comfort from her after his father's unexpected
death; Zachary, a rich friend whose suicide attempt had
inadvertently caused Leo's father's death, tries to make her
responsible for his well-being; and Adam, a student of
marine biology, discovers that she has telepathic powers that
can aid in his experiments with wild dolphins. All the while,

Vicky's minister grandfather is dying of leukemia. As his condition deteriorates, Vicky struggles to overcome her confusion and grief through reading and her own poetry. The book's title (short for "a great ring of pure and endless light") and another line from Henry Vaughan's poetry—"a deep but dazzling darkness"—offer metaphors for eternity that portray the spiritual and moral dimensions underlying life processes. Characters, events, and meanings are skillfully evoked through sensitive writing and careful detail by a prolific and respected writer for children as well as adults.

LeShan, E. *Learning to say good-by: When a parent dies.* New York: Macmillan, 1978. Nonfiction. Age 10 and over. This family counselor and writer speaks to children in a simple, straightforward manner about the problems they face when losing a parent and how these problems may be overcome. The main thrust throughout this helpful and comforting book is the acceptance of the griever as a person who is suffering much pain and disorientation but who is healthy and will be capable of coping by expressing and sharing her or his feelings in open communication with interested and caring adults. The book is well-written, and examples are used to amply illustrate a situation or clarify a point. An informative, nonthreatening, supportive book.

Levit, R. E. *A short life long remembered.* New York: Bantam, 1974. Nonfiction. Age 12 and over. In the midst of her parents' struggles with their own separation, 15-year-old Ellen is diagnosed as having bone cancer. The book is the mother's personal account of her daughter's last two years of life, interspersed with letters and poetry written by Ellen during her illness. Not a literary piece but a believable portrayal.

Lifton, R. and Olson, E. *Living and dying.* New York: Praeger, 1974. Nonfiction. Age 15 and over. The authors discuss the ways in which North Americans have written death out of their culture and sought "immortality" through various symbolic modes of escape. They also note the attitudinal transformation growing out of nuclear fears and national self-confrontation brought on by Vietnam, the assassinations of the 1960s, and other traumatic events. The authors espouse the philosophy that it is better to confront death, risk loss, and live well than to evade life's challenges, sorrows, and joys. They consider experiential transcendence as a means of coping with time and death. A profound and provocative book. Intellectually demanding. Although not specifically written for youths, mature young readers will be challenged and stimulated.

Little, J. *Home from far.* Boston: Little, Brown, 1965. Fiction. Ages 9-12. Jenny's twin brother, Michael, is killed; and soon after the accident Jenny's parents bring two foster children into the home. One of them, named Mike, is Jenny's age. Jenny is deeply hurt and bitterly resents her parents for having brought these other children into their home. She believes her parents have forgotten Michael, and so she withdraws. The period that follows is a difficult one for the family and also for the foster children Hilda and Mike, whose own mother has died. The author sensitively portrays the feelings of grief, loss, anger, and fear of abandonment and shows how sharing one's feelings make them more bearable. Especially valuable for children who have difficulty expressing grief.

Lowry, L. *A summer to die.* Boston: Houghton Mifflin, 1977. Fiction. Ages 10-15. The themes of birth and death are juxtaposed in this story of 13-year-old Meg, her pretty 15-year-old sister Molly, and their parents, who move to the country so that their father can write a book. Lonely at first and jealous of her popular, lively sister, Meg meets and befriends an elderly neighbor and a young couple living nearby. She also begins to recognize and develop her own talents. The sense of tranquility, however, is shattered when Molly becomes terminally ill. As Molly weakens, Meg's overwhelming interest becomes the baby expected by the young neighbors. It is through the drama of their baby's birth at home, with Meg sharing in the experience, that the poignant link between birth and death is made.

Lowry, L. *Autumn Street.* Boston: Houghton Mifflin, 1980. Fiction. Ages 10-14. This, the most recent book by the author of *A summer to die,* demonstrates perhaps even better the author's ability to enter and move freely in the child's worlds of thoughts, dreams, worries, anxieties, and fears. Elizabeth is six years old. Her father has gone off to fight in World War II; and Elizabeth, her mother, sisters, and baby brother go to live with her grandparents on Autumn Street in a small Pennsylvania town. The street ends in a wood that is declared forbidden territory by the adults; it both terrifies and attracts Elizabeth and her friend Charles. One day, humiliated by a gang of boys in the park, Charles wants to demonstrate his courage to Elizabeth and runs toward the woods. Elizabeth tries unsuccessfully to persuade him to stay away, returns home with a fever and a sore throat, and is put to bed. When Charles does not return by nightfall, everyone begins to worry, and he is reported missing. Then the shocking news arrives: Charles has been murdered. Violent death is a reality, and the author has the courage to deal with it and does it sensitively. The story shows in a cryptic yet moving way the extent and quality of comfort given to children by caring adults, even if their worlds may be far apart.

Lundgren, M. *Matt's grandfather* (A. Pyk, Trans.; F. Hald, Illus.). New York: Putnam's, 1972. Fiction. Ages 6-8. Matt and his parents are on the way to visit the little boy's grandfather on his 85th birthday. Grandfather lives in a nursing home; and Matt's parents try to explain that grandfather is senile ("he is almost like a baby again"), that he forgets things and needs nurses to take care of him and the other old people, who may walk in the park but are not allowed out because they might get lost. When Matt arrives, he has his first surprise: the nursing home is like a huge castle with spires and towers, and ivy, and the park is beautiful. When he gets to Room 115, Matt has his second surprise. Grandfather does not look so old at all, and he certainly does not act like a baby. The third surprise remains a secret between Matt and Grandfather. It is an ingenious way Grandfather had discovered to get out of the park and go down to the boats for a while each day and to be back before anybody misses him. This story is simply written, but it speaks eloquently of the problems facing some old people, and it portrays with great tenderness the mutual closeness and warmth possible

between the very young and the very old. The colored
illustrations are vivid and add greatly to the mood of the
story.

Lutters, V. A. *The haunting of Julie Unger.* New York: Atheneum, 1977. Fiction. Age 12 and over. Thirteen-year-old Julie
Unger is "haunted" by Papa, her father who has died
recently of a heart attack. Julie and Papa had been very
close. He had been a photographer, and photography is
Julie's hobby. The "haunting" Julie experiences is benign.
She copes with her loss by revisiting the places where she
and her father had spent time together, such as the river
bank on which they had sat, talking and taking pictures of
Canada geese. Julie secretly takes up photography again and
is angry at her family for "spying" on her in the darkroom.
In fact, she does not get along with her family at all,
especially not with her grandparents. Julie Unger copes well
with her father's death, but she needs to do her grieving
alone. After a time, her family begins to understand this,
and harmony is reestablished.

Madison, A. *Suicide and young people.* New York: Seabury/
Clarion, 1978. Nonfiction. Age 14 and over. This book
discusses possible causes for the rising rate of suicide among
young people. The approach is journalistic, with frequent
stylized case examples and occasionally confusion over inter-
woven questions of euthanasia. The concluding list of suicide
prevention centers is not comprehensive. On the whole,
however, a readable book.

Madison, W. *A portrait of myself.* New York: Random House,
1979. Fiction. Age 14 and over. Pressure from a broken
home and a favorite teacher's rejection can drive a high
school student to suicide. Catherine d'Amato is a sensitive,
artistic 16-year-old whose father left their Connecticut home
four years earlier and whose mother wants her to be popular
and to take practical courses. Her large Italian family
sometimes seems to stifle her individuality. Catherine is an
artist who wants to be someone other than herself and who
mistakenly thinks a cool, Nordic gym teacher would be a
good role model for her. When the imitation fails and the
pressures become too great, Catherine attempts suicide but

does not succeed. This leads to a visit with her immigrant grandparents, who remind her of her own good qualities and who give her an example of the courage to be oneself. This is good writing for young people, a well-delineated sketch of character without clichés or false emotions.

Mann, P. *There are two kinds of terrible.* New York: Doubleday, 1977. Fiction. Ages 9-12. The first kind of terrible, breaking one's arm just as summer vacation starts, is shown to be far easier for a grade school child than the illness and death of a parent. During his mother's hospitalization, Robbie Farley gets little information or support from his uncommunicative father. An only child, Rob has always been very close to his mother. Now, father and son each withdraw into isolation, which only intensifies anxieties and anguish and makes them almost unbearable to each other. Only after his mother's death can Robbie and his father reach out to each other and share their loss and warm memories of the woman they both loved. A very effective portrait from the child's viewpoint, by the author of many other books including the well-known story of divorce, *My dad lives in a downtown hotel.*

Mazer, N. *A figure of speech.* New York: Delacorte, 1973. Fiction. Age 8 and over. This poignant story is about Jenny, a young girl, and her grandfather whom she loves deeply. When she overhears her parents discussing plans to send him to a nursing home, Jenny reports the discussion to her grandfather, and both run away. This results in grandfather's death, which cause the estrangement of Jenny from her parents. Recommended only with parental guidance and discussion of the book, particularly its ending, to reassure the young reader of his or her parents' unconditional love.

McLendon, G. H. *My brother Joey died.* New York: 1982. Nonfiction. Ages 8-11. Simply and sensitively told first-person account of a 9-year-old girl's reactions to the illness and death of her brother, how she tried to cope with this loss, and how family and friends helped. Photographs enhance this moving story.

Miles, B. *The touble with thirteen.* New York: Knopf, 1979. Fiction. Ages 9-13. This story is about two girls turning 13, the difficulties they encounter, and the adjustments they have to make. Mostly, it is about losses and how to cope

with them. Rachel's parents are getting a divorce, and
Rachel's mother will be moving to New York City to find
work. Rachel is going to live with her mother, which means
leaving her girl friend Annie. Just as Annie is trying hard to
prepare herself for Rachel's leaving, she discovers Nora, her
dog, lying helpless under a lilac bush. The dog had begun to
cough a few days earlier, and Father did not think it was
necessary to take Nora to the verterinarian. But now Nora is
wheezing, her body is jerking and twitching in Annie's arms;
and no amount of comforting helps. As Nora thumps her
tail, trying to please, and looks sadly into Annie's eyes, she
gives a quick little gasp and dies. The author relates sensitively how Nora is buried and memorialized and how Annie
copes with her anger at Father, her grief and sorrow, and
how she is comforted by her parents, brother, and friends.
We all experience losses as we grow and change, but good
memories can be cherished. An engrossing, well-written
story.

Miles, M. *Annie and the old one.* Boston: Little, Brown, 1971.
Fiction. Ages 8–12. This is the moving story of Annie, a
nine-year-old Navajo girl, and her grandmother who is making preparations for her death. When Annie's grandmother
explains that when the new rug is woven and taken from the
loom she will be ready to "go to Mother Earth," Annie tries
desperately to stop the rug from getting finished. She is told
by her grandmother in a gentle way that the "earth from
which good things come is where all creatures finally go."
This helps Annie see how the entire family, including herself,
are part of this life cycle and that death is a part of life.
Carefully detailed, beautifully written.

Molloy, A. S. *The girl from two miles high.* New York: Hastings
House, 1967. Fiction. Age 12 and over. After her mother's
death, 13-year-old Phoebe lives with her father, a mining
engineer in the Peruvian mountains. Phoebe loves her father
deeply and needs his love particularly since her mother's
death. Then one day her father is killed in an avalanche.
Phoebe feels that she is left all alone. She is put on a plane
to go live with her grandmother. The story tells rather
sensitively how Phoebe learns to cope with the loss of her

parents and how both she and her grandmother learn to adjust to one another and eventually come to love each other. The reader will find it easy to identify with Phoebe's loss, grief, loneliness, and eventual reestablishment in a new environment. Love is a basic need all people have, young or old. And love helps heal wounds. Good reading.

Moody, R. *Life after life.* St. Simons Island, Ga.: Mockingbird, 1975. Nonfiction. Age 16 and over. In this fascinating book the author reports the results of his interviews with 150 people with near-death experiences. Most had been resuscitated following cardiac arrests. The accounts of out-of-the-body experiences and experiences of meeting dead relatives and a "being of light," all accompanied with an experience of indescribable peace and beauty, are truly amazing. Scientists are still trying to explain these experiences physiologically and psychologically. A courageous book.

Morgan, E. *A manual of death ecucation and simple burial.* Burnsville, N.C.: Celo, 1980. Nonfiction. Age 14 and over. This is the ninth edition of a concise, plainly written pamphlet that provides information about death education; about relating to dying people; and most particularly about memorial societies and their functions; simple burial or cremation; and body, organ, and tissue donation. The author is one of the founders of the Continental Association of Funeral and Memorial Societies. Although not written specifically for youthful readers, this book answers many practical questions that adolescents often ask, and it is written in clear and simple language, making it a valuable resource for them.

Naylor, P. R. *To walk the sky path.* Chicago: Follett, 1973. Fiction. Ages 10–13. Ten-year-old Billie, a Seminole Indian, knows he is a link between two very different worlds. Yet he feels torn between living the traditional way of his grandparents and enjoying the modern conveniences of the white people. He learns all of the Indian stories and legends that he can, but he also feels that going to school is important. When his grandfather dies and is buried in the traditional Indian manner, the boy realizes that an important part of his life is gone. He cherishes the memory of his grandfather and his heritage.

Ness, E. *Sam Bangs and moonshine.* New York: Holt, 1966. Fiction. Preschool to age 9. Samantha, called Sam, is a fisherman's daughter who envelops herself in a world of fantasy in which her dead mother becomes a mermaid living in a cave; in which Bang, her cat, can talk and have conversations with her; and in which she has a baby kangaroo as a pet. Her father helps Sam to confront reality and distinguish it from moonshine (her fantasy world). A beautiful, imaginative story, winner of the 1967 Caldecott Medal.

Norris, G. B. *The friendship hedge* (D. Payson, Illus.). New York: Dutton, 1973. Ages 6–9. When Claire receives a guinea pig for her birthday, she is so enthralled that she neglects the nine girls at her party and even forgets the cake. No one is allowed even to touch the guinea pig. Claire's best friend, Alice, is angrier than the others, and she seeks revenge. The story tells of the jealousy Alice feels, how her revenge accidentally leads to the death of the guinea pig, how Claire copes with the loss of her new pet and Alice with her feelings of guilt and remorse. The two girls bury the guinea pig by the Friendship Hedge, and their friendship survives. A well-told story. The illustrations are appealing.

Orgel, D. *Mulberry music.* New York: Harper, 1971. Fiction. Ages 8–12. The efforts of Libby's parents to protect her from the harsh reality of her beloved grandmother's impending death result in turmoil both within the girl and around her. Jenny, searching for Grandma Liza, breaks into her grandmother's home. Sitting down at the piano, she plays the favorite pieces she and Grandma Liza had shared and finds comfort in doing so. After her grandmother's death, a home memorial service is held during which her grandmother's favorite music is played. This is a realistic story that depicts the parents' good intentions as well as their willingness and courage to admit that they made a mistake in the way they handled a crisis. Well written and well worth reading. Also recommended for parents.

Patterson, K. *Bridge to Terabithia.* New York: Crowell, 1977. Fiction. Ages 9–11. Ten-year-old Jess Aarons is a loner, far too talented and sensitive to fit easily into a traditional, isolated, rural Virginia lifestyle. The Burke family moves into the community to escape the rigors of city life, and Jess and Leslie become close friends. Leslie appreciates Jess's art and teaches him that imagination, caring, and love for learning are nothing to be ashamed of. Together they create Terabithia, a private, secret kingdom in the woods where their imaginations rule. The joy turns to tragedy as Leslie is killed in an accident on her way through the woods. Jess's subsequent dealing with her death is realistically and sensitively described.

Peck, R. N. *A day no pigs would die.* New York: Knopf, 1972. Fiction. Age 12 and over. Robert Peck, a 13-year-old Vermont farm boy, has been given a small pig, which he raises as a pet. Haven Peck, Robert's father, is ill and knows he has not long to live. When fall comes and the pig has not had her first heat, Robert recognizes that the family cannot afford to keep the pig. Mr. Peck, a hog butcher by trade, and Robert kill the pig. When Robert understands the difficulty his father had killing the pet, he realizes how much he loves and admires his father. Shortly afterward, Mr. Peck dies. Robert must arrange his father's funeral and he must learn to cope with the sadness and pain he experiences at his father's death.

Pevsner, S. *And you give me pain, Elaine.* New York: Seabury/ Clarion, 1978. Fiction. Age 12 and over. Andrea, 13, has a 16-year-old sister, Elaine, and a brother, Joe, a college sophomore, whom she loves in a special way. Elaine is a troublemaker who monopolizes her parents' attention. Just when things settle down, Joe is killed in a motorcycle accident. The family's grief and later events are briefly sketched. Life is rebuilt and goes forward.

Potter, L. L. *When someone you love dies—A book to share feelings.* Lincoln, Neb.: Word Services, 1979. Nonfiction. Ages 7-9. This 26-page volume talks to the young reader about dying, death, religious beliefs, and bereavement. The writing style is crisp, the illustrations are soft, and the basic message is of the continuity of life—a reason to enjoy and celebrate it. Probably best read together with parents.

Pringle, L. *Death is natural.* New York: Four Winds, 1977. Nonfiction. Ages 8-12. Using as a theme the death of a rabbit hit by a car, the text explains how the rabbit's body is recycled through scavengers and decay. Death is shown as necessary so that elements and atoms can be passed on to other forms of life. Characteristics, genes, extinct species, and the balance of nature are discussed. This book emphasizes death as a natural part of the life cycle—as it affects the world as a whole rather than the individual—and it points at the interdependence of various forms of life. The book does not merely inform by giving the reader a hint of the larger picture; it does much more. It inspires awe.

Rabe, B. *The girl who had no name.* New York: Dutton, 1977. Fiction. Ages 9-12. It is 1936 in southeast Missouri, and Girlie Webster is 12. Following her mother's death, Girlie is sent by Papa to live with one after another of her nine older sisters. Girlie's story traces her efforts to discover why she cannot live with Papa and why he refused to give her a proper name when she was born. There is comedy and mystery in this tale of a young girl's determination and maturation.

Rabin, G. *Changes.* New York: Harper, 1973. Fiction. Age 12 and over. In this keenly perceptive and realistic first-person narrative, Chris, who still grieves over his father's death, must make adjustments to a move, a change in lifestyle, and entirely new feelings and emotions signifying adolescence. In addition to all this, Chris's grandfather dies. A helpful account not only of the loss of loved ones but of other changes occurring as a result and of how an adolescent learns to cope, recover courage, and discover new strength in the process of growing up.

Rawlings, M. K. *The yearling* (E. Shenton, Decorator). New York: Scribner's 1938. Fiction. Age 8 and over. Jody Baxter is the last surviving child of Ory and Penny Baxter. The Baxters live in Florida on a high rise of ground called Baxter's Island. Jody's only friend is a physically malformed young boy named Fodderwing. Life is difficult and death not far from most every door in the bush of Florida's interior during the time of the story; but Jody has not been personally touched, for his brothers and sisters died when he was very young and his mother does not permit animals as pets. For some time Jody has been unable to visit his sickly friend, Fodder-wing, because Jody's father has been bitten by a snake and Jody must help around the house. When Jody eventually gets to Fodder-wing's house, he is met by Buck, Fodder-wing's older brother, and told that Fodder-wing is dead. At first Jody cannot comprehend what is being said. Buck leads him to the room where Fodder-wing lies covered in a sheet up to his chin. Buck invites Jody to speak to the dead boy even though Fodder-wing would not hear him. Jody whispers "Hey," and when Fodder-wing does not answer, Jody understands that death is silence. Later, Jody's fawn, Flag, has to be killed because it is eating the crops and the family will starve unless something is done. All attempts to prevent Flag's destroying the crops fail, and Jody is devastated. During the terrible moment that Jody experiences in his grief over Flag, he compares Flag's death to that of Fodder-wing. Fodder-wing had died, and that was terrible; but the awfulness passed, and the awfulness of Flag's death would pass, too. But the knowledge that his father had gone "back on him," when he ordered the death of the fawn, is intolerable. Betrayal leaves no one to turn to in grief. Thus, the death of Flag becomes more difficult to bear. Eventually Jody and his dad become reconciled, and Jody emerges from all his pain with a more mature understanding of life and its purposes. This timeless classic is a must. It appeals to the young and not so young alike.

Rhodin, E. *The good greenwood.* Philadelphia: Westminster, 1972. Fiction. Age 12 and over. This tense and moving story is about Mike, who has lost his good friend Louie. Time passes slowly, but eventually Mike comes to realize that Louie is really dead and is not going to reappear around the next corner. Although he still grieves, he now begins to remember Louie for the clown and dreamer he was and for the good times they had together. These memories help him overcome his sorrow and pain. Good.

Roberts, J. *Emir's education in the proper use of magical powers* (L. Cherry & E. Friede, Illus.). New York: Delacorte, 1979. Fiction. Age 9 and over. Emir is a young prince who lives in a brand-new kingdom, with beautiful people, creatures, and plants—just about everything except seasons. People can live forever if they want to, and they do not look old because they do not know they are supposed to. Emir's father, the king, decides to send Emir on a long journey around the kingdom instead of sending him to school. He is to seek out the land of the gods for answers to the problems of the kingdom. Emir's journey is full of surprises. He invents the first lie and finds that it is just as easy to invent truth. He meets conscience and inspiration, leaves his body for the first time, and invents the idea of death. This symbolic tale contains an important message. The author says: "Emir is that part of me and of everyone who at some time has to question the meaning of life and death, and don't we each think of ourselves as the center of our own kingdom as Emir does?" A very unusual, creative, and effectively crafted story that is deceptively simple. The meanings are profound.

Sanderlin, O. *Johnny.* Cranbury, N.J.: A. S. Barnes, 1968. Nonfiction. Age 12 and over. A mother's account of her son, who at the age of 11 is stricken with leukemia. The book describes the boy's courageous struggle to lead a normal life for almost five years until his death. A tribute to the strength of the human spirit, especially in one so young. Moving.

Schoen, B. *A place and a time.* New York: Crowell, 1967. Fiction. Age 12 and over. This is a believable narrative of a girl's nurturing family life and of her steadily growing understanding of herself and others. Although death is not a major theme in this story, it is nevertheless worth sharing in Josie's reaction to and eventual acceptance of her beloved grandmother's death. The loss, grief, and working through are shown as an important part of the girl's growth to maturity.

Shotter, R. *A matter of time.* New York: Collins & World, 1979. Fiction. Age 14 and over. In coping with grief, there is an opportunity for self-discovery and the development of a better sense of one's own identity. Lisl Gilbert is 16, and her mother is dying of lung cancer. Lisl's mother had always been the special person in the family—busy, vivacious, a superstar. As she moves toward death, Lisl realizes that behind all this activity her mother is insecure and lonely. In one important moment, Lisl and her father are finally able to let her mother know that they do love her and that they know she loves them. By the time her mother dies—on the day of Lisl's high school graduation—Lisl has realized that she is free to use her own time to become a special person herself. Surprisingly for a book of this kind, a social worker appears as a prominent character who helps Lisl and her family to grow during these difficult few months.

Segerberg, O., Jr. *Living with death.* New York: Dutton, 1976. Nonfiction. Age 14 and over. The subject of death is discussed from anthropological, theological, historical, and thanatological perspectives. The author asks teen-agers to philosophize and probe. The coverage includes such topics as euthanasia, psychic research, North American views of death, attempts to avoid death through cryonics, and the work of Elisabeth Kübler-Ross. This is a broad survey of the subject of death. Informative, challenging.

Shotwell, L. R. *Adam Bookout.* New York: Viking, 1967. Fiction. Age 12 and over. Adam avoids acknowledging the deaths of his parents by pretending they are still alive. In his grief, he runs away from well-meaning guardians. When he reaches his destination, he meets a number of people from different backgrounds with many kinds of problems. He realizes that he is not the only one with problems. He learns, too, that problems are not left behind when people run away. Valuable.

Shreve, S. *Family secrets: Five very important stories* (R. Cuffari, Illus.). New York: Knopf, 1979. Fiction. Ages 7-9. In these five stories, eight-year-old Sammy tells about his experiences with the death of his dog, the divorce of his aunt and uncle, the suicide of his best friend's brother, his 70-year-old grandmother who has cancer and has recently moved in with Sammy's family, and cheating on a math test at school. Sammy's viewpoint is simple and insightful; he has the great advantage of sensitive and supportive parents.

Simon, N. *We remember Philip* (R. Sanderson, Illus.). Chicago: Whitman, 1979. Fiction. Ages 7-10. The text and pictures describe the responses of Sam and his classmates to the accidental death of their teacher's son, Philip. The children exchange feelings; and the class, with the help of the principal, offers support to the teacher as he works through his grief. The students urge their teacher to show pictures of Philip to the class, and the children plant a tree in his memory. Somewhat contrived and cool in tone.

Simon, S. *Life and death in nature.* New York: McGraw-Hill, 1976. Nonfiction. Ages 6–11. This is a valuable book. It deals with death from a scientific-experimental perspective. Experiments with earthworms grown and put into crowded or uncrowded environments to study their survival are described. The reader learns about decomposition, ecology, overpopulation, and the balance of nature. Although the book does not deal with the emotional aspects of the death of loved ones—people or pets—the young reader will not only be fascinated but perhaps comforted to discover that nutrients contained in living things today may once have been part of a rose petal, a dinosaur, or a human being of an earlier era. This recognition of the continuity of life is awe inspiring and may offer some reassurance at a time of loss. This book is instructive and causes the reader to reflect on the question of life and death and our part in it.

Slote, A. *Hang tough, Paul Mather.* Philadelphia: Lippincott, 1973. Fiction. Ages 9–12. Paul Mather, a sixth grader, loves baseball, and he is good at it, especially pitching. But Paul also has leukemia and is in his third remission when the story begins. His parents have moved twice, hoping to find the hospital that can cure their son. Now they have arrived in Michigan, and the Little League of baseball teams in the new neighborhood need Paul. He is needed as a pitcher for the Wilson Dairy team, and when his parents refuse to give permission until he has seen his new doctor, Paul fakes his parents' permission and plays anyway. His father is irate; his mother, frightened. Paul has trouble convincing his parents how much he needs to play baseball in order to keep up his hope. Paul's new doctor, Tom Kinsella, turns out to be of critical help. He is open, informal, understanding, and becomes personally involved. When Paul is hospitalized, he visits three or four times a day. Twice, when Paul had vomited, he helped the orderly clean up. But most of all, in

Paul's own words, "He knew how to break bad news better than any doctor I ever had." In this deeply moving book, the author tells of the courageous struggle of a young boy to cope with his illness, with his parents' protectiveness, and eventually with the knowledge that he has little time left to live. The author has an uncanny ability to evoke emotions by a style of writing that is full of understatements and has a simplicity that speaks eloquently. Inspiring.

Smith, D. B. *A taste of blackberries.* New York: Crowell, 1973. Fiction. Preschool to 6. A little boy is confronted with loss, grief, and guilt when his best friend, Jamie, dies from being stung by a bee while the two are picking blackberries. The feeling of guilt is natural enough. Jamie had a way of kidding around, so that, when he rolled on the ground after the bee sting, his friend thought he was only joking. After a time, the boy comes to accept his friend's death. The story is simply and sensitively written and richly illustrated. The book won a Child Study Association award.

Sperry, A. *Call it courage.* New York: Macmillan, 1956. Fiction. Ages 10-14. This is the story of "Mafatu, the Boy Who Was Afraid," who lived on a South Sea Island and battled with Moana, the Sea God, for a peaceful existence with the sea. Mafatu wins the battle with his own fear of the sea, which he projects onto the sea god. As the story goes, Mafatu was three when he and his mother were caught by a hurricane while on a reef fishing for sea urchins. As the winds and rain beat on the canoe, it capsized, so the child held on to his mother as she tried to swim to the shore of Tekoto, an uninhabited islet. Sharks circled them at one point, and the boy sensed that Moana was reaching up to pull them down into the sea. They made shore, but the mother died after pressing some coconut meat to her weakened child's lips. The boy's father, who was the island chief, had named him Mafatu—Stout Heart—but this incident created such fear of the sea in Mafatu that he was ridiculed. The other boys his age excluded him from their games. The girls laughed, for what kind of husband would he make, afraid, as he was, of the sea by which they all lived. The older people blamed the ghost spirit. When Mafatu is an adolescent, he slips away one

night in a canoe to "do battle with the sea"—his fear. He
finds himself on an uninhabited island that is visited periodically by headhunters; and during this time, he becomes a
man, conquers his fear, builds a canoe, and sails back to his
island, where he collapses in his proud father's arms. A
highly readable book of adventure, fear and courage, life,
and death.

Stein, S. B. *About dying.* New York: Walker, 1974. Fiction.
Preschool to 9. This sensitively written book is designed for
both children and parents, with separate texts for each
group. Vivid photographs accompany the children's texts,
which deal with the death of Snow, a pet bird, and with
Eric's, Michael's, and Jane's grandfather. The children have a
funeral for Snow and participate in their grandpa's funeral.
The parents' text serves as a resource for handling the
children's questions. Death is dealt with in an honest and
straightforward, but low-keyed, manner and with deep sensitivity.

Stevens, M. *When Grandpa died.* (K. Ualand, Photographer).
Chicago: Childrens Press, 1979. Fiction. Preschool to 7.
Fourteen brightly colored and strikingly beautiful photographs face pages with a brief first-person narrative text
telling about a little girl's relationship with her grandfather,
his assistance in helping her to talk about death and to bury
a dead bird that they found, and her efforts (with help from
her parents) to cope with his illness and subsequent death. A
simple story, directly told.

Stolz, M. *By the highway home.* New York: Harper, 1971.
Fiction. Age 12 and up. When her brother Beau is killed in
Vietnam, 13-year-old Catty and her family are dejected.
Only after her father loses his engineering job and her family
moves halfway across the nation to help run a family inn, do
its members begin to come to terms with their loss. For the
family, going on with life without regrets and self-recrimina-
tions is a major achievement. The characters are realistically
drawn.

Stolz, M. *The edge of next year.* New York: Harper, 1974.
Fiction. Ages 11–14. Orin and Vic Woodward are in the
family car when the accident in which their mother is killed

happens. Orin, 14, takes on the housework, the care of his younger brother, and the worry about his father, who tries to drown his grief by drinking. The story graphically describes both the shock and pain the mother's death causes the family and the problem of alcoholism. Eventually the father joins Alcoholics Anonymous, thus providing a hopeful note. This is a gripping and realistic story.

Stull, E. G. *My turtle died today.* New York: Holt, 1964. Preschool to 8. When Boxer, a little boy's pet turtle, dies, the boy and his friends have a funeral and get into a discussion of the meaning of being alive and dead. As the children look at new kittens, they realize that "they have to live first before they die." The story is rather contrived and didactic. Despite this shortcoming, the concepts of life and death are presented in a simple and understandable manner.

Talbot, T. *Dear Greta Garbo.* New York: Putnam's, 1978. Fiction. Ages 12–14. Thirteen-year-old Miranda and her grandmother are both stricken by the sudden death of her grandfather. When Grandma moves into the bedroom in their New York City apartment that Miranda was to have inherited from her older college-bound sister, both of their lives are further disturbed, and each finds herself at a crossroads. The two console and support each other, but it is only when they are again able to assert their independence— Grandma by taking a job as a part-time cashier at the movie theater and moving back to her own apartment, and Miranda by cutting her hair short in the style of Greta Garbo—that they begin to recover and to be able to help Miranda's mother deal with her own grief. A well-told tale of cross-generational similarities in grief and growth.

Thomas, I. *Hi, Mrs. Mallory!* (A. Toulmin-Rothe, Illus.). New York: Harper, 1979. Fiction. Ages 6–8. A young black girl, Li'l Bits, describes her special friendship with her neighbor, Mrs. Mallory. They share fun and fantasy together, but one day Mrs. Mallory is no longer home. She is dead and Li'l Bits is sad, though Mrs. Mallory's dog comes to live with her. The death is abrupt and unexplained; its consequences are not as well developed as is the predeath relationship.

Tobias, T. *Petey.* (S. Shimin, Illus.). New York: Putnam's, 1978.

Fiction. Ages 7–9. Emily is a little girl who has a pet gerbil named Petey. One day when she comes home from school, Emily finds Petey sick. By the next morning he is dead. This is a first-person narrative interspersed with memory flash-backs. The author very capably helps the reader empathize with Emily's feelings of anger, sadness, and love as she grieves her pet's death and comes to accept her loss. The story is warm and sensitive, as are the drawings.

Tolan, S. S. *Grandpa—and me.* New York: Scribner's, 1978. Fiction. Ages 9–14. In this first-person narrative, 11-year-old Kerry Warren tells how she, her older brother Matt, and her parents are trying to cope with her 80-year-old grandfather's senility. The account is given from the perspective of a mature, loving, and caring granddaughter. It does not spare the reader the troublesome, embarrassing, and painful details of her grandfather's confusion, loss of memory, and loss of bodily functions. The family's routine is disrupted; Grandpa needs constant supervision. At a family meeting they discuss whether to place Grandpa in a nursing home. The children rebel at the thought of such an arrangement. During brief periods of lucidity, Grandpa is frustratingly aware of his condition. Then early one morning he packs his things in boxes, marks them for family members, walks to the park, and drowns himself in the swimming pool. This story is gripping; the problems with which it deals are realistic; and its style is straightforward and unsentimental. A must.

Tresselt, A. *The dead tree* (C. Robins, Illus.). New York: Parents' Magazine Press, 1972. Fiction. Preschool to 7. This unusual book depicts poetically and through illustration the life cycle of an oak tree. Death is portrayed as a natural and necessary part of this life cycle. It is shown that in nature nothing is ever wasted and nothing completely dies—a hope-ful message for the young reader. Instructive.

Turner, A. *Houses for the dead: Burial customs through the ages.* New York: McKay, 1976. Nonfiction. Age 12 and over. This book presents a carefully researched history of burial customs, funeral vehicles, exposure of bodies, scavengers, and the like. Sometimes a case history is told at length; at other times, the work jumps from culture to culture, from century to century, to make a point. In this respect, the book is somewhat uneven. The author's descriptions are vivid. Included is rich material about loss and how the beliefs of various cultural groups affect their rituals.

Uchida, Y. *The birthday visitor.* New York: Scribner's, 1975. Fiction. Ages 7-9. This beautiful story is about Emi, a Japanese-American girl, and what happens at her birthday party. A baby sparrow has fallen from the nest on Emi's birthday. The birthday celebration includes a funeral for the dead bird and a burial under a peach tree. A Japanese minister is the birthday visitor after whom the book is titled. The language is simple and direct, and characters and events are vividly portrayed.

Viorst, J. *The tenth good thing about Barney.* New York: Atheneum, 1971. Fiction. Ages 5-9. When the little boy's cat, Barney, dies, his mother helps him prepare for the funeral and offers comfort by asking the boy to think of 10 good things about Barney. He can only think of 9. But with the help of his father he is able to add the 10th good thing: "Barney is in the ground and he's helping grow flowers." Although many very young children may not understand the concept of Barney's role as fertilizer, the language is generally simple and concrete. The story is gentle and hopeful and portrays parents who are deeply sensitive to children's needs and capable of giving them comfort.

Vogel, I. M. *My twin sister, Erika.* New York: Harper, 1976. Fiction. Ages 6-9. This is the story of Erika and Inge, who are identical twins. Inge is jealous of her exuberant and more creative twin sister and often tells her that she hates her and wishes she were dead. Erika, too, sometimes wishes her twin, Inge, were dead. Erika bosses Inge because she is the "big" sister—older by 30 minutes. Both jealously outdo themselves in their friendship with Magda next door. Then one day Erika becomes feverish and is put to bed. At first Inge enjoys her status of being the one up and about. She even feels more loved when her bed is moved into her parents' bedroom. But Erika is very sick and one night she dies. Inge's parents tell her, "You are the only one now." The story very perceptively deals with the special identity problems that identical

twins often have and how important it is for parents to be
alert and to help twins achieve a sense of uniqueness. The
death of the twin sister in this story causes special problems
for Inge. At first, having been so closely identified with
Erika, she feels like only the part "left over," until she
begins to develop her own separate identity and realize that
she is loved. Inge also has to overcome her strong feelings of
guilt about having wished her sister dead and her fear that
perhaps she, through the magic power of her wish, actually
brought about her twin's death. A young reader might
falsely assume that the death of an identical twin can
facilitate the other's independence. With parental guidance,
this book is recommended. Most young readers who have
siblings can relate well to the problems of jealousy, which
are realistically portrayed. The black-and-white drawings are
highly appealing and sensitive.

Walker, M. *Year of the cafeteria.* Indianapolis: Bobbs-Merrill,
1971. Fiction. Age 12 and over. This is a first-person
narrative that skillfully portrays the development of a warm,
if complex, relationship between a teen-age girl and her
grandmother. When her grandmother dies, she refuses to
believe it until she hears the principal of the school where
Grandma had worked announce the sad news to the students. Now the girl is no longer able to turn to her grandma
for help and companionship. The girl's grief and mourning
are sympthetically, sensitively, and realistically described.

Warburg, S. *Growing time.* Boston: Houghton Mifflin, 1969.
Fiction. Ages 7–10. The central character in this story is
Jamie, whose old dog King dies, leaving the boy lonely,
angry, and sad. His parents rush to replace King with a new
puppy, which Jamie rejects at first. Different family members explain to the little boy what happened to King after
he died. An uncle tells Jamie that King's body becomes part
of the rich earth that feeds us. Grandmother talks about
King's spirit that never dies because it is stored in a loving
heart. Jamie is comforted and accepts his puppy when he
recognizes how helpless and in need of care the puppy is.
The story is carefully crafted and vividly and beautifully
written. It offers comfort as well as information about the
finality of physical death.

Watts, R. G. *Straight talk about death with young people.* Philadelphia: Westminster, 1975. Nonfiction. Ages 12 and over. Aimed toward helping young people, this book grew out of the author's experience in discussion groups with seventh and eighth graders. It explores facts and feelings about death and dying, grief, funerals, and hopes by which people live and die. A frank and honest book that avoids romanticizing and minimizing issues, facts, and feelings.

Wersba, G. *The dream watcher.* New York: Atheneum, 1968. Fiction. Age 12 and over. Albert's entire life has seemed empty, and his relationship with his family has not been good. Then he meets Mrs. Woodfin, an eccentric old lady who encourages Albert to see himself as an acceptable, interesting human being. She tells Albert that she had been a famous actress when she was young, but when she realized that fame and fortune do not bring happiness, she gave up acting. Unexpectedly, Mrs. Woodfin dies of a heart attack. Albert learns that she had been a lonely old woman on welfare who had never been able to hold a job because she drank too much. At first he is angered, but when he remembers all she has meant to him, he continues to cherish her in his memories.

Wersba, B. *Run softly, go fast.* New York: Atheneum, 1970. Fiction. Age 16 and over. David Marks, 19, has just returned home from his father's funeral. He hates his father and decides to write a journal about their relationship. He remembers that when he was young his father was the most important person in his life. Slowly, his feelings had changed. This may have started when Dave discovered that his dad was having an affair with another woman; it may have been a reaction to his father's dislike of Dave's poetry and paintings; or it may have been when Dave realized what a ruthless businessman his father was. The final break came when his father accused Dave's best friend of "being a queer." Dave then moved out of the house to live in the "hip" community. He rarely spoke to his father. When his father was in the hospital dying of cancer, Dave came to visit him, however. Nearing the end of the journal, Dave recognizes errors in his recollections, gains a new perspective, and is able to perceive his father differently. A believable

story to which young people can relate well. It deals with
the difficulties adolescents and youths have in accepting
their parents as human beings with faults. Writing a journal
helped David resolve his anger and facilitated his grieving for
his father.

White, E. B. *Charlotte's web.* New York: Harper, 1952. Fiction.
Ages 8–11. This beautiful and popular story is about Wilber,
a pig; Templeton, a rat; and their friendship with Charlotte,
a spider. Charlotte's death and the subsequent rebirth of her
children help explain how the cycle of life continues through
children. The story also describes the grief and sorrow one
experiences after the death of a close friend and shows how
memories of a dead friend can be kept alive in a healthy
manner. A classic.

Whitehead, R. *The mother tree.* New York: Seabury, 1971.
Fiction. Ages 8–12. When Tempe's mother dies suddenly, the
10-year-old girl quite suddenly has to take care of her
4-year-old sister Laurie and help with the household chores.
To make matters worse, Laurie continually asks, "When will
Mother come back?" Tempe's own impulses to play and be
free of this burden of responsibility make her feel guilty.
But the patience and kindness Tempe shows toward her little
sister help Laurie to face the fact that her mother is dead
and cannot return. At the end of a long summer, Tempe is
rewarded by her father's praise and gratitude. This is a
moving story.

Winthrop, E. *Walking away.* New York: Harper, 1973. Fiction.
Age 11 and over. Emily has come to spend another summer
with her grandparents on their farm, a place she loves to
visit, a world that does not change. Emily and her grandfather are especially close and have many serious talks about
people and situations, and about death. After Grandpa injures
himself, Emily finds that the farm is not well kept, and this
disturbs her greatly. When Nina, her friend, comes to visit,
Emily's loyalties are torn between her unpredictable friend
and her steady grandfather. Grandpa dies that winter, but
Emily remembers their talks and is comforted by this
memory. Well written, with an easy flow of dialogue and
sensitive portrayal of life, death, and changing relationships.

Woodford, P. *Please don't go*. New York: Dutton, 1972. Fiction.
Age 14 and over. This is a story about a 15-year-old English
girl who, after spending her summer vacation in France,
faces the many problems of growing up—problems of self-
acceptance, keeping a friendship with a girl friend whose
personality tends to drive people away, infatuation with an
"older man," and finally the problem of accepting the death
of a young man of whom she has grown fond. A sensitive story.

Young, J. *When the whale came to my town* (D. Bernstein,
Photographer). New York: Knopf, 1974. Fiction. Ages 6–12.
This is a moving account of a boy's encounter with a whale
who has beached itself at the tip of Cape Cod. The boy
stays with the dying whale for three days while other
children, townspeople, sailors, the coast guard, and several
doctors come and go. All efforts fail to persuade the whale
to go back into the water. The boy, sitting with the whale
late into the night, is awed and forced to ponder the
question of life and death. The photographs add vividness to
the story, which is based on the author's personal experience. Powerful and tender.

Zim, H., and Bleeker, S. *Life and death*. New York: Morrow,
1970. Nonfiction. Age 9 and over. In this pioneering book
the authors discuss in plain language the biologic, physical,
and chemical facts of life and death and the naturalness of
the life cycle for plants, animals, and humans. In addition,
the authors deal with people's attitudes toward death and
with various death and funeral customs in different cultures;
they bring the reader up to our present best definition and
determination of medical death. This is a scientific and
dispassionate account, yet not at all insensitive. What im-
presses most is that this little book contains a great many of
the answers to children's questions about death that often
are not available to them through interaction with adults.
This information-packed volume is most valuable because it
will help in avoiding misconceptions and fantasies about
aspects of death that are unpleasant and distasteful to many
adults. The book has a hopeful conclusion: it suggests that
people who lead useful and happy lives are likely to come to
an acceptance of all life, including its end. Outstanding.

Zindel, B., & Zindel, P. *A star for the latecomer.* New York: Harper, 1980. Fiction. Age 12 and over. Brooke Hillary is 17 and lives on Long Island, but she commutes into New York City to attend a school for youngsters seeking a theatrical career. Her mother—who is 46 and has advanced bone cancer—wants Brooke to be something special, and Brooke tries hard to become a star before her mother dies. For herself, Brooke likes dancing, but she really would rather just have a boy friend and be like other girls. This could have been little more than a tale of intergenerational conflict, but the authors know that real life is more complex than that. Mother and daughter do love each other, but each must seek her own freedom and fulfillment.

Zindel, P. *The pigman.* New York: Harper, 1968. Fiction. Age 12 and over. This is a moving story about two young people who come from homes where love is largely absent. They pursue a destructive course, caring little for anyone but themselves, finding excuses for their behavior, and blaming others for their own ineptitudes. When their friend, Mr. Pignanti, nicknamed Mr. Pigman, dies, however, they finally recognize the tragic consequences of their behavior. The story ends leaving the impression that Mr. Pigman's death and its irreversibility will bring about positive changes in the young people's behavior.

Zolotow, C. *My grandson Lew.* (W. Pene Du Bois, Illus.). New York: Harper, 1974. Fiction. Preschool to 8. Four years have passed since Grandfather died. Now Lewis is six and suddenly tells his mother that he misses his grandfather. His mother had assumed Lewis had been too young to remember his grandfather. Now, to her surprise, she finds that Lewis remembers many experiences with great clarity, such as the scratchy beard when Grandpa kissed him, the time he took him to the place that had many pictures to look at, and the time Grandpa let him warm his hand around the pipe. Lewis confides to his mother that he has missed Grandpa and has been waiting for him to return. Lewis's mother, in turn, tells the little boy that she has missed him, too. Sharing their memories of Grandpa make Lewis and his mother a little less sad. This story, a work of art in which each sentence is written with restraint and charm, provides evidence of the author's deep insight into the world of a child. Du Bois's pictures are vivid and project the same kind of warmth and love that characterize the text.

AUDIOVISUAL RESOURCES

RICHARD A. PACHOLSKI

Presented here is the most thorough mediagraphy to date on children and death, a collection of 154 annotated items. The entries are numbered for convenience in using the topical index on p. 245, and are arranged alphabetically by title. Initials following the title suggest audiences for which the item would be appropriate.

GS: grade school
MS: middle school
HS: high school
A: adults—general audiences, undergraduates, and professionals in training
P: professionals with specialized interests

Following the discussion of the content of the item is the name of a distributor and other factual information such as kind of medium (film, videotape, filmstrip, audiocassette), running time, and release or publication date if known.

Distributor identification and addresses given have been checked and rechecked against all current directories and catalogs, but users of audiovisuals should be alert to unexpected changes. It is important to realize, too, that in most cases the distributor listed for each item is not the only one handling the item; it is simply the one we have used or have seen advertised nationally. Users of audiovisuals should be alert to distributors or other sources of media in their own areas or communities and should remember that not-for-profit media libraries—in medical schools, colleges and universities, clinics, hospitals, public libraries, schools, churches, or funeral homes—often make materials available for substantially lower cost than do commerical distributors. In addition, organizations like the American Cancer Society, Leukemia Society of America, National Association for Mental Health, and National Sudden Infant Death Syndrome Foundation maintain large audiovisual collections, especially in topics of interest, and should be consulted. Write for catalogs of available audiovisuals and ask to be put on mailing lists for information about new releases.

I have decided not to include the rental or purchase prices and terms of audiovisual materials because such information changes rapidly. If one is operating on a limited budget, one must double check with the distributor in any event and must be sure to search out alternative sources of supply, perhaps with the aid of librarians or media specialists. Users certainly can save money on audiovisuals by combining careful consideration of alternative media on a given topic with a judicious search for and selection of distributors. I recently taught a four-week course using 23 films and videotapes, all critically acclaimed, available from four local sources. The only expense involved was return postage for eight of the items.

A topical index to this chapter is located on page 245. Topics and subtopics in the area of children and death are suggested and annotated; then the numbers of relevant audiovisual items are listed under each heading. Many audiovisuals, of course, appear in several categories. Teachers and others searching for appropriate materials should find the index a helpful tool in making their choices.

For information on additional audiovisuals and other resources on all death and dying topics, refer to H. Wass, C. A. Corr, R. A. Pacholski, & C. M. Sanders, *Death education: An annotated resource guide,* Washington: Hemisphere, 1980. See also H. Wass & C. A. Corr (Eds.), *Childhood and death,* Washington: Hemisphere, in press.

List of Audiovisuals

1. *Adolescent Suicide: A Documentary* (A). Dr. Herman Farberow and other staff members at the Suicide Prevention

Center in Los Angeles discuss factors in the alarmingly high rate of adolescent suicide, the effects on survivors, and possible methods of prevention and intervention. Included are interviews with youths who have attempted suicide. The Charles Press, Bowie, MD 20715; audiocassette, 54 minutes; 1973.

2. *After Our Baby Died: Sudden Infant Death Syndrome* (A). This well-made, impressive film, winner of a blue ribbon in mental health at the 1976 American Film Festival, was created to help professionals and others who come in contact with SIDS parents to understand the syndrome better. Parents are interviewed and offer telling lessons and insights for care givers. Free loan from the National SIDS Foundation, Room 1904, 310 S. Michigan Ave., Chicago, IL 60604; color; 20 minutes; 1976. Write the foundation for information on several other audiovisuals available.

3. *All the Way Home* (HS, A). The novel on which this fine film is based, *A Death in the Family,* is one of the most profoundly moving, most searching, and best written analyses of family reactions to the death of a member in all literature. Particularly important are the many cameo portraits of grief: the dead man's wife, his two very young children, and various other relatives. Religious belief—or lack of it—as a conditioning factor in responding to death is studied in minute detail. The novel is essential reading for everyone trying to understand death, and the film also makes a major contribution. Films, Inc., 1144 Wilmette Ave., Wilmette, IL 60091; black and white; 103 minutes; 1963.

4. *American Association of Suicidology, Proceedings of the Conference, 1978: A Set of Presentations on Adolescent Suicide* (P). Titles include "Suicide and Children," "Suicide Methods and Potential in Ages 4–12," "Intent and Death Attitudes of Adolescents," and "Mobilizing Help in Adolescent Suicide," Highly Specialized Promotions, 391 Atlantic Ave., Brooklyn, NY 11201; four audiocassettes.

5. *American Cancer Society, National Conference on Childhood Cancer: Meeting Highlights* (A, P). American Cancer Society, 777 Third Ave., New York, NY 10017; film; 2 hours; 1974.

6. *And We Were Sad, Remember?* (HS, A). In a 2-minute dramatized episode, a small family group (mother, father, and two young children) reacts to Grandmother's death. Then there is a 10-minute discussion involving various children and adults about what it is like to lose a parent. The major point made is that it is not easy but that children must always know the truth. This well-made and informative program is one of a series called "Footsteps," sponsored by the U.S. Office of Education, on approaches to parenting. A viewer's guide to the whole series may be obtained from Consumer Information Center, Pueblo, CO 81009. The film is available from the National Audiovisual Center, Order Section, Washington, D.C. 20409; color; 30 minutes.

7. *Anna and Poppy* (A). Faced with the death of her grandfather, Poppy, young Anna comes to learn that memories of shared love and happy times together can overcome the effects of sadness. This film can foster discussion and sensitize audiences to death in the family and to the nature and function of the bonds of love. University of Illinois, Visual Aids Service, 1325 S. Oak St., Champaign, IL 61820; color; 15 minutes; 1977.

8. *Annie and The Old One* (GS, HS). Annie, a Navajo girl, loves her grandmother, the Old One, very much. When the grandmother tells Annie she expects to "return to the earth" when a new rug she is weaving is taken from the loom, Annie tries to delay its completion. Based on a book by Miska Miles, the film is a beautiful portrayal of death and the meaning of the generations from a child's point of view. University of Illinois, Visual Aids Service, 1325 S. Oak St., Champaign, IL 61820; color; 16 minutes; 1976.

9. *But Jack was a Good Driver* (HS, A). His schoolmates begin to suspect that Jack's death in an auto accident may have been a suicide. Subsequent discussion shows the students considering their own attitude toward suicide, dispels some myths, presents the warning signs to look for, and offers suggestions on relating to and working with suicidal people. University of California at Berkeley, Extension Media Center, 2223 Fulton St., Berkeley, CA 94720; color film; 15 minutes; 1974.

10. *A Call for Help* (A). This is a training film for police officers, rescue workers, and emergency room personnel, although a general range of care givers will find it valuable. Specific lessons are offered for dealing with cases of SIDS. A study guide is available. Free loan from National SIDS Foundation, Room 1904, 310 S. Michigan Ave., Chicago, IL 60604; color; 20 minutes; 1976.

11. *Chickamauga* (HS, A). Based on the Ambrose Bierce short story, the film graphically portrays the terror and the folly of war from the perspective of a six-year-old deaf mute. Viewfinders, Inc., Box 1665, Evanston, IL 60204; black and white; 33 minutes.

12. *Childhood Cancer: Emotional Effects* (P). This videotape is available for medical professionals. M. D. Anderson Hospital and Tumor Institute, Medical Communications Department, University of Texas System Cancer Center, Houston, TX 77025; color; 58 minutes, 1975.

13. *Children and Death* (A). When children experience the death of someone close, their special needs demand knowledgeable and honest intervention. The topic is explored with an audience of parents, teachers, counselors, medical personnel, and clergy in mind. Wolfelt Productions, 814 W. Charles St., Muncie, IN 47305; color filmstrip (or slides) and audiocassette; discussion manual; 15 minutes; 1979.

14. *Children and Death* (A). Included in this program are discussions about children's experiences with death, their perceptions and questions about it, and a series of related suggestions for adults. J. A. B. Press, Box 213-J, Fairlawn, NJ 07410; three audiocassettes.

15. *Children and Death* (A). Dr. Simon Yudkin gives an overview of essential aspects of this topic: the importance of death education for children, the significance of religious training, and the need to allow children to participate in death rituals and mourning. Communications in Learning, 2280 Main St., Buffalo, NY 14214; audiocassette; 40 minutes.

16. *Children and Death: A Guide for Parents and Teachers* (A). This program provides general answers to a number of questions: How does one tell a child about death? What should one say and not say? What form should death

education take, and when? Should children be allowed to attend funerals? Allied Memorial Council, P.O. Box 30112, Seattle, WA 98103; audiocassette; teacher's guide. See also *Understanding Death Series.*

17. *Children and Dying Conference, University of Chicago, 1977: Proceedings* (A, P). Audiocassettes are available on these topics: "Care for the Caregivers," "The Child and Sudden Death," "What Shall We Tell the Children?," "The Dying Child at Home," "The Dying Child in the Hospital," and "Parental Loss and Childhood Bereavement." Highly Specialized Promotions, 391 Atlantic Ave., Brooklyn, NY 11201; available as a set or individually.

18. *Children Die Too* (P). See *Physician's Role with the Dying Patient.*

19. *Children in Crisis: Death* (A). The titles of the five filmstrips in this series accurately suggest the content: "Death as a Reality of Life," "Expressing Grief," "Ages of Understanding," "Explaining Death to Children," and "The Importance of Funerals." Reviewers (for example, *Death Education,* 1977, *1*, 351-353) suggest the program may have value for general audiences or beginning death educators but lacks depth. Parent's Magazine Films, Dept. F, 52 Vanderbilt Ave., New York, NY 10017; color, with audiocassettes or record; scripts and discussion guide.

20. *Children's Conceptions of Death* (A, P). This critically acclaimed program is well organized and informative. Children at various ages—under 5, between 6 and 9, and 10 and older—have different and developing attitudes toward death and differing needs in the face of it. Teachers, care givers, and parents will find these lessons most helpful. University of Wisconsin-Milwaukee, School of Nursing, Box 413, Milwaukee, WI 53201; color videotape; 40 minutes; teacher's guide: 1974.

21. *A Child's Eyes: November 22, 1963* (A). This short film provides valuable insights into the minds of children and into basic human questions of life and death. A number of five- and six-year-olds react to the assassination of President Kennedy through crayon drawings and their own narrative. Julian Morris Agency, 1350 Avenue of the Americas, New York, NY 10019; color; 9 minutes.

22. *Cipher in the Snow* (HS, A). This excellent film tells a moving story of a school boy's sudden and unexplained death and how he had been written off as a zero (or so he felt) by his parents, classmates, and teachers, none of whom, as they realize after the fact, really knew the boy. Is it possible to die physically as well as emotionally from lack of love? Saying yes in a convincing but not maudlin way, the film could trigger discussion of the essential relationship between love and life. Brigham Young University, DMDP Media Business Services, W 164 Stadium, Provo, UT 84602; color; 25 minutes; 1974.

23. *A Conference on the Dying Child* (P). A pediatric head nurse, a nursing supervisor, and a nursing instructor share their experiences and opinions about working with dying children. Emotions are a major issue, for nurse and family alike. Also discussed are children's concepts of death and their origins; how nurses should respond in given situations; and how, when, and whether the truth should be told. American Journal of Nursing Company, 267 W. 25th St., New York, NY 10001; film or videotape; black and white; 44 minutes; 1967.

24. *Coping* (A). This film documents a series of interviews between a doctor, a young boy terminally ill with leukemia, and his parents. What is remarkable about the boy and his family is the level of acceptance of the disease and of death that they have reached together; they understand the prognosis and discuss it openly and honestly. The film demonstrates the great value of healthy familial relationships when someone is dying. University of California at Berkeley, Extension Media Center, 2223 Fulton St., Berkeley, CA 94720; 22 minutes; 1974.

25. *Coping with Death and Dying: Emotional Needs of the Dying Patient and the Family* (A). Here perhaps is the "essential Kübler-Ross," at least in audiocassette format. This 180-minute tape series is certainly the longest and most detailed presentation of her views outside of her writing and follows the format of argument and explanation familiar to readers of *On Death and Dying.* On Tape 1, "The Fear of Death: Verbal and Nonverbal Symbolical Language," Küb-

ler-Ross reports how her research began and the early
distrust and hostility of her medical colleagues. Then she
explains that many patients see death as an impersonal,
catastrophic force and that care givers should be able to
pick up on verbal and nonverbal expressions of these
attitudes and feelings. Clinical examples are used to illustrate. Tapes 2 and 3 present the now-familiar stages of
dying in considerable detail and with a wealth of illustrative
case studies. Children and death is the topic of Tape 4.
Again citing case studies, Kübler-Ross treats the basic concerns of truth telling, problems caused by denying parents,
helping parents cope, children's conceptions of death, and
how these conceptions develop during the process of dying.
On Tape 5, sudden death is discussed from the viewpoint of
emergency room personnel. How does one tell the waiting
survivors or others injured in the same accident? How does
one give such information on the telephone? Should emotional outpouring be encouraged? Do survivors need to see
the body? What of the emotional needs of medical professionals, after their efforts have failed? *Psychology Today*
cassettes, P.O. Box 278 Pratt Station, Brooklyn, NY 11205;
five audiocassettes; 30 minutes each; 1973.

26. *Counseling the Terminally Ill* (A, P). Medical care givers are
the primary audience for this detailed film introduction to
the physical and psychological needs of dying patients, both
adults and children, in the clinical setting. The emphasis is
on effective communication on matters of diagnosis, prognosis, treatment regimen, and involvement of family members. Write Charles A. Garfield, Ph.D., 106 Evergreen Lane,
Berkeley, CA 94705; color; 55 minutes.

27. *Crib Death: Or Sudden Infant Death Syndrome* (P). This is
a videotaped lecture by a physician, Barbara Bruner. Georgia
Regional Medical Television Network, Emory University
School of Medicine, 69 Butler St. S.E., Atlanta, GA 30303;
black and white; 47 minutes; 1972.

28. *Crib Death: Sudden Infant Death Syndrome* (A). In this
round-table discussion, Dr. John Coe reviews current research and statistics on SIDS. Nurse Carolyn Szybist and
parents who have lost children to SIDS discuss their bad

experiences—the fears, the guilt, the ignorance of outsiders—
as well as great benefits offered by the National SIDS
Foundation and its self-help activities. Additional suggestions for care givers are offered. The Charles Press, Bowie,
MD 20715; audiocassette; 59 minutes; 1972.

29. *Crisis: The Hospitalized Child* (A). A chaplain, a 16-year-old
cystic fibrosis patient, and her family discuss the disease,
treatment methods, and the inevitable outcome. Communications in Learning, 2280 Main St., Buffalo, NY 14214; audiocassette, 37 minutes.

30. *A Cry for the Children* (HS, A). This short film has much to
offer: insights into the effects on fire fighters of witnessing
the deaths of children in fires; chilling warnings of the lethal
nature of house fires; information about fire awareness and
prevention; and, focusing on children, reminders of what life
is all about. A fine film to trigger discussion, well made and
fast paced. Film Communicators, 11136 Weddington St.,
Hollywood, CA 91601; color; 11 minutes; 1977.

31. *The Day Grandpa Died* (HS, A). David comes home from
school one afternoon and is told that his beloved grandfather has died. "I don't want Grandpa dead," he cries.
Then his mind gradually fills with happy memories of
shared experiences. David's father is particularly helpful and
understanding: "You've lost your grandpa and your friend,
but I've lost my father," beautifully making an essential
point about generations. The graveside ceremony helps
David come to terms with the fact of the death so he can
resume living, rich in his memories. University of California
at Berkeley, Extension Media Center, 2223 Fulton St.,
Berkeley, CA 94720; color film; 12 minutes; 1970.

32. *A Day in the Death of Donnie B* (A). Donnie B. is a young
inner-city drug addict, and his death at the end of a short,
miserable life is a foregone conclusion. Voice-over commentary on the drug problem by mothers, doctors, police
officers, ex-addicts, and members of the clergy adds chilling
irony to the reality of Donnie's dying. National Institute of
Mental Health, Drug Abuse Film Collection, National Audiovisual Center, General Services Administration, Washington,
D.C. 20409; black-and-white film; 18 minutes.

33. *The Dead Bird* (GS, HS, A). Cartoon pictures and voice-over narration tell the Margaret Wise Brown story of a group of children who discover, bury, and mourn a dead bird. There are insights here into children's attitudes toward death. Indiana University, Audio-Visual Center, Bloomington, IN 47401; color film; 13 minutes; 1972.

34. *Dealing with Loss and Grief* (A, P). See *Death and Dying: Closing the Circle*.

35. *Dear Little Lightbird* (A). The subject, an incurably ill "blue baby," is the three-year-old son of the film maker. Viewfinders, Inc., Box 1665, Evanston, IL 60204; color; 19 minutes.

36. *Death—A Natural Part of Living* (GS). In addition to making the key point referred to in the title, this program surveys a variety of contemporary death-related issues and examines attitudes toward death in other lands and at other times. Marsh Film Enterprises, P.O. Box 8082, Shawnee Mission, KS 66208; filmstrip (65 frames) and audiocassette or record; teacher's guide; 1977.

37. *Death and Dying: Closing the Circle* (A, P). This extensive introductory program on death and dying consists of five color filmstrips, with accompanying audiocassettes or records and a discussion guide and study outline. Consultants are Robert Jay Lifton, M.D., and Professor Austin H. Kutscher. In Part 1, "The Meaning of Death," Lifton surveys death in our society. Part 2, "A Time to Mourn, a Time To Choose," examines death, burial, and memorial rites and society's underlying beliefs, assumptions, and attitudes about them. In Part 3, "Walk in the World for Me," Doris Lund retells her son Eric's five-year struggle with leukemia. Part 4, "Dealing with the Critically Ill Patient," features an interview with a man with cardiovascular disease. He relates his reaction to his disease, and suggestions are offered for care givers working with high-risk patients. Part 5, "Dealing with Loss and Grief," consisting of interviews with survivors of a young cancer victim, provides commentary and analysis of the nature of grief. This set of programs is one of the better introductory surveys in the field. Guidance Associates, Communications Park, Box 3000, Mount Kisco, NY 10549.

38. *Death and Dying: When a Child Dies* (A, P). Dr. C. Charles Bachmann interviews a mother who has lost several of her children to a genetic disease. Communications in Learning, 2280 Main St., Buffalo, NY 14214; audiocassette; 43 minutes.

39. *Death and the Child* (A). Dr. Edgar Jackson tells parents, health professionals, and teachers to be honest, truthful, and realistic in teaching children about death, in answering their questions, and in helping them through death crises. Anything less can cause emotional problems. Specific approaches, resources, and skills are suggested. The Charles Press, Bowie, MD 20715; audiocassette; 45 minutes; 1972.

40. *Death and the Family: From the Caring Professions' Point of View* (A, P). Professor Delphie Fredlund lectures on effective treatment of dying children and on the preparation and responsibilities of care givers of the dying. The Charles Press, Bowie, MD 20715; audiocassette; 30 minutes; 1972.

41. *Death Be not Proud* (HS, A). This is a film version of John Gunther's famous 1949 memoir of the dying and death of his 17-year-old son, victim of a brain tumor. Learning Corporation of America, 1350 Avenue of the Americas, New York, NY 10019; color; 99 minutes; 1976.

42. *Death, Drugs and Walter* (HS, A). The protagonist of this story is a 12-year-old heroin addict. His short and unhappy career is followed to the end, to the toilet in a Harlem tenement where, wearing a Snoopy T-shirt, he finally overdosed. Interviews with Walter's grieving aunt and his friends raise many points for discussion about the dangers of drugs, the unmet needs of children, and the kind of society in which this sort of thing can happen. Viewfinders, Inc., Box 1665, Evanston, IL 60204; color film; 13 minutes.

43. *Death Education* (HS). George Daugherty, author of a variety of death education materials for school use, talks about different courses already implemented in grade and high schools. Excerpts from various visual presentations used in those courses are shown. Allied Memorial Council, P.O. Box 30112, Seattle, WA 98103; color videotape or film; 30 minutes.

44. *Death: How Can You Live With It?* (GS, HS). This 19-

minute clip from the Walt Disney film *Napoleon and Samantha* focuses on the reaction of a young boy to the dying of his grandfather. The producers believe the film would be effective in triggering discussion, a guide for which is included. Walt Disney Educational Media Company, 500 S. Buena Vista St., Burbank, CA 91521; color; 19 minutes; 1977.

45. *Death in Literature* (HS, A). This program presents a great variety of literature, from Psalm 104 and Ecclesiastes through Shakespeare to John Gunther, Tom Stoppard, and Simone de Beauvoir. Commentary introduces each piece of literature and its historical and cultural context. In addition, certain themes like the loss of friends and suicide are developed in the literary selections. Guidance Associates, Communications Park, Box 3000, Mount Kisco, NY 10549; two color filmstrips and audiocassettes or records; teacher's guide.

46. *Death in the Family* (A). Eda LeShan, author of *Learning to Say Goodby,* discusses the pain and the grief of survivors. Children, too, experience great suffering. Ms. LeShan analyzes their emotions and suggests ways of helping them cope. Psychology Today Cassettes, P.O. Box 278, Pratt Station, Brooklyn, NY 11205; audiocassette.

47. *Death of a Gandy Dancer* (HS, A). This brilliant little film story explores how the dying of Grandfather Ben affects other members of the Matthews family. Ben's daughter and son-in-law are concerned and loving, but both want to hide the truth. Grandson Josh is the focal point of Ben's last days and, as it turns out, the best hope that the grandfather's principles and ideals will live on in his progeny. Casting and acting are superb, and the story is rich in insight for students of death education. Family dynamics in the dying trajectory, the importance of memory and progeny, truth telling, and the advantages of choosing one's manner of dying are just a few topics that discussion can explore. Learning Corporation of America, 1350 Avenue of the Americas, New York, NY 10019; color; 26 minutes; 1977.

48. *Death of a Newborn* (A, P). Presented in this program is an

interview with a young couple who lost their firstborn infant at age four weeks. Valuable insights are offered into parental needs, problems, grief and mourning, and into intervention techniques that do and do not work. Polymorph Films, 118 South St., Boston, MA 02111; color film or videotape; 32 minutes; brochure; 1976.

49. *Death of a Sibling* (A). Beginning with an actual case of a child's accidental death in a house fire, the film portrays and interviews the parents as they struggle to tell the surviving sibling and work through their fears, guilt, and other emotions. Then two physicians review these events and generalize about anticipated emotional and other problems in such cases, questions for care givers to expect, and what methods of helping would be most appropriate. Network for Continuing Medical Education, 15 Columbus Circle, New York, NY 10023; color videotape; 19 minutes; 1972.

50. *Death of the Wished-for Child* (A). Dr. Glen W. Davidson, Professor of Thanatology at Southern Illinois University School of Medicine, interviews a mother who lost a wished-for child at birth and who developed emotional problems because of errors in intervention made by her care givers. Davidson makes quite clear what should be done and said in such situations. OGR Service Corporation, P.O. Box 3586, Springfield, IL 62708; color film; 28 minutes.

51. *Death Themes in Literature* (HS). See *Perspectives on Death: A Thematic Teaching Unit.*

52. *Death Themes in Music* (HS). See *Perspectives on Death: A Thematic Teaching Unit.*

53. *Death through the Eyes of the Artist* (HS). Presented on this 87-frame color filmstrip are photographs of masterpieces of world art treating death in various ways. Audiocassette commentary analyzes the themes of death illustrated in each work and generalizes about the universality of death and its portrayal in art. Educational Perspectives Associates, P.O. Box 213, DeKalb, IL 60115; see also *Perspectives on Death: A Thematic Teaching Unit.*

54. *Depression/Suicide: You Can Turn Bad Feelings into Good Ones* (HS, A). The subject of this film is teen-age suicide.

Young people who have attempted suicide are interviewed, and they explain what motivated them. They now successfully control remaining suicidal urges and are putting their lives back in order. University of California at Berkeley, Extension Media Center, 2223 Fulton St., Berkeley, CA 94720; color; 28 minutes; 1976.

55. *Dying Child* (A). Dr. Elisabeth Kübler-Ross addresses herself in this videotaped lecture to the problems and needs of dying children, their parents and care givers. She offers several specific suggestions on ways of getting children to express their feelings about their deaths: poetry, play therapy, and art activities, for example. Medical College of South Carolina, Division of Continuing Education, 80 Barre St., Charleston, SC 29401; color; 42 minutes; 1975.

56. *The Dying Patient and his Family* (A). Presentations by four experts at a critical-care medicine symposium were recorded: Dr. P. G. Gaffney, "The Dying Child"; Dr. Ned Cassem, "The Dying Adult"; Ms. Margaret Wynn, "The Social Worker's Role"; and Rev. G. E. Jackson, "The Clergyman's Role." University of Pittsburgh, School of Medicine, 1022 H. Scaife Hall, Pittsburgh, PA 15261; four audiocassettes; 1974.

57. *Emily: The Story of a Mouse* (GS). A simple story designed to introduce the concept of death at the elementary level, the film tells the life of a field mouse growing from a child to an adult, raising her children, then dying. Even in her death, life goes on, for her body provides warmth and nourishment for new life. Viewfinders, Inc., Box 1665, Evanston, IL 60204; 5 minutes; 1975.

58. *Emotional Support for Dying Patients* (A). Dr. Jimmie Holland lectures on common attitudes toward and conceptions of death and provides helpful suggestions for dealing with dying children and their families. Communications in Learning, 2280 Main St., Buffalo, NY 14214; audiocassette and slides; 38 minutes.

59. *Epitaph: The Lingering Heart* (HS, A). A young father is diagnosed as having leukemia, approaches his death, and dies within 15 months. At the same time, the film studies his wife and daughters and records their grief, bereavement,

then readjustment to a new life. WKYC-TV, Public Affairs Department, 1403 E. Sixth St., Cleveland, OH 44114; color; 25 minutes; 1975.

60. *Explaining Death to Children* (A). Rabbi Earl Grollman, who has written extensively on this subject, offers essential introductory concepts. Available from Allied Memorial Council, P.O. Box 30112, Seattle, WA 98103; color film or videotape; 30 minutes; 1974.

61. *Extending Life* (MS, HS). This brief survey of the moral and social implications of scientific advances in "life extension" would be useful to introduce the topic to school children. BFA Educational Media, 468 Park Ave. South, New York, NY 10016; color film; 15 minutes; 1976.

62. *The Family of the Dying Patient* (A, P). Nationally known nursing consultant Virginia Barckley addresses an audience of nurses, though all care givers will find her remarks useful. She observes that the families of dying patients must be well understood, too, and handled with the same thoughtful care as the patients. Different problems arise when the dying person is a child, a parent, or an aged spouse. Whatever the case, family members have particular needs influenced by lifestyles and family customs. A number of positive suggestions are offered. American Cancer Society, 777 Third Ave., New York, NY 10017; 23 minutes; discussion guide; 1972.

63. *Family Reactions to Stillbirth* (P). This lecture-presentation urges medical professionals to deal more sympathetically with such situations and offers useful background information and suggestions. Communications in Learning, 2280 Main St., Buffalo, NY 14214; audiocassette; 16 minutes.

64. *Father* (HS, A). Starring Burgess Meredith, this fine little film is based on a short story by Anton Chekhov. Ned Kelly, a hansom cab driver in New York's Central Park, alone in the world since the recent death of his son, tries to share his grief with passengers in his cab but is coldly rebuffed or ignored. The point is made beautifully but painfully that grief must be shared. University of California at Berkeley, Extension Media Center, 2223 Fulton St., Berkeley, CA 94720; black and white; 1971.

65. *Feelings of a Father* (A). A father discusses his grief at the loss of his child. The Compassionate Friends, P.O. Box 1347, Oak Brook, IL 60521; audiocassette.

66. *The Following Sea* (HS, A). At the funeral of his father, an old fisherman, Charles recalls his father's life and realizes the legacy of wisdom and insight left behind, which now, like a following sea, continues to move the lives of his survivors. McGraw-Hill Films, 1221 Avenue of the Americas, New York, NY 10020; black and white film; 11 minutes.

67. *Gale is Dead* (A). A 19-year-old girl dies of a heroin overdose, and this award-winning documentary film attempts to reveal the causes of her addiction, not simply the effects. Framed at beginning and end by scenes from her funeral, the film interviews teachers and acquaintances, explores her early years and formative experiences, and suggests that in many ways society and its institutions, not simply the addict's own psychological condition, are at least partly to blame; they could have done more for her. Films, Inc., 1144 Wilmette Ave., Wilmette, IL 60091.

68. *The Garden Party* (HS, A). Based on the Katherine Mansfield short story, the film juxtaposes upper- and lower-class attitudes, assumptions, misinformation, and fears about death and postdeath rituals, as it portrays in depth the effects of death on a young girl. This is excellent for discussion purposes. AIMS Media, Inc., 626 Justin Ave., Glendale, CA 91201; 24 minutes.

69. *Graduation Day* (HS, A). A probation officer manages to help a suicidal teen-ager back to a healthy sense of reality. The point is made that a worthwhile life must be based on a sense of personal identity and inner freedom. Paulist Productions, P.O. Box 1057, Pacific Palisades, CA 90272; color film; 27 minutes; 1973.

70. *Grief Therapy* (A). Originally produced as part of the CBS-TV "60 Minutes" series, this film presents several on-camera grief therapy sessions. Dr. Donald Ramsey leads a mother to "let go," to face the facts and separate herself from her daughter, whose accidental death she has been mourning intensely for over 2½ years. Insights into the

nature of grief are graphically presented. Carousel Films, 1501 Broadway, New York, NY 10036; color; 20 minutes; 1976.

71. *Handling Holidays* (A). The title refers to the special problem faced by parents wo have lost a child, and this audiocassette offers practical advice from people who have had the experience. The Compassionate Friends, P.O. Box 1347, Oak Brook, IL 60521.

72. *Help Me! The Story of a Teenage Suicide* (HS, A). Based on the story of one young girl who becomes a suicide statistic, this film explores behavior patterns of suicide-prone people and offers suggestions for effective intervention. S.L. Film Productions, P.O. Box 41108, Los Angeles, CA 90041; color; 25 minutes.

73. *How Death Came to Earth* (MS, HS, A). For classes interested in the cross-cultural study of death, this well-made little film with attractive musical accompaniment may be valuable. It retells an East Indian folk tale about a time when there were two suns and two moons and no one died. When one of each pair fell in love with each other and came to play on earth, people were afraid of the fire, so a hunter was sent to kill them both. Thereupon storms, rain, and death descended upon the earth. McGraw-Hill Films, 1221 Avenue of the Americas, New York, NY 10020; color; 14 minutes; 1971.

74. *How Do You Explain Death to Children?* (HS, A). Use of this film is free to classroom teachers and death educators. Write for information and make booking well ahead of time. Walter J. Klein Co., Ltd., 6301 Carmel Rd., Box 220766, Charlotte, NC 28222; color; 28 minutes; 1976.

75. *I Never Saw Another Butterfly* (A). This is a film record of a fascinating set of children's drawings, which include depictions of the happiness and joy of houses, toys, and flowers as well as vivid renderings of funeral scenes and death by gallows and lightning. What is special are the artists, inmates of a Nazi concentration camp in World War II. Macmillan Films, 34 MacQuesten Parkway South, Mount Vernon, NY 10550; color; 15 minutes.

76. *Just Hold My Hand* (A, P). Two middle-aged women, both

dying of cancer, are filmed during the last six months of
their lives. One is a widow, a mother of seven, whose "most
horrifying thought is having to leave my family." Pressures,
problems, and conflicts in the family group and in the
individual children are revealed. The other woman, a professional research biologist, is especially troubled by her inability to work and the concomitant (for her) loss of human
dignity; thus she decides to stop her chemotherapy treatments. Both women discuss euthanasia at some length. The
mother of seven would never consider interfering with the
plan of God, but the scientist disagrees: "I say I'll never do
it, but I know it's in my medicine cabinet. Maybe I
will. . . . " The overall theme of this impressive and very
moving filmed documentary is how two people overcome
great odds to live their last months meaningfully. Doctors
Ned Cassem and Melvin Krant, involved in the care of these
patients, comment. Write Mr. Howard Finkelstein, Boston
Broadcasters, Inc., 5 TV Place, Needham Br., Boston, MA
02190; color videotape; 60 minutes.

77. *Last Rites: A Child's Reaction to Death* (MS, HS, A). At his
mother's funeral, a young boy cannot grasp the meaning
and the reality of his loss. He retreats into fantasy until a
stranger is able to get through and to help the boy accept.
This new film on "the mystery of death and its incompre-
hensibility to a child" has been described as an excellent
teaching tool. Filmakers Library, 133 E. 58th St., Suite 703
A, New York, NY 10022; color; 30 minutes; 1979.

78. *Leukemia Panel Discussion* (A). Parents of leukemic children
and their doctors discuss the psychological and emotional
effects of the disease on the families. Stanford University,
School of Medicine, Division of Instructional Media, M 207,
Stanford, CA 94305; color videotape; 32 minutes; 1975.

79. *The Life That's Left* (A). A number of people who have
experienced a loss—an elderly widower, a young widow, a
sibling, parents, and the mother of a stillborn baby—describe
their feelings in interviews. Great Plains National Instructional Television Library, Box 80669, Lincoln, NE 68501;
color film or videotape; 29 minutes.

80. *The Magic Moth* (HS, A). Based on the book by Virginia

Lee, the film portrays the illness, death, and funeral of Maryanne, the middle child of five, and the reactions of her family and friends. The family is a model (perhaps somewhat unrealistic) of healthy relationships characterized by open discussion and honest acceptance of the reality of death. Their frankly stated Christian beliefs and point of view may be objected to by some as simplistic. As Maryanne dies, the beautiful moth of the title springs from a cocoon given to her earlier by her brother. The acting is, at times, only fair. Centron Educational Films, P.O. Box 687, 1621 W. Ninth St., Lawrence, KA 66044; color; 22 minutes; 1977.

81. *Marek* (A). Marek is a seven-year-old boy who must undergo dangerous cardiac surgery to correct a birth defect. The doctors advise the parents of the risks involved and counsel the family attentively. The surgery is performed, but there are complications and Marek dies. The parents are then helped through the shock of the loss. Produced by BBC-TV, the film is well made and impressive. Films, Inc., 1144 Wilmette Ave., Wilmette, IL 60091; color; 45 minutes; 1978.

82. *Mongoloid Infant: Should We Operate?* (A, P). A panel of doctors at the University of Virginia Medical School breaks this question down into its more specific medical and ethical components and discusses the varying types and prognoses of mongoloidism, the "quality of life" concept, and the extent of parental rights in determining treatment. University of Virginia, School of Medicine, Charlottesville, VA 22904; black-and-white videotape; 60 minutes; 1973.

83. *My Grandson Lew* (MS, HS, A). When, how, and what to tell children about a death in the family are questions raised by this film, based on the book by Charlotte Zolotow. Lew is thinking about his grandfather and wonders when he will visit again. Mother tells Lew that the grandfather died and that she was afraid to tell him earlier because he was too young. They then share happy memories of grandfather. Barr Films, P.O. Box 5667, 3490 E. Foothill Blvd., Pasadena, CA 91107; color; 13 minutes; 1976.

84. *My Son, Kevin* (A). Kevin, a "thalidomide baby," has no

arms or legs, but he rises above misfortune to attend a community school and be a loved and loving person. This film would interest discussion groups on policies and attitudes toward malformed fetuses, abortion, and birth defects. Viewfinders, Inc., Box 1665, Evanston, IL 60204; color; 24 minutes.

85. *My Turtle Died Today* (GS). The book on which this cartoon is based tells the story of a pet turtle getting sick, dying, then being mourned by three children until they realize that life continues. BFA Educational Media, 468 Park Ave. South, New York, NY 10016; color film; 5 minutes.

86. *A Need to Know: A Family Faces Death* (A, P). Part of the video tape series "Interventions in Family Therapy," this program presents an interview between Lois Jaffe, M.S.W., a leukemia patient herself, and the family of a child with the same disease. ETL Video Publishers, 1170 Commonwealth Ave., Boston, MA 02134; color; 60 minutes; 1975.

87. *Nine-year-olds Talk about Death* (GS, HS, A). School teachers and others interested in understanding children's attitudes toward death will find this short film informative and stimulating. The format is straightforward. A group of fourth graders are filmed as they answer questions about death posed by a teacher who is off-camera and comment on one another's responses. Here is yet another valuable illustration of the sometimes profound wisdom of children. International Film Bureau, 332 S. Michigan Ave., Chicago, IL 60604; black and white; 15 minutes; 1977.

88. *Nursing Management of Children with Cancer* (A, P). The purpose of this film is to illustrate the skills, commitment, and rewards involved in pediatric cancer nursing. The procedures demonstrated include infusions, mouth care, control of infections and fevers, ostomy care, and play therapy. The need for emotional support for patients and their families is explained, as is the nurse's teaching responsibility in aiding parents to help and treat their children at home. Statistical information is provided that suggests that the prognosis of many childhood cancers is improving. American Cancer

Society, 777 Third Ave., New York, NY 10017; color; 22
minutes; 1974.

89. *One in 350: Sudden Infant Death* (A). Perhaps one of the
most serious problems faced by parents who have lost a
child to SIDS is the tactless ignorance of family, friends,
and well-meaning care givers. Education on the nature of
the disease and on the fact that so little is known about it,
can help parents and the public alike. In this film, parents
share their experiences and their particular kind of grief.
National SIDS Foundation, Room 1904, 310 S. Michigan
Ave., Chicago, IL 60604; black and white; 30 minutes.

90. *Parents and the Dying Child* (A, P). Eugenia Waechter, a
counselor of dying children and their families, describes the
principles she follows in her practice and the lessons she has
learned. Big Sur Recordings, P.O. Box 91, Big Sur, CA
93920; audiocassette; 90 minutes; 1974.

91. *Perspectives on Death: A Thematic Teaching Unit* (HS).
Widely used in secondary schools, this program consists of
an anthology of readings, a student activity book, teacher's
resource book, and four audiovisuals. "Funeral Customs
around the World" (a 110-frame color filmstrip and audiocassette) is a cross-cultural survey. "Death through the Eyes
of the Artist" (an 87-frame color filmstrip and audiocassette) shows the work of such masters as Michelangelo,
Rembrandt, Bosch, and Picasso and explains how style,
color, and symbolism can "capture the face and mood of
death." Narrators read from selected works of Shakespeare,
Poe, London, Wilder, and others in "Death Themes in
Literature" (audiocassette, 20 minutes); and musical selections like "Danse Macabre," Mozart's "Requiem," "Die Erl-
Konig" by Schubert, "Taps," and "Deep River" are played
in "Death Themes in Music" (audiocassette, 18 minutes).
Components of the unit are available separately. Educational
Perspectives Associates, P.O. Box 213, DeKalb, IL 60115.

92. *Physician's Role with the Dying Patient* (P). Three programs
make up this series aimed at helping practicing physicians
improve their work with dying patients. "Children Die Too"
offers suggestions on treating dying children and relating

effectively with family members. "Maintaining Integrity of the Profession" offers guidelines for physician-patient exchange at various stages in the dying process. "The Philosophy of Dying" discusses legal, social, and emotional factors in the dying situation. University of Arizona, Health Sciences Center, Division of Biomedical Communications, Tucson, AZ 85724; three color videotapes; 50–57 minutes each; 1974.

93. *Poetry of Death* (HS, A). A number of well-known poetic treatments of death, ranging from Shakespeare to contemporary song lyrics and including such chestnuts as Robert Louis Stevenson's "Requiem" and William Cullen Bryant's "Thanatopsis," are read to the accompaniment of guitar music and evocative photographs. Spectrum Educational Media Service, Box 611, Matoon, IL 61938; two color filmstrips and audiocassettes, with text; 1974.

94. *A Question of Values* (A). Down's syndrome (DS) is explained, and moral issues related to keeping and caring for Down's syndrome and other handicapped infants are raised. Patients (three infants and three children, aged 5–21) and their families are introduced to illustrate commentary on the widely varying physical and psychological traits found in the DS population. This presentation tries to counter the film *Who Should Survive?* which presents the case of a DS infant, unwanted by parents, who was allowed to die without corrective surgery. Edward Feil Productions, 4614 Prospect Ave., Cleveland, OH 44103; color film; 28 minutes; 1972.

95. *Rabbit* (GS, HS, A). A 9-year-old boy learns that taking care of three pet rabbits given as an Easter present is more of a chore than he thought. Finding homes for two of them, he releases the third in the woods and then is filled with sadness and guilt when he discovers it dead. His first encounter with death is complicated by the burden of responsibility. The film is a sensitive, insightful portrait of the child's responses to loss and death. Viewfinders, Inc., Box 1665, Evanston, IL 60204; color; 15 minutes; 1974.

96. *Reactions of Children to Serious Illness, Death, and Natural Catastrophe* (P). This is a videotaped lecture to a medical

audience by Dr. Howard Hansen. University of Washington Audiovisual Services, Seattle, WA 98195; 60 minutes.

97. *Reinvestment-Reorganization-Recovery* (A). The words outline a program of therapeutic action for parents who have lost a child. The Compassionate Friends, P.O. Box 1347, Oak Brook, IL 60521; audiocassette.

98. *Richie* (HS, A). The theme of this story is teen-age drug addiction and its impact on a family. Richie's parents cannot comprehend his increasing dependency on drugs and his resulting behavior changes. Disintegrating communication results in increasingly hostile confrontations in the home, climaxing in the father's shooting of Richie. This program is an edited selection from the feature film *The Death of Richie*, based on a book by Thomas Thompson. Learning Corporation of America, 1350 Avenue of the Americas, New York, NY 10019; color film; 31 minutes; 1978.

99. *Rick: An Adolescent Suicide* (A). A 17-year-old high school senior committed suicide. The film tries to recreate events and to investigate Rick's mental and emotional state before the fact. Medical Media Network, Room 514, 10995 LeConte Ave., Los Angeles, CA 90024; black and white; 29 minutes; 1969.

100. *The Role of the Schools in Death Education* (A). Schools at all levels should offer death education, argues Dr. Dan Leviton. He offers specific commentary on curricula as well as teacher and parent preparation in the subject matter, which should include crisis intervention. The Charles Press, Bowie, MD 20715; audiocassette; 27 minutes.

101. *Ronnie's Tune* (GS, HS). The film is a carefully detailed, realistic portrait of complex family reactions following the death of a teen-age son. Only with painful difficulty is it revealed to a visiting niece, Julie, that her cousin Ronnie's death was a suicide and that Ronnie's father has left his wife as a result. Ronnie's mother makes a great effort and is finally willing to talk freely about her response to the death and to share her grief. After tears, grieving, and much thought of her own, Julie decides to learn to play

Ronnie's banjo. Wombat Productions, Little Lake, Glendale Road, P.O. Box 70, Ossining, NY 10562; color; 18 minutes; 1978.

102. *Sandcastle* (GS, MS). This program for ages 10-12 presents a conversation between a father and his children on the unexpected death of their mother. Image Publications, Miles-Samuelson, Inc., 15 E. 26th St., New York, NY 10010; color filmstrip and audiocassette or record; 1971.

103. *A Small Statistic* (A). This film records the reactions of a young couple to the death of their first child. Association Instructional Materials, 866 Third Ave., New York, NY 10022; color; 27 minutes. (Recent correspondence with the distributor indicates that the film is now "withdrawn from circulation by sponsor.")

104. *Some Days It's Harder To Say Yes: Suicide in the Classroom* (HS). Offered here are interviews with two high school students who are suicidal, together with related information and insight into teens and suicide. Highly Specialized Promotions, 391 Atlantic Ave., Brooklyn, NY 11201; color videotape; 30 minutes; teacher's guide; 1979.

105. *A Special Kind of Care* (A). This film has two main purposes: (1) to dramatize the effects on a family of a mother slowly dying of cancer and the related problems of truth telling and (2) to highlight the nature and functions of the National Cancer Foundation and its service arm, Cancer Care, Inc. With the counseling of Cancer Care, the father is finally able to meet the needs of his children and of himself in the crisis situation. Association Films, 866 Third Ave., New York, NY 10022; color; 14 minutes; 1968.

106. *The Street* (HS, A). Mordecai Richler's fine little book is turned into a delightfully moving animated film. A grandmother dies slowly in her son's home; and the family, especially her grandchildren, reacts to her passing. The urban poor, ethnic Jewish atmosphere is faithfully reproduced. A nine-year-old grandson, loving but totally realistic and irrepressible, provides the main point of view. Living and dying in this family are real, ordinary, serious, and comic. These are individual people beautifully portrayed,

experiencing death in their own way. National Film Board of Canada, 16th Floor, 1251 Avenue of the Americas, New York, NY 10020; color; 10 minutes.

107. *Sudden Infant Death Syndrome* (A). A brief introduction to the topic. National Audiovisual Center, Order Section, Washington, D.C. 20409; color film; 4 minutes; 1976.

108. *Sudden Infant Death Syndrome and the Pediatrician* (P). Directed at physicians, this program presents guidelines for working with parents of SIDS-prone children, reports on recent research into the syndrome, and surveys parental responses to SIDS deaths. University of Arizona, Health Sciences Center, Division of Biomedical Communications, Tucson, AZ 85724; color videotape; 43 minutes; 1974.

109. *Suicide: Causes and Prevention* (HS, A). This presentation for a high school audience includes issues and case studies carefully presented to foster discussion. Sunburst Communications, 39 Washington Ave., Pleasantville, NY 10570; two color filmstrips and audiocassettes or records; teacher's guide; 1976.

110. *Suicides: Causes and Prevention* (A). Suicide among high school and college students is the focus of these two programs. Causal factors and varying scholarly theories about them are treated in the first program. In the second, the emphasis is on prevention and intervention. Human Relations Media Center, 175 Tompkins Ave., Pleasantville, NY 10570; two color filmstrips with audiocassettes or records.

111. *Suicide: Who Will Cry for Me?* (HS, A). This new sound filmstrip set focuses on the growing problem of teen-age suicide. It surveys and corrects a number of myths about suicide, analyzes reasons why the teen-age population is particularly at risk, offers detailed analysis of warning signs, and in general offers much useful information for teens themselves and for parents and care givers. Learning Arts, P.O. Box 179, Wichita, KS 67201; three color filmstrips and audiocassettes; teachers guide; 1979.

112. *The Syndrome of Ordinary Grief* (A, P). In an interview, a sophomore medical student describes his reactions to the accidental death of his only child, a two-year-old boy,

some weeks earlier. Included is a scholarly paper on this
case history. University of Texas Medical Branch, Videotape Library of Clinical Psychiatric Syndromes, Galveston,
TX 77550; color videotape; 32 minutes.

113. *Talking to Children About Death* (A). Dr. George C.
Williams argues that of course children should be taught
about death. They almost automatically adopt parents'
attitudes, so parents must straighten themselves out and
then share openly with children. Otherwise children may
have emotional problems in later life. Concrete suggestions
for parents are offered. The Charles Press, Bowie, MD
20715; audiocassette; 57 minutes; 1972.

114. *A Taste of Blackberries* (MS). See *Understanding Death
Series.*

115. *Teen-age Suicide: A National Epidemic* (A). Joseph Teicher
lectures. Psychology Today Cassettes, P.O. Box 278, Pratt
Station, Brooklyn, NY 11205; audiocassette; 1977.

116. *Terminal* (A). Members of the Open Theatre Ensemble of
New York City perform in a frankly experimental production that combines acting, dancing, chanting, and panto-
mime. The theme is death and a wide variety of related
issues, attitudes, and customs. Funeral ritual and hospital
treatment of patients, for example, come in for a good
measure of satire. Courses approaching death through
literature and the other arts or through philosophy or
psychology will find this useful. Foundation of Thanatology, 630 W. 168th St., New York, NY 10032; black-and-
white videotape; 30 minutes; 1970.

117. *That Undiscovered Country* (HS). The country "from
whose bourn no traveler returns," as Hamlet tells us, is
death. The audiocassette portion of this program presents
readings of seven popular poetic interpretations of death,
with muscial background. An accompanying booklet contains these texts and other classic literary statements on
death and dying. A detailed teacher's guide with many
suggestions for use is included. Perfection Form Company,
1000 N. Second Ave., Logan, IA 51546; audiocassette;
reader; teacher's guide.

118. *Themes in Literature: Death* (HS, A). Professional readings

from many authors—Chaucer, Shakespeare, Donne, Boswell, Gray, Wordsworth, Browning, Tolstoy, Dickinson, Synge, Millay, Gunther, Steinbeck, Agee, Stoppard—demonstrate a multiplicity of attitudes to human mortality. Guidance Associates, Communications Park, Box 3000, Mount Kisco, NY 10549; two color filmstrips and audio-cassettes or records.

119. *Things in Their Season* (HS, A). Members of the Gerlach family, working a dairy farm in southern Wisconsin, were growing apart until the day that wife Peg was diagnosed as having leukemia. In the face of this tragedy the family forced itself back together, facing truth, finally speaking the unspoken, reevaluating their relationships, and eventually finding a measure of happiness. This is a fine film portrayal of the dynamics of death in the family situation. Learning Corporation of America, 1350 Avenue of the Americas, New York, NY 10019; color; 79 minutes; 1975.

120. *To Be Aware of Death* (HS, A). This film surveys a number of young people on their feelings about death and their experiences with it. The commentary is made more attractive by means of accompanying color photography, still pictures, and folk music. University of Minnesota, AV Library Service, 3300 University Ave. S.E., Minneapolis, MN 55414; color; 13 minutes; 1974.

121. *Two Daughters* (A). In this evocative Swedish film, a mother mourns the death of her young daughter and remembers her own mother's death. This is a fine study of relationships and of generations and an effective stimulus to discussion. University of California at Berkeley, Extension Media Center, 2223 Fulton St., Berkeley, CA 94720; color; 22 minutes; 1976.

122. *Uncle Monty's Gone* (GS). Fat Albert and the Cosby Kids react to the death of someone close. Undine's Uncle Monty, a long-time entertainer, agrees to help the kids stage a fund-raising show. When he dies suddenly, Undine is crushed and angrily withdraws from her friends. Then her mother tells her more about Uncle Monty, his zest for life, and how he would have wanted them all to live with enthusiasm and joy. The show must go on, and with

Undine and her friends back together, it does. University
of Illinois, Visual Aids Service, 1325 S. Oak St., Champaign, IL 61820; color film; 16 minutes; 1976.

123. *Understanding Changes in the Family: Playing Dead*
(GS, MS). This one of a series of filmstrip programs asks
an audience of children to role-play. In the process,
someone recalls the death of a grandfather, and discussion
takes up the idea. Guidance Associates, Communications
Park, Box 3000, Mount Kisco, NY 10549; color filmstrip
and audiocassette or record; 5 minutes.

124. *Understanding Death: A Basic Program in Death and
Dying* (MS, HS). Six filmstrips and three accompanying
audiocassettes make up this introductory series on the
subject for the schools. "Thinking about Death" gives
general background and encourages students to examine
their own experiences with and attitudes toward death.
"Mourning," the second filmstrip, discusses grief as a
normal human emotion, and one not exclusively associated
with death. "Practical Guidelines," the next program,
explains death certificates, wills, organ bequests, and so on.
"Death's Moment and the Time that Follows" explains
why "death" is so difficult to define in precise medical
and legal terms and that scientific advances constantly
force changes in society's conception of death and of life.
The fifth program, "Dying Occurs in Stages," builds on the
theories of Kübler-Ross. Finally, "The Gift of Life"
examines various types of "symbolic immortality" and
argues that a well-spent life can rob death of some of its
sting. Eye Gate Media, 146-01 Archer Ave., Jamaica, NY
11435; six color filmstrips (about 50 frames each) and
three audiocassettes, available as a set or singly; 1976.

125. *Understanding Death Series* (MS). Included in this series
are four programs especially designed for middle school
students, with an accompanying program for parents and
teachers. In "Life-Death," death is presented as a natural
part of the life cycle; natural, too, are feelings of grief.
Causes of death and a number of other topics are covered.
In both "Exploring the Cemetery" and "Facts about
Funerals," a boy pays visits and gets background informa-

tion from, respectively, a cemeterian and a funeral director. The fourth program, "A Taste of Blackberries," is adapted from a book by Doris Buchanan Smith. A boy loses his best friend, then works through his grief to an awareness of death as a natural part of the human experience. Finally, "Children and Death: A Guide for Parents and Teachers" offers advice on truth telling, death education, the changing stages and levels of children's understanding of death, and other matters. Educational Perspectives Associates, P.O. Box 213, DeKalb, IL 60115; five color filmstrips and audiocassettes, also available separately.

126. *Very Good Friends* (MS, HS, A). When her 11-year-old sister dies suddenly, a 13-year-old is tortured by grief, anger, and guilt. Her parents help her sort through her feelings, accept the loss, and rest more comfortably with her memories. This fine study of a death in the family can stimulate discussion. Learning Corporation of America, 1350 Avenue of the Americas, New York, NY 10019; color film; 20 minutes; 1977.

127. *Walk in the World for Me* (A, P). See *Death and Dying: Closing the Circle.*

128. *Warrendale* (A). This documentary film is mainly the study of an institution for emotionally disturbed children, but its conclusion is of particular interest to death educators. One of the cooks at the institution, a favorite of the children, dies suddenly and unexpectedly. The children's grief reactions are astounding, from angry self-destructive activities to severe depression. Here are many aspects of grief that, in "normal" people, often do not surface or that appear in more "acceptable" guises. Film Division of Grove Press, 196 W. Houston St., New York, NY 10014; 105 minutes.

129. *Where is Dead* (A). A six-year-old girl, grieving at the accidental death of her brother, comes to understand death as part of the cycle of life and can then be happy with her memories of her brother. The film is a fine study in the dynamics of grief, especially in the child. While the reactions of the adult family members are not emphasized, the adult-child relationships surrounding the death are

healthy. The acting and the whole production are first rate. Encyclopaedia Britannica Educational Corporation, 425 N. Michigan Ave., Chicago, IL 60611; color; 19 minutes.

130. *Who Should Survive?* (A). The film opens with the birth of a baby, a diagnosis of Down's syndrome, the parents' refusal to permit life-saving abdominal surgery, and the subsequent starvation of the infant in the hospital. A 19-minute panel discussion then argues various legal, ethical, and scientific aspects of the case. A teacher's guide and bibliography are available. University of California at Berkeley, Extension Media Center, 2223 Fulton St., Berkeley, CA 94720; color; 26 minutes; 1972.

131. *Who Speaks for the Baby?* (A). The case of a newborn mongoloid infant who will die without corrective surgery is dramatized here. When the parents refuse their consent, the physician seeks a court order to operate. In a panel discussion, professionals offer their responses to the question of the title. See also *A Question of Values* and *Who Should Survive?* Network for Continuing Medical Education, 15 Columbus Circle, New York, NY 10023; color videotape.

132. *With His Playclothes On* (A, P). At 21 months, Jerry dies suddenly of causes that, even after autopsy, are not completely understood. The immediate emotional responses of the parents and three older brothers are vividly presented. Two months after the death, the family is still torn by unresolved shock, anger, and conflict, as the family members react on different levels and from incompletely shared points of view. This study of grief in the family, one of the best available on the subject, includes extensive analytical commentary by Dr. Glen Davidson, Professor and Chief of Thanatology, Department of Psychiatry, Southern Illinois University School of Medicine. OGR Service Corporation, P.O. Box 3586, Springfield, IL 62708; color filmstrip and audiocassette; 47 minutes; 1976.

133. *You Are Not Alone* (A). SIDS is the topic of this program. Parents who have lost children to the disease, care givers, and general audiences are reminded that causes of the

syndrome are largely unknown and that little can be done to prevent an attack. Specific advice is offered on dealing with emotional and other responses of parents, siblings, relatives, and friends. The cases of several couples are dramatized. National SIDS Foundation, Room 1904, 310 S. Michigan Ave., Chicago, IL 60604; color film; 25 minutes; 1976.

134. *The Young Man and Death* (HS, A). Unique among audiovisual materials on death is this ballet danced to music of J. S. Bach by Rudolph Nureyev and Zizi Jeanmaire. The ballerina in the role of Death acts alternately as a destroyer and as a temptress. The Young Man, first fleeing, then falling victim to her blandishments, gives himself up to her. Having won her victory, she scornfully turns away from him and offers him a noose. This film would be very effective in classes studying death in the arts or as a stimulus to discussion. Macmillan Films, 34 MacQuesten Parkway South, Mount Vernon, NY 10550; color; 16 minutes; 1976.

135. *You See—I've Had a Life* (HS, A). At 13, Paul Hendricks is diagnosed as having leukemia. After some initial attempts at denial, the parents decide to tell Paul. The whole family shares the experience with him, working to enhance the quality of his life in the time remaining. The film records Paul's continuing school and athletic activities, treatments by medical staff, the care-giving activities, and the personal reactions of the parents and of Paul himself. This is a moving, well-made story of one family's togetherness in the face of death and of one child's courage. The words of the title, which accurately suggest the essence of his character and the quality of his response to death, are spoken by Paul to reassure a friend who came to offer sympathy. Viewfinders, Inc., Box 1665, Evanston, IL 60204; black and white; 32 minutes; 1973.

136. *The Youth Killers* (MS, HS). Leading causes of death in this age group are discussed in this program. A teacher's guide is included. Audiovisual Narrative Arts, Box 398, Pleasantville, NY 10570; two color filmstrips and audiocassettes or records; 1975.

Appendix

But He Was Only Seventeen—The Death of a Friend (HS, A).
Six months after Steve is killed in an automobile accident,
his friends and high school classmates try to sort out their
feelings. Guided by an understanding teacher, they begin to
face up to their feelings, to understand the complex nature
and effects of grief. Each person's grief is unique, they learn,
and in the process deepen their understanding of themselves
and others. Their grief teaches them the difference that their
friend Steve has made in their lives. Sunburst Communications, 39 Washington Avenue, Pleasantville, New York
10570; 3 filmstrips and audiocassettes, teachers's guide,
1981.

Can't It Be Anyone Else? (HS, A). Three children dangerously ill
with leukemia share their experiences, feelings, and fears
with one another, with their family members, and with the
filmmaker. Typically, children have much wisdom and
courage and hope to offer the rest of us; this film, in
poignant fashion, can provide large quantities of insight and
inspiration to parents of seriously ill children and to professional caregivers. Pyramid Films, Box 1048, Santa Monica,
California 90406; color film or videotape, 54 minutes. 1980.

The Compassionate Friends (A). The history, goals, and operating methods of this self-help organization for bereaved
parents are introduced. The Compassionate Friends, P.O.
Box 1347, Oak Brook, IL 60521; color filmstrip and audiocassette; 1980.

Fighting Back (HS, A). This moving and uncompromising documentary film records the cases of 4 children, ages 9 to 13,
stricken with leukemia, at the War Memorial Children's
Hospital in London, Ontario. Their treatments, their reactions, their remissions, their relapses are presented realistically. The emotional reactions of the parents and the children
themselves make for enlightening, moving and painful viewing—only one child survives into a hopeful remission at the
end of the film. This prize-winning film would be useful for
general adult audiences as well as allied health and counselor

education programs. Documentary Films, 3217 Trout Gulch Road, Aptos, California 95003; color film, 90 minutes, 1981.

Going Home (A, P). Returning home from the hospital can present patients and family with monumental problems, particularly when the medical condition, cancer for example, is serious and chronic. This major, comprehensive program, consisting of 13 videotapes and a 131-page instructional manual, is designed especially to prepare patients, their families, and home health-care professionals for the tasks ahead. Individual program titles include Recreation, Positioning in Bed, Ostomy Care, Emergencies, Massage, and Pain Medication. This program was developed under the supervision of Ernest H. Rosenbaum, M.D., by three cooperating institutions: Mount Zion Hospital and Medical Center, San Francisco Regional Cancer Foundation, and the Marshal Hale Memorial Hospital. Videotapes and manual are available separately or, at a special rate, as a set. Bull Publishing Company, P.O. Box 208, Palo Alto, CA 94302; 13 videotapes ranging in length from 5 to 14 minutes.

I Want to Die (HS, A). At a Thanksgiving dinner, Bill, a college student, is deeply depressed; he is going to quit school, he says, and is planning to kill himself. The balance of the film reveals what it is about his relationship with his family that had led to Bill's decisions. At the root is a failure of communication between parents and child. A closing commentary by movie star Kirk Douglas asks viewers to be prepared to help such people. University of Illinois, Visual Aids Service, 1325 S. Oak St., Champaign, IL 61820; color; 27 minutes; 1977.

Jocelyn (HS, A). The protagonist of this film portrait is 17 and is dying of cancer. What sustains her is her tremendous—and authentic—spiritual strength. She *is* blessed with good family and good friends, but her faith and her poise come from inside her. Perhaps the best use for this film is to share it with seriously ill patients who need encouragement and motivation. Jocelyn has so much to share. Filmmakers Library, 133 East 58th Street, Suite 703A, New York, NY 10022; color film or videotape, 28 minutes.

A Last Cry for Help (HS, A). This film dramatizes the attempted suicide of an apparently happy and healthy teenage girl, the shocked reactions of family members, and the only partly successful attempts of a psychologist to correct the family situation. This open-ended approach is designed to encourage audience discussion; in the film itself, many insights into suicidal thinking, causative factors, techniques of intervention and so on are offered to enhance audience awareness of the complexities of the growing national problem of teenage suicide. The dramatization is very well acted, and the factual content detailed and forcefully presented. Learning Corporation of America, 1350 Avenue of the Americas, New York, NY 10019; color film, 32 minutes. 1980.

Old Friends, New Friends—Gerald Jampolsky, M.D. (A). This new film brings together some very special people in a very special way. Arthur Barron, the filmmaker who brought us the story of the dying of Albro Pearsall (Death: see *Death Education: An Annotated Resource Guide* (1980, p. 173), spotlights the special approaches to dying children taken by Dr. Jampolsky, and features a visit to the Doctor's Center for Attitudinal Healing by Fred Rogers. Family Communications, 4902 Fifth Avenue, Pittsburgh, PA 15213; color film or videotape, 29 minutes, 1980.

Preventing Teen Suicide: You Can Help (HS, A). "Jennifer is 16, pretty, bright, popular, talented—and a suicide." This new program first outlines causal factors in Jennifer's decision: the divorce of her parents, her break-up with her boy friend, her rejection by the college of her choice. These are all common enough occurrences, but in this case, because no one heeded danger signals, their cumulative effect was another teen suicide. The program then shows the family, teachers, and friends as they consider what they might have said and done for Jennifer—and lessons are drawn for the viewer. Sunburst Communications, 39 Washington Ave., Pleasantville, NY 10570; three color filmstrips and audio-cassettes or records: teachers guide; 1980.

Stillbirth (A, P). A mother who delivered a stillborn baby agreed to be interviewed, and reveals her feelings of guilt, anger, frustration, failure and grief. She makes us both know and *feel* how empty and cruel are the usual consolations offered at such times: "it's not like losing a real person," or "you can always have another." Great Plains National Instructional Television Library, Box 80669, Lincoln, NE 68501; color film or videotape, 20 minutes.

Talking about Death with Children (GS, MS). Rabbi Earl Grollman, an authority on this topic, explains death and the funeral to an audience of children. Batesville Management Services, P.O. Drawer 90, Batesville, IN 47006; color filmstrip and audiocassette; 11 minutes; 1980.

Time to Come Home (A, P). In some situations a dying child is better cared for at home than in the hospital. This film builds on the team concept—physician, nurses, and parents—but focuses on the instruction of parents as primary care givers. Lessons for physical care of the child are given, and both the benefits and risks of bringing the dying child home are discussed. Department of Physical Medicine and Rehabilitation, University Hospital, 860 Mayo, Box 297, 420 Delaware St. S.E., Minneapolis, MN 55455; color; 24 minutes.

Valley of the Shadow—A Journey through Grief (A). This probing yet deeply sensitive study of grief, produced by Bill Goveia (Death of a Wished-for Child), focuses on a father who has lost two children, ages 5 and 8, in an auto-train accident. The father's grief initially was mismanaged, resulting in adverse physical effects and illness. The film explores the biochemistry of grief and explains how that situation was resolved. National Funeral Directors Association, 135 West Wells Street, Milwaukee, WI 53203; color film or videotape, 38 minutes, 1980.

We Can Help (A, P). This film describes a multifaceted family-oriented care-giving program for children with cancer, a program combining medical treatment with personal, academic, and vocational counseling. The patients and their family members are interviewed. Polymorph Films, Inc., 118 South St., Boston, MA 02111; color film or videotape; 20 minutes.

When a Child Dies (A). In candid interviews with three bereaved couples, each of whom lost their child in different circumstances, insights into grief and suggestions for helping are offered. The particularly destructive nature of parental grief is explained, as well as the attendant rage and frequent loss of religious faith. Reasons for the high rate of divorce following the death of a child are highlighted. Recalling their experiences, the interviewees offer suggestions on dealing helpfully with bereaved parents, whether one is a family member, friend, neighbor, or medical or mental health professional. This prize-winning film (Mental Health Film Festival; American Film Festival) was funded by, and is available from, the National Funeral Directors Association, 135 West Wells St., Milwaukee, WI 53203; color film, 24 minutes, 1979.

When Disaster Strikes: Coping with Loss, Grief and Rejection (HS, A). Typical human responses to life crises like serious illness, death, and the loss of a loved one are outlined in stages: shock, anger, and acceptance. Variations in individuals are noted, as are related physical and emotional effects. Then coping strategies and grief work are explained, and the complex healing process is clarified. Dramatized illustrations make the subject matter concrete. Sunburst Communications, 39 Washington Ave., Pleasantville, NY 10570; three filmstrips and audiocassettes; teachers guide; 1980;

Winning Battles: A Film about Children with Cancer (A, P). This short film highlights a pediatric cancer program at Stanford University Children's Hospital, in which all caregiving staff are committed to the creation of a warm, supportive atmosphere for the children and their families. Filmmakers Library, 133 East 58th Street, Suite 703A, New York, NY 10022; color film of videotape, 8 minutes. 1979.

TOPICAL INDEX TO "AUDIOVISUAL RESOURCES"

Numbers refer to entry numbers.

Bioethical issues, birth defects,
82, 84, 94, 130, 131

Cancer:
Family reactions, 24, 41, 78, 86,
135
In children, 5, 12, 21, 24, 78, 86,
88, 135
Caring and care giving for the dying
child (This heading identifies
those many audiovisual
materials developed to teach
understanding of the nature
of the dying experience,
thoughtful sympathy for the
dying patient, and the ability
to relate with and effectively
meet the needs of the patient
and family members, whether
those needs are medical,
emotional, psychological,
social, spiritual, or practical.
Each item is labeled for
potential audience appeal,
but the reader will have to
assess her or his own needs
and experience in making
choices. Some items
obviously appeal to
sophisticated medical
professionals with specialized
interests, but most of these
audiovisuals, even those

ostensibly addressed to care
givers, have value for any
audience of mature adults who
want to relate better to the
dying. By the same token, many
audiovisual items addressed to
general adult audiences have
much to offer medical
professionals who have not had
occasion to acquire the relevant
skills or experience.), 12, 17, 18,
23–26, 29, 30, 40, 41, 55, 56,
58, 62, 78, 80, 81, 86, 88, 90,
92, 96, 135
Children's attitudes and responses to
death
General, 14–16, 19–23, 25, 33, 39,
41, 75, 80, 85, 95, 96, 106,
120, 129
Of someone close—parent, grandparent, sibling, other relative,
friend, 3, 6–8, 17, 31, 44, 46,
47, 49, 66, 76, 77, 79, 80, 83,
102, 106, 114, 122, 125, 126,
128, 129, 132
Cystic fibrosis, 29

Death themes
In art, 53, 91
In literature for children
Fiction, 3, 8, 11, 33, 64, 68, 73,
80, 106, 114, 125
General, 45, 51, 91, 93, 116–118

TITLE INDEX TO "BOOKS FOR CHILDREN"

Numbers refer to page numbers.

247

INDEX